# MANAGING STRESS IN FAMILIES

*Managing Stress in Families* deals with the use of well-researched psychosocial strategies in working with families under stress. This includes households where one or more members experience major mental or physical health problems, learning disabilities, as well as marital and family stresses. It takes a structured problem-solving approach that builds on the efforts of all members living together to manage their stresses in the best way they know.

Designed as a practical workbook to assist in the training of therapists from all clinical disciplines, the book describes in detail the strategies that are effective in working with families, and the therapist skills required in order to employ these interventions. The authors, who have all worked with families in community settings, describe in a clear step-by-step manner how to employ a variety of techniques including communication skills training and training in the use of problem-solving skills. They use case studies to illustrate their practice and to cover problem areas such as dealing with crises and the difficulties that arise in therapy.

*Managing Stress in Families* is an invaluable practical handbook which gives a clear idea of what to do in therapy sessions. It will be of immense help to all mental health and social service practitioners, particularly those working in community settings.

**Ian Falloon** and **Victor Graham-Hole** are Co-directors of COMMEND, an NHS consultancy for the development of effective community mental health services; **Gráinne Fadden** is Principal Clinical Psychologist with the Buckingham Mental Health Service; and **Marc Laporta** is Assistant Professor of Psychiatry at McGill University, Montreal.

# STRATEGIES FOR MENTAL HEALTH
## Series editor
Reinhard Kowalski
*Principal Clinical Psychologist and Psychotherapist,*
*East Berkshire Health Authority and the Cardinal Clinic, Windsor,*
*Berkshire*

STRATEGIES FOR MENTAL HEALTH is a series of guide books for the mental health practitioner. It will introduce practitioners to relevant therapeutic approaches in a practical 'hands on' way. Over recent years numerous psychological therapy approaches to mental health have been developed and many of them have become well-established methods in the field. The dilemma that practitioners and students face is how to obtain an up-to-date practice-oriented introduction to a particular method without having to work their way through a mass of research literature.

The books in this series are written by experienced practitioners and trainers. Style and content are practice-orientated, giving readers the knowledge, skills, and materials needed to plan, set up, and run projects in their particular area of mental health work. Those who want to acquire a deeper knowledge of the theoretical foundations will find up-to-date references with each of the titles.

*Already published*

## ANXIETY AND STRESS MANAGEMENT
*Trevor J. Powell and Simon J. Enright*

## REHABILITATION AND COMMUNITY CARE
*Stephen Pilling*

## ASSERTION TRAINING
*Shân Rees and Roderick S. Graham*

*Forthcoming title*

## SELF-DISCOVERY
*Reinhard Kowalski*

# MANAGING STRESS IN FAMILIES

## Cognitive and behavioural strategies for enhancing coping skills

*Ian R. H. Falloon, Marc Laporta,*
*Gráinne Fadden and*
*Victor Graham-Hole*

*London and New York*

First published in 1993
by Routledge
11 New Fetter Lane, London EC4P 4EE

Simultaneously published in the USA and Canada
by Routledge
a division of Routledge, Chapman and Hall Inc.
29 West 35th Street, New York, NY 10001

©1993 Ian R. H. Falloon, Marc Laporta, Gráinne Fadden and
Victor Graham-Hole

Typeset in Linotron Baskerville by
J&L Composition Ltd, Filey, North Yorkshire
Printed and bound in Great Britain by
Biddles Ltd, Guildford and King's Lynn

*British Library Cataloguing in Publication Data*
A catalogue record for this book is available from the British Library.

*Library of Congress Cataloguing in Publication Data*
Managing stress in families : cognitive and behavioural strategies for
enhancing coping skills / Ian R. H. Falloon ... [et al.].
p.    cm. – (Strategies for mental health)
Includes bibliographical references and index.
1. Family psychotherapy.    I. Falloon, Ian R. H.    II. Series.
RC488.5.M334    1992
616.89′156–dc20
92–12221
CIP

ISBN 0–415–07192–5
0–415–07193–3 (pbk)

# CONTENTS

# ILLUSTRATIONS

## TABLES

## FIGURES

# PREFACE

Over the years mental health services have struggled with a variety of strategies that aimed to enhance the quality of family life. Many of these efforts have resulted in confrontation with family members, particularly when the obvious distress of families burdened with the care of their disturbed relatives has been considered a potential cause of major mental disorders. It is now clear that persisting high levels of stress place people who are prone to stress-related health and mental health problems at a high risk of succumbing to episodes of those disorders. It is also clear that households with the ability to manage stress in a highly effective and efficient manner not only assist in reducing acute episodes of these disorders, but probably contribute substantially to full and sustained recovery from many disabling conditions.

This book is based upon the premiss that family care is the greatest natural resource for the clinical management of all health problems. The behavioural family therapy (BFT) approach described is a well-researched series of modules that have been developed over 30 years with the primary aim of building on the efforts of all family members living together to manage their stresses in the best way that they know. We realize that modern society provides minimal training in stress management strategies for dealing with the complexity of family living, and that considerable stress results in most families in the course of everyday living together. When one or more members of the household is stricken with a potentially disabling health or psychosocial problem, few families are equipped to manage the stress that inevitably arises from the added burdens. As a result, their best efforts at coping may prove relatively ineffective in providing the calm, supportive environment that is the basis for all health care. Furthermore, the added burdens associated with care of a disabled person may lead to a breakdown in the health of the carers, further compounding the family problems.

Behavioural family therapy is a very straightforward method of helping family members to adopt methods that facilitate mutual expression of needs and desires, and to assist all members of the household to resolve their everyday problems and achieve their personal goals, even when they have the misfortune of suffering from or caring for a disabling disorder. It is derived from the principles of learning, and employs educational training methods throughout. These include assessment of the specific assets and deficits of each household member and the group as a whole, education that provides a logical explanation for each component, skill training through repeated practice and supportive coaching, and, most important of all, application of strategies in everyday life situations with further coaching and refinement until the family are satisfied that they have developed stress management strategies that are effective in their household and have become an intergral part of their lifestyle.

The book is designed as a practical workbook to assist in the training of professional therapists from all clinical disciplines. Ideally this training should be part of specific course in behavioural family therapy under the guidance of qualified tutors. However, most mental health professionals who have received basic training in cognitive-behavioural approaches may be able to learn the BFT strategies from studying this book. Worksheets and guides to assessment and training modules are provided in the Appendices. Chapters 2 to 6 provide more detailed descriptions and examples of the major strategies. Some repetition of strategies, such as assessment, real-life practice, and the six-step problem-solving approach, is employed throughout. This aims to prompt the therapist to build upon previous modules, and to see that each module continues to be employed continuously, and is not forgotten as soon as that step has been mastered by the family. Chapters 7 to 9 describe specific applications of problem solving to the management of family crises, specific mental health problems, and difficulties that the therapist may encounter in applying the BFT approach.

Once again the key components of the structured problem-solving approach are the main ingredients that are applied to deal with these issues.

Although this book is primarily written to aid the training of professional therapists in behavioural family therapy methods, the strategies are described in sufficient detail that many families may find it helpful to read about the methods themselves. While it is doubtful that all the skills could be incorporated into a family lifestyle without some assistance from a professional therapist, some principles of problem solving and goal achievement could be readily used.

A brief history of the development of behavioural approaches to families is outlined in Chapter 1. Several key figures in the field are cited, but many more who are not mentioned in this summary have been responsible for the development and refinement of this approach, which is now the most effective treatment approach for dealing with aggressive children, adolescent disturbance, marital discord, and, in combination with optimal drug therapy, schizophrenic disorders. The particular approach described in this book was pioneered by Ian Falloon, Robert Liberman, Francis Lillie, and Edward Harpin at the Maudsley Hospital in 1975, and became the basis for the psychoeducational approaches that have been widely researched and applied in the mental health field in recent years. Notable contributions to the development of this approach have been provided by Christine McGill, Jeffrey Boyd, Kim Mueser, Shirley Glynn, Gina Randolph, Marvin Karno, Susan Gingerich, Susan Rappaport, Jeffrey Boyd, Jane Taylor, Jurella Poole, Trudi Pass, Teresa Konieczna, Loren Mosher, Julian Hafner, Gayla Blackwell, Thad Eckman, Nina Schooler, Christine Vaughn, Michael Crowe, Max Birchwood, Joanne Smith, Jeri Doane, Nicholas Virgo, Per Borrell, June Dent, Lynne Norris, Pamela Jenkinson, Ian Heath, Terry Pembleton, Tilo Held, Lorenza Magliano, Kurt Hahweg, Michael Goldstein, David Miklowitz, Leona Murray, Olga Piatkowska, Gerard McCann, William Shanahan, Nick Tarrier, and Charles Brooker. In addition we have learned from all the hundreds of students of the approach whom we have supervised over the years, and those who have conducted research into the approach.

Above all, the many people who have been participants in courses of behavioural family therapy, to assist them with the many stresses in their lives, have provided the feedback that has helped us to shape this approach and improve its effectiveness and efficiency. We are hopeful that this book will lead to many more people deriving benefits from the approach, and we hope that both they and their therapists will continue to provide us with information, not only about the benefits they derive, but also about any major difficulties they encounter with this method, preferably after problem solving their own strategies for countering such problems!

# 1

# COPING WITH STRESS
## The role of the family

The family in its many guises constitutes the greatest natural resource for the management of the wide range of stresses associated with life in our communities, and in the maintenance of both mental and physical health. It is all too easy to criticize the role of the family when breakdowns in this vital role appear to contribute to major health or psychosocial problems, albeit owing to poor nutritional habits, inadequate caring, or a lack of skills in dealing with major life crises, such as bereavement, childbirth, or relationship breakup. In contrast to these dramatic events, the everyday efforts that families contribute to the quality of life of their members may be readily overlooked. However, recent developments in research on the way people cope with stress suggests that the role of the family is crucial in helping people to manage to resolve major stresses in their lives. Furthermore, a series of studies has shown that the way in which a family helps its members to cope with stress may be a major factor in their recovery from physical and mental disorders (Falloon and McGill 1985).

## WHAT IS STRESS?

Stress may be defined as an individual's response to threat. These responses may be psychological, e.g. recognition and emotional response; behavioural, e.g. escape or avoidance responses; physiological, e.g. autonomic arousal, hormonal and biochemical responses; or combinations involving all three systems. In everyday terms, a person may realize that a situation is likely to be stressful, feel apprehensive about it, try to find ways to avoid dealing with it, and find that his or her blood

1

pressure, heart rate, and adrenal hormones are all higher than usual.

However, no two people react in exactly the same way to the same stress (Cooper *et al.* 1985). There is substantial variation in the patterns of stress responses, even when the stresses are of a similar nature, such as the death of a parent. It is likely that each person's response to stress is multidetermined, with bio-genetic factors determining physiological response patterns, and psychological factors, such as personality, conditioning to past experiences, coping skills and being prepared for an expected occurrence, all determining the individual's actions in response to the specific stress. Thus, one person may react to a stressor by producing excess stomach acid leading to heartburn, while another may react to the identical stressor by becoming quiet and socially withdrawn, and yet another with feelings of frustration, and yet another may not experience any undue reaction to the situation.

Although patterns of stress responses vary widely from person to person, each individual tends to develop his or her own characteristic pattern. Where that response is excessive it may lead to a mental or physical disorder, such as a peptic ulcer or a depressive disorder, or a maladaptive psychosocial response, such as an aggressive outburst or self-destructive action (Kety 1984). Health problems are more likely to be triggered when a person is highly vulnerable to a specific disorder. This may be because of an inherited weakness, previous episodes of a major illness, or current poor health status.

It is postulated that the risk of stress-related episodes of impairment is increased where stress exceeds an individual's vulnerability threshold (see Figure 1.1). The level of this threshold is determined by a person's overall vulnerability at any point in time. Exceeding this threshold is associated with a high risk of impaired health. Two types of stressor have been extensively researched.

**Ambient stress** is the stress experienced in dealing with the day-to-day hassles of life in the community. It is an accumulation of stresses in the household, social and leisure pursuits, and in the work environment (DeLongis *et al.* 1982). Such a wide range of stressors is extremely difficult to quantify (Cooper *et al.* 1985). However, household stress has been measured by indices such as 'expressed emotion' (Vaughn and Leff 1976b) and 'family

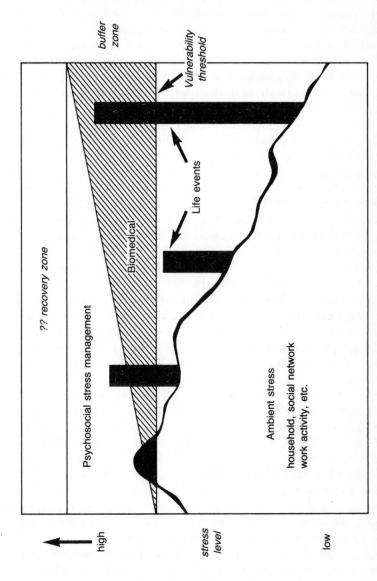

*Figure 1.1* Stress, vulnerability, and clinical management in the determination of outcome of major health problems

burden' (Grad and Sainsbury 1963). Work-related stress and stress in social relationships, including the stresses associated with home-making, childcare, unemployment, and interpersonal relationships, have been less readily measured, yet they are undoubtedly as important as family relationships as sources of ambient stress. Indices of ambient stress have predicted the risk of recurrent episodes of major mental disorders (Leff and Vaughn 1985; Miklowitz *et al.* 1988; Brown and Harris 1978), as well as many physical disorders (Cobb and Rose 1973; Friedman and Rosenman 1959).

**Life events** are more discrete stressors, such as the loss of a job, the death of a close associate, or the breakup of an intimate relationship. Life events that lead to long-term increases in ambient stress have been associated with the onset of major health problems (Brown and Harris 1978; Brown and Birley 1968; Ambelas 1987; Tennant and Andrews 1978; Holmes and Masuda 1973; Edwards and Cooper 1988). It seems likely that, regardless of the specific origins of stress, the longer a person's overall stress level remains above their stress threshold, the greater their chance of succumbing to the major health problems to which they are most vulnerable.

The **coping behaviour** of an individual will modify the level of stress experienced as a result of any stressor. This includes all efforts to resolve the problems associated with the stressor and people's immediate responses to it, and encompasses the problem-solving capacity of the person's intimate social network, particularly the family unit (Pearlin and Schooler 1978; Billings and Moos 1981). Where a person is able to communicate readily with other people in his or her social system, and together they are able to assist in developing efficient strategies for handling the key problems, the risk of a detrimental outcome is likely to be minimized (Falloon and McGill 1985). This is summarized in Figure 1.2. It should be noted that all members of the household may experience increases in their stress levels as a result of shared concern about a major stress that impinges most directly upon one member of the living group (such as a member losing his job; another having a baby; or one person sitting important exams), and that the everyday tensions in the household itself may exceed some people's stress thresholds at times. Thus, as well as dealing with the more dramatic life events, effective family management of stress involves dealing with everyday

4

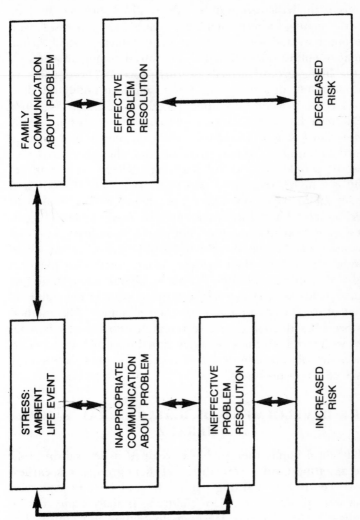

*Figure 1.2*   The roles of family communication and problem resolution

hassles and tensions and the problems of all members of the household, not merely those most vulnerable to health disorders.

It is concluded that the family, or alternative intimate living group, is the basic care unit in industrialized societies. It is the natural setting where members share their stresses with one another, and seek assistance in its effective and efficient management. Considerable skill is required among all members of the living group to facilitate this process. Those skills are seldom taught in a systematic way in modern family development. This probably accounts for the high rate of family breakdown, family violence, and perhaps even contributes to the higher rates of morbidity associated with mental and physical disorders found in industrialized societies when compared with those of people living in tribal settings, where stress management is a highly structured part of everyday life (Falloon and McGill 1985). Certainly where one member of a household develops a disabling disorder of any kind, exceptionally efficient stress management is essential, not merely in assisting with that person's rehabilitation, but also in enabling the other household members to sustain their efforts towards their own personal goals (McCubbin *et al.* 1980). This handbook will outline one approach to assisting families to acquire skills in managing all forms of stress that impinge upon their members. This method has been based upon extensive research into the way families cope with stress, and has been developed over a 20-year period in a series of carefully designed research studies with a wide range of target problems.

## THE DEVELOPMENT OF BEHAVIOURAL FAMILY THERAPY

Behavioural family therapy has developed in several different clinical settings, with several different client groups. The earliest efforts centred on assisting parents to find ways to cope with behaviour problems in their children. Initially many of the children suffered severe learning disabilities and autism, but later developments focused on using similar methods to deal with a variety of conduct disorders. Problems included aggressive behaviour, temper tantrums, bed-wetting, and children with speech and learning difficulties. Parents were trained

6

to administer straightforward rewards and punishments in a highly systematic way when their children displayed specific unwanted behaviours. These initial efforts to apply simple behaviour modification strategies proved somewhat limited in their effectiveness, particularly when efforts focused exclusively on eliminating unwanted behaviours rather than on the development of a more effective repertoire of interpersonal problem-solving skills for *both* the parents and the children. Gerald Patterson and John Reid, two psychologists from Eugene, Oregon, pioneered these methods, and over the past two decades have continued to develop increasingly effective family interventions for families who seek help for their difficulties in coping with disturbed behaviour in their young children (Patterson 1971; 1988).

The second major figure in the development of family-based stress management was Robert Liberman (1970). He applied similar detailed analysis of the contingencies surrounding ambient stress in family households and their association with psychosocial and health problems. His work as a community-based psychiatrist involved adults as the target population and emphasized the need for each family member to define clearly his or her personal goals and to obtain mutual support from other household members in the pursuit of those goals. These approaches were highly consistent with the development of systemic theories of family interaction that were being proposed by family theorists at that time. Richard Stuart, a social worker, extended the reciprocity concepts in his development of behavioural marital therapy (Stuart 1969). He noted how marital distress appeared to develop as couples began to focus increasingly on each other's negative responses and paid minimal attention to the everyday exchanges of positive feelings. He found that helping couples to restructure their interaction patterns so that they began to increase their acknowledgement of mutually rewarding interaction, no matter how brief and seemingly insignificant, provided a milieu in which major disagreements could be resolved more readily than where marital counselling focused exclusively on solving the conflicts that couples initially targeted for therapy. Stuart had derived these ideas from Thibaut and Kelley (1959), who postulated that 'the exact pattern of interaction that takes place between spouses is never accidental; it represents the most rewarding of all the available alternatives ... it represents the best balance which each can achieve between individual and mutual rewards and costs' (p. 12).

This is the theoretical basis for much of the subsequent development in behavioural interventions with families. Family members are considered always to select the responses to specific situations that at each point in time represent their 'best' efforts to resolve the problems that they confront. This applies even when the chosen responses appear destructive rather than constructive to harmonious relationships. Thus, behavioural family therapists have always acknowledged the problem-solving *efforts* of all family members rather than their *achievements*, and attempted to build upon the strengths of individuals, rather than focus on their all too obvious defects.

This focus on enhancement of positive communication often led to conflict resolution, particularly in couples where the main source of conflict was a lack of mutual reinforcement for everyday events. However, where the family conflicts centred on disturbed behaviour in children or the disabilities associated with severe mental or physical disorders, it was apparent that enhancement of communication did not necessarily resolve major stressors. This led to the addition of problem-solving strategies to the intervention approach. Family members were trained to employ approaches that incorporated brainstorming techniques in an attempt to structure their conflict resolution into systematic discussions that would lead to clearly defined plans, rather than acrimonious rows. These methods were pioneered by therapists working with a wide range of client groups, including marital distress (Jacobson and Margolin 1979; Weiss 1980); premarital counselling (Markman and Floyd 1980); childhood conduct disorders (Griest and Wells 1983); adolescent conflict (Alexander and Parsons 1982; Foster *et al.* 1983); developmentally disabled (Harris 1983); adult mental disorders (Falloon *et al.* 1984) and dementias (Zarit and Zarit 1982). Most of these applications have been supported by controlled trials that clearly demonstrate their effectiveness in clinical practice (Falloon 1991).

The increasing sophistication of intervention strategies has been accompanied by similar advances in the assessment processes. Rather than merely counting the numbers of positive and negative responses observed during problem-related discussions, methods of examining sequences of family inter-action were developed. The methods of Hahlweg and his colleagues (Hahlweg *et al.* 1984) enabled the development of heated arguments to be mapped, and contrasted with construc-tive expressions of unpleasant feelings that contributed to effec-tive conflict resolution. It was established that the expression of unpleasant feelings in a manner that assisted in the clear definition of a specific problem, rather than through coercive nagging or hostile comments, was a crucial first step to conflict resolution.

A final component of behavioural intervention strategies has been the incorporation of a range of specific strategies that have been demonstrated as highly effective in dealing with specific problems. These strategies have included interpersonal skills training, anxiety management, cognitive restructuring, in addition to the operant reinforcement methods employed in the early behavioural approaches. Where families have been caring for a person with a disabling disorder, specific education has been provided for the person and family to enhance their under-standing and enable them to participate fully in the long-term care process (Falloon *et al.* 1984).

The high rates of successful application of these methods have somewhat obscured the problems associated with the approach, including the people who fail to derive any benefits. While it has been accepted that some families are slower to learn than others, it has been assumed that, given sufficient time, all families will acquire the skills and use them to manage the stresses they experience. However, in recent years greater emphasis has been placed on those people who have major problems incorporating these communication and problem-solving strategies into their everyday lives (Birchler 1988). At the moment there is little research to support the use of any particular strategies for enhancing adherence to the relatively small, but highly significant, changes in lifestyle that these methods seek to achieve. However, there is evidence that the training methods employed by therapists may play an important role (Patterson 1988). This has led to the development of methods of assessing the competence of therapists in the application of behavioural interventions with families (Laporta *et al.* 1989).

## WHAT IS A FAMILY?

Most family therapies address the needs of the typical western middle-class family of Mom, Dad, and two children, preferably one boy and one girl. However, households consisting of such stereotyped family arrangements are found less and less frequently. There are numerous combinations of families, such as multigenerational, single parent, multiparent, multifamily, adopted parental, sibling or avuncular households. In addition many people live in family-style households who are not blood relatives. These include young adults sharing households, gay relationships, residential schools and training centres, hostels, boarding homes, and lodgings.

Furthermore, family care extends well beyond the confines of the family home, with continued and extensive support being provided for family members when they are residing in households other than the family home. Vast improvements in telecommunications and modern transportation have enabled people to remain in close contact while at different ends of the earth. The concept of the intimate social network that provides both emotional and physical support for an individual on an everyday basis probably encompasses the notion of a 'family' much better than that tied solely to people sharing a living space, or those related by birth. Even the homeless person sleeping on the streets may have a close support network of fellow itinerants who are deeply concerned for his or her day-to-day welfare. It is a sad reflection that sometimes people in such situations may receive greater supportive human contact than those living in mansions with relatives, or in the splendid social isolation of modern housing estates.

The definition of a family used in behavioural family therapy is a broad one that requires one of two features to be present:

- *either* those people who live in the same household living unit, sharing the everyday responsibility for the organization and maintenance of that unit;
- *or* those people who are the key providers of emotional support for an individual on an everyday basis, regardless of the location of their residence.

Throughout this book we will be using the term 'family' according to this definition. The approaches to therapy that we will be

10

*Table 1.1* Problems likely to benefit from behavioural family therapy strategies

| | |
|---|---|
| PSYCHOSOCIAL | * children's conduct disorders<br>* learning disabilities and autism<br>* adolescent behavioural disturbance<br>* marital and family conflict<br>* sexual dysfunction<br>* drug and alcohol misuse<br>* family violence and child abuse<br>* premarital counselling<br>* divorce mediation<br>* eating disorders<br>* suicide prevention<br>* residential care: homes, hostels, etc.<br>* criminal offending problems |
| BIOMEDICAL | * depression<br>* bipolar disorders<br>* schizophrenia<br>* anxiety disorders<br>* relapse prevention<br>* chronic physical health problems<br>* dementias<br>* prevention of stress-related disorders in high-risk groups |

outlining have been employed successfully with a multitude of households and social network groups. The typical group numbers two to six participants, with groups of ten or more proving somewhat unwieldy. However, many therapeutic units are structured around even larger numbers living in the same household, and these approaches have been adapted to assist in the management of stress in these households.

## CONCLUSIONS

It is concluded that behavioural family therapy provides a structure for assisting people living together in small, shared living groups to enhance the quality of their efforts to assist each other in coping with the multitude of stressors that they encounter in their everyday lives, as well as those less frequent major life crises. This is achieved mainly through improving the efficiency of the problem-solving functions of the group through enhancement of interpersonal communication skills combined with clearer structuring of regular problem-solving discussions. The overall aim is to minimize periods of high stress that threaten to overwhelm the coping capacity of members of the household, particularly those members who may be highly vulnerable to stress-related health or psychosocial problems. Additional strategies, including the full range of cognitive and behavioural strategies, psychoeducation, and targeted pharmaco-therapy, may all be combined with this approach to provide a comprehensive plan of care for serious psychosocial and health problems. The range of problems likely to benefit from the application of behavioural family therapy is summarized in Table 1.1.

# 2

# ENGAGING FAMILIES IN BEHAVIOURAL FAMILY THERAPY

In order that an intervention programme succeeds in improving the efficiency of stress management in a household it is necessary for all members of that household to be committed to the programme. In behavioural family therapy (BFT) it is assumed that adherence to all aspects of the programme requires some special effort and that, unless each participant perceives that the short-term and long-term benefits are greater than the efforts that they expend, they are unlikely to participate fully in the process. Specific measures must be undertaken with every family to maximize adherence to all aspects of the programme. These measures begin with the initial contacts with household members and continue throughout the entire course of the intervention with each family.

The major aim of the therapist is to assist *every participant* to attain his or her chosen personal goals. The family unit is a powerful resource to assist members to achieve their desired benefits, and to reduce the stress that they may encounter along the way. The problems encountered by any participant usually affect every other person in the household. Each problem issue is taken at face value, carefully evaluated and an action planned with the assistance of the entire family group. Specific problem-solving or goal achievement strategies are individually tailored to different problems in different households. Unlike some family-based therapies, they are not preconceived according to theoretical notions, and offer maximal flexibility.

We will describe the various strategies employed to ensure that effective engagement is initiated and then maintained as a cooperative and therapeutic alliance throughout therapy.

## OUTLINE OF THE BFT INTERVENTION

BFT is designed so that in every aspect, including the beginning and ending of therapy, it contributes to engaging and fostering self-help skills in the family.

The overall outline of BFT includes:

(a) Initial meetings with the household members.
(b) Meetings with each participant individually.
(c) Training in specific skills to enhance stress management efficiency of the household.
(d) Disengagement of the therapist.

This chapter will focus on the specific strategies employed to engage with all household members, and to ensure that the disengagement process is successfully negotiated. Subsequent chapters detail individual assessments and the skill training procedures.

### Getting started: the initial meeting with the family

At the outset of therapy, before BFT is embarked upon, a first meeting with the family is scheduled. This meeting is different in some ways from other sessions in the course of therapy. Both for the family and the therapist, meeting for the first time is an important moment. Each person comes with his or her expectations and wishes, and this meeting is a golden opportunity for each person to understand how therapy can fulfil these. In the first meeting, after getting to know the family, the therapist sets out to outline clearly the following issues about therapy:

– the goals of the family intervention;
– the role of the therapist;
– the expectations of all the participants;
– how sessions and the therapy as a whole unfold.

The therapist introduces the meeting by saying:

'I am very pleased to see you all here for this meeting. The purpose of meeting with you all at this stage is to give you some information about the methods we use to assist families and to answer your questions as best I can, so that you know exactly what is involved. We find that when people can make sense of the things that we may ask them

14

to do they benefit more than when they do not feel they are involved in the process. At the end of our discussion I will give you a sheet that summarizes the key points that I am going to make, so don't worry if you cannot remember everything that we talk about right now (see sample guide sheet, 'Guidelines for Family-Based Treatment' pages 222–8).

'The points I would like to cover are the following: 1. What are the goals of this approach?; 2. What is my role?; 3. What would I like each of you to do?; and 4. What is going to happen in future meetings that we hope to have? I would like you to be very clear about all these points. Please feel free to stop me at any time and ask clarifying questions about any aspect.'

It is seldom possible to provide more than an overview of the BFT approach at this initial meeting. Further details are provided at each subsequent phase of the programme, and revision about key points may be conducted at any stage, particularly at times when important components of the approach are not adhered to. A common issue concerns the lack of real-life practice, and the rationale for this may need to be outlined repeatedly.

The *goals of the family intervention* are:

1 To assist every participant to achieve the *personal goals* considered most important to him or her.
2 To help each person become efficient at dealing with the stresses that he or she is experiencing, and able to work together to help every other member of the household resolve his or her stresses. The family is a great resource for helping individuals to manage their stresses and burdens. The programme aims to harness that resource and to maximize its effectiveness. This is achieved mainly through regular family meetings in the home where a structured problem-solving approach is employed routinely.
3 To enhance the *clinical management* of any stress-related disorder to which any household members are highly vulnerable. This can be accomplished through increased understanding of the disorder to prepare better for major episodes; efficient stress management to prevent episodes that may be triggered by stress; specific strategies to cope with problems that might arise during the course of the disorder; compliance

15

training and understanding of optimal drug treatment where indicated.

The *therapist outlines his role* as follows:

1 To *assess* the major strengths and weaknesses of the family in managing their stresses and achieving their goals. Detailed assessment will be done initially with each participant. This will be reviewed briefly at the beginning of each session, with major reviews every three months.

2 To *teach* families strategies that may assist them in improving their current best efforts at stress management and goal achievement. Family strengths are used as a starting point for all training.

3 To employ methods that are essentially *educative*, to give training in skills; these training methods are different from many other family therapy and psychotherapy approaches that participants may have experienced.

4 To encourage participants to practise new ways of managing real-life situations during the sessions with coaching from other participants as well as the therapist.

5 To disengage from active participation at the earliest possible time and to sit on the sidelines to coach and encourage participants. This facilitates real-life performance of newly acquired skills.

6 To be available for crisis consultation on a continuing basis. Arrangements for after-hours consultations are outlined with phone numbers and specific guidelines provided in writing.

7 To respect individuals' specific needs for confidentiality, and to apply any statutory duties, such as reporting of child abuse or criminal activities.

8 To acquire permission to record sessions for supervision. Sign consent forms regarding this when necessary.

*Participants* are expected to take specific *responsibilities:*

1 To maintain active involvement in defining the nature and content of all issues dealt with throughout the programme. Participants are the experts on the difficulties they experience and the solutions that appear most likely to resolve them. The therapist can coach them in problem-solving skills, but cannot take responsibility for their problem resolution.

2 The success of the approach depends entirely on household

members' application of problem-solving skills in their every-day lives. To assist them in this task specific real-life practice will be assigned at the end of every session.

3 Each household is expected to convene a *family meeting* every week, during which time they coordinate their goal achievement and problem-solving efforts without the assistance of the therapist.

4 *Attendance* of all household members at both therapist-led sessions and family meetings is essential to attaining the goals of the intervention. Where absences cannot be avoided the therapist or family may be able to reschedule sessions.

5 Taking drugs or alcohol, physical violence, or other major disruptive behaviour is *not permitted* during sessions. Sessions will be stopped immediately and members ejected if necessary.

6 For home-based sessions, plans may need to be made to minimize disruptions from telephone calls, visitors, and meal preparation, etc.

The *format of sessions* can be outlined in the following manner:

1 The *duration* of sessions is expected to be one hour. This may vary according to need. For example, where a major crisis is being resolved the session may be extended, and where the family have acquired good problem-solving skills sessions may be completed in 30–40 minutes.

2 The *structure* of each session consists of essentially four parts:
   (a) assessment of progress and difficulties with personal goals, review of family meeting, review of status of specific disorders;
   (b) review of real-life practice based on the previous sessions;
   (c) training in specific skills;
   (d) assignment of real-life practice to incorporate skills into everyday lives.

3 The *number of sessions* likely to be needed will be agreed after the assessment of the family, and may vary from one or two to regular meetings extending over several years. The usual programme involves around 10–12 sessions at weekly intervals during a three-month period, followed by several booster sessions at monthly intervals. The initial contract is made for the first three months only, with further plans being based upon the review of progress at each three-month point.

4 BFT is considered as a long-term commitment with the aim

17

of enhancing problem-solving efficiency indefinitely. However, the therapist aims to disengage at the earliest possible time, and to provide the minimal amount of intervention to ensure that efficient problem-solving activity is maintained. The timing of disengagement from regular training sessions is based solely upon evidence that the family has incorporated the problem-solving skills into everyday life to the best of their ability. However, continued monitoring is usually necessary, with plans for revision sessions made according to the needs of each household. In a sense the therapy is never considered 'complete', and the therapist and his or her team may provide continual monitoring for some families, particularly those where one or more members are vulnerable to major stress-related disorders.

## Who attends sessions?

One question that is frequently asked is 'Who should come to the sessions?'. The stress management approach aims to encompass all those individuals who form the core social network for each vulnerable person, or all those who may be able to make a substantial contribution to the stress management of the household. The following people may be considered for assessment, and subsequent attendance at training sessions:

- all members of the household;
- all those involved in major caregiving roles for a vulnerable person;
- intimate (i.e. close) friends or family members not resident in the household.

Children may be included provided that they are able to attend to, and understand, the training process. Most children who are 10 years old will have little difficulty, but many younger children are also capable of making valuable contributions.

The optimal size of the training group is no more than six participants. Thus in residential settings with larger households it may be more effective to run a number of small groups than attempt to establish training a large household group. The above criteria for including people in the training may assist in determining the membership of these sub-groupings.

Participation of individuals will be difficult when their

concentration is disrupted by symptoms of their disorders. When a person is experiencing an exacerbation of schizophrenia, a manic episode, or is severely slowed with depression he or she may find it difficult to attend to training. The same may be true for people with persistent learning deficits or psychotic symptoms. Initial training sessions are best delayed until all key members are able to attend to the best of their ability, and special strategies (see page 160) may need to be used to assist those who remain persistently disabled. However, the highly structured nature of the sessions allows many people with attentional difficulties, who would not be considered for other therapeutic approaches, to participate in BFT sessions.

### Incorporating skills into everyday life

Behavioural interventions ensure that the interpersonal skills rehearsed in the sessions are incorporated into each participant's everyday life. Specific strategies are employed to ensure that this transfer of skills occurs as efficiently as possible. These include:

- *Home-based sessions.* Learning skills in the same setting as they will be applied in real-life facilitates generalization. For this reason sessions are conducted in the home, whenever this is feasible. It has been estimated that this 'on-the-job' training almost doubles the efficiency of the approach, with skills being incorporated into the family lifestyle in half the time it would take if sessions were office-based. Although efforts to re-enact issues in a realistic way are feasible in settings outside the home it is seldom possible to replicate all the relevant aspects. For example, in sessions in the office, Pam was able to practise requesting help with preparing meals in the kitchen. Yet she was consistently unable actually to perform this skill at home in between sessions. When her therapist transferred sessions to the home it became clear that the kitchen was in an enclosed space, and that the television was usually on in the living room. When she went to the next room to request help, she could not make good eye contact with those watching the screen, and did not speak loudly or assertively enough to be heard over the loud background television sound. Specific ways of making eye contact and being heard included turning down the volume of the television and standing in full view of those watching to request some help. In the week after the home-based session, she was able to get help as wished by applying the specific techniques practised in the session.

- *Re-enactment of real-life performance.* In addition to conducting training in the home or other real-life locations (e.g. job centres, restaurants, coffee shops, pubs, shops), participants practise dealing with the stressful situations that are of concern to them by re-enacting the situations in precisely the manner they occurred. In the above example, Pam practised making a request with her family engrossed in the television in exactly the same way as on the occasions when she had failed to gain their assistance. Such re-enactments may appear to take more time than a mere discussion or a less elaborate role play. However, such practice facilitates the transfer process, and is usually an excellent investment in therapy time.

- *Real-life practice.* At the end of each session, the therapist and family carefully agree on specific assignments to ensure that they practise the skills they have learned in the sessions in their everyday lives. These assignments are carefully explained and examples given before the end of a session. Specific worksheets are provided for each set of communication and problem-solving skills. This real-life practice is reviewed at the beginning of the next session, with feedback, re-enactment, and further training when needed.

- *The family meeting.* In order to ensure that the locus of family problem solving and goal achievement remains within the household group a weekly meeting of all household members is convened in addition to the therapy. The meeting lasts approximately 30 minutes, and is arranged at a regular time and location, and employs a business-like structure. A chairperson and a secretary are elected from among the participants, and reports are made at the beginning of each session with the therapist. The agenda is set by participants, who use this meeting to deal with their own goals and problems. It is hoped that these sessions will be incorporated into family life and will continue long after the training has been completed. The family meeting may not seem necessary when therapist-led sessions are held at weekly intervals. However, they do enable the therapist to focus on the *structure* of interpersonal communication and problem solving rather than on the current 'hot' issues, which may be addressed during the family meetings.

As training progresses the therapist hands over more and more of the structuring of the sessions to the family chairperson and secretary, so that the two sessions become identical in all respects, and the therapist eventually becomes redundant, unless a major crisis arises. This is another example of the way BFT aims to foster real-life practice.

- *Booster sessions.* Even when skills have been incorporated into the daily routines of the household it is likely that there will be a decrease in the efficiency with which they are applied over time. It is helpful to recognize this fact and to plan one or more booster sessions over the ensuing months and years. These sessions provide a review of current goal achievement and problem-solving functions and revision as needed.

### Focus on structure rather than content

The behavioural family therapy approach focuses on the way in which living groups structure their goal achievement and problem resolution interactions, rather than on the particular goals and problems that participants encounter. Only rarely, when major crises arise, does the therapist concern himself with the issues that are the targets for the family problem-solving efforts. In all other circumstances the therapist provides training in the manner in which people express their feelings, concerns, and needs to each other, and the manner in which they go about resolving those issues.

At times the content of an issue may interfere with the ability of participants to learn communication or problem-solving skills. This is usually a 'hot' issue that arouses considerable emotional responses in one or more participants. The therapist should endeavour to steer families away from addressing such issues in the early phases of their training when they are

21

learning ways of enhancing their skills. At times when an argument appears imminent, the therapist may need to stop the discussion assertively and get the group to choose a less stressful topic so that learning the steps of a particular skill can be facilitated during the session. The 'hot' issue can be dealt with during the family meeting, although the therapist may recommend that it be deferred until the family acquires more effective problem-solving skills enabling the issue to be resolved with minimal stress. Of course, some issues cannot be deferred, and the therapist may need to take a break from the training agenda to provide crisis intervention. This will also apply when participants deviate from the guidelines laid down for the sessions, particularly those relating to unacceptable behaviour.

## Focus on effort rather than achievement

Throughout the assessment and training the therapist focuses upon the efforts that each participant makes to enhance the quality of life of the household, even when these efforts are relatively minor and produce minimal achievements. Feedback is always directed to note these efforts and ensures that they are noted and rewarded by all participants. It is acknowledged that each person's responses to any situation represent their *best efforts* to function within the constraints imposed upon them by their personal resources, such as intelligence, past experience, skills repertoire, health problems, as well as interpersonal and social resources, such as their perceptions of the responses of others, availability of work, recreation, housing, or financial opportunities, etc. Thus, even when performance appears far from optimal it is never simply a matter of a person 'not trying', or deliberately behaving in an 'inappropriate' manner. It is assumed that if we were placed in an identical situation, with identical skills and resources, we would probably respond in a similar manner. This level of empathy is something all behavioural family therapists strive to achieve. Furthermore, the approach aims to facilitate similar empathic feedback among all participants.

Major deficiencies in interpersonal performance are subsequently addressed from a supportive learning perspective, where the participants re-enact the scenarios and attempt to respond in alternative ways that may provide greater benefits.

22

The repeated consistent application of this approach to enhancing interpersonal effectiveness throughout all aspects of the programme is considered a major component in the development and maintenance of a therapeutic alliance with every participant.

## Disengagement

Ending a programme of BFT may be perceived as a stressful life event for many participants. It will be more likely to prove highly stressful if the therapist's departure is precipitous and unprepared. However, if effective plans have been made for this event the stress is less likely to provoke a crisis. As we have noted, the therapist aims to make himself redundant from the beginning of the programme, and the duration of training is determined by the time expected for this process to be completed. At such a point participants will have developed sufficient self-help skills to be expected to be able to sustain the key benefits of the intervention programme in their everyday lives together. Nevertheless it is useful to have some guidelines to assist in coping with the anticipated stress of ending regular therapist contacts. These include the following:

1 Contract a fixed number of sessions, or fixed time period when you initially engage a family in treatment.
2 Remind them at regular intervals of the number of sessions (time) completed, and of sessions (time) remaining.
3 Plan your interventions so that you hand over the responsibility of problem solving to them from the earliest sessions. Adopt the role of 'coach'; avoid becoming 'team captain'. Sit on the sidelines and assist the participants in trying out new strategies.
4 Remind participants that you will be leaving them in the future and ensure that they take responsibility for conducting their own family meetings as well as playing a prominent role in structuring problem-solving discussions during the training sessions.
5 Avoid acting as a friend. Do not 'help out' by finding information for the family, when they can seek that information for themselves. They will value learning how to deal with the various social or health agencies themselves, especially when you are no longer available to 'help out'.

6 Several weeks before your agreed date of termination, suggest that the family conduct a problem-solving discussion on the issue of ending BFT sessions. Let them define their own stresses, strategies, and plans.

7 If sessions are to continue in some format, such as booster sessions or a support group, prepare participants for this change. Educate them about the nature, goals, and expectations of the alternative sessions.

8 Review progress on personal goals, residual stresses, and goal achievement and problem-solving skills during the penultimate session. Highlight constructive changes and emphasize the work they have done to achieve these changes. Assist participants to define their future goals and to commit themselves to continue their family meetings on a permanent weekly basis.

9 Leave the final session free for any important unfinished business. Allow the family to structure this session in the manner they desire.

## CONCLUSIONS

The range of specific strategies that form the basis for the therapeutic alliance between participants and therapists engaged in behavioural family therapy has been outlined in this chapter. It is evident that considerable effort is made to ensure that people are informed about the precise nature of the approach before committing themselves to a course of therapy. A written summary of the points is provided for each participant which they can refer to later. Some therapists have found it useful to structure this as a contract between the therapist and each participant. However, at the time of the initial meeting it is not clear what the assessment process will reveal, and therefore the precise form that the intervention is likely to take. It is even possible that the assessment will reveal that the strengths of the household are such that no training is indicated.

The initial overview provides a general idea about the nature of the approach. Further discussion will be provided as each phase of the training unfolds. Some therapists have found that demonstrations of key aspects of the approach, such as how a scene may be re-enacted, or how a family meeting is structured, may prove helpful. The use of brief videotaped examples of key aspects of the approach may be useful and may reassure anxious participants, some of whom may have found previous experiences of psychotherapeutic interventions somewhat traumatic. However, we have found that the vast majority of people are readily engaged in this approach when it is carefully explained to them. Moreover, once engaged their participation is sustained with minimal difficulty. Specific strategies for managing instances where adherence to the approach is suboptimal are addressed in Chapter 8 (pages 160–73).

# 3

# ASSESSMENT OF THE FAMILY UNIT

## INTRODUCTION

The sources of stress in families are extremely varied. They reflect the conflicts between personal aspirations of individual household members and the wide range of constraints placed upon them by their social habitat. The assessment of family functioning from a behavioural perspective focuses upon the efficiency of the household as a problem-solving unit. This is summarized in Table 3.1. The strengths and weaknesses of the household group in resolving the problems associated with stresses that impact upon the biomedical and psychosocial vulnerabilities of each member while they are attempting to pursue their life goals are a major consideration in this approach. It is assumed that each household member may contribute both to the stress and to the problem-solving capacity of his or her social milieu, and that no person is invulnerable to the effects of stress. Thus, the approach aims to facilitate stress management, while at the same time enhancing the quality of life of *every* member.

It is assumed that at all times people are responding with their best efforts to resolve problems and achieve goals. However, at times the 'best' efforts of one person may create problems for others in his or her intimate social circle. Thus, problem solving is usually most effective when carried out in a mutual manner that includes all those people who are closely involved with the issue or its potential solutions. Where one or more members of an intimate household group are highly vulnerable to a major disabling health problem, the household may need to become super-efficient in the everyday management of stress, not merely to assist those vulnerable members to reduce the risks of recurring episodes of their disorders, but also to enable all household members to continue to pursue their personal goals without restriction. A crucial component of this highly efficient problem-solving capacity is the ability of all members of the living group to communicate effectively with each other so that they can sit down together and discuss their problems and goals in a direct, open, and supportive manner that facilitates the problem-solving process. However, merely enhancing the interpersonal communication between family members may not result in better problem solving. Additional structuring of the discussions may improve the quality of problem-solving functions and enable effective plans to be implemented to reduce stress and achieve goals with maximum efficiency. Thus, the assessment of the family involves an exploration of the way in which the living group conducts their communication and problem solving to facilitate the achievement of each member's personal goals. This assessment is a continuous process that guides the precise choice of intervention strategies throughout clinical management.

## GOALS OF ASSESSMENT

The assessment process aims to achieve the following goals:

1 To develop a therapeutic alliance with every household member.
2 To define each member's understanding of the nature and clinical management of any disorders to which he or she and others are highly vulnerable.
3 To define the specific personal goals of each household member.
4 To define specific problems that may need to be resolved for each person to achieve specific personal goals.
5 To define the strengths and weaknesses of each household member that may contribute to or detract from mutual problem solving.
6 To define the strengths and weaknesses of the household group as a problem-solving unit.
7 To devise a method of monitoring progress towards greater problem-solving efficiency, stress management, and goal achievement.

*Table 3.1* Behavioural analysis of a family system

| Targets | Methods | Primary goals | Secondary goals |
|---|---|---|---|
| 1. Individual family members | Interviews<br>Questionnaires<br>Self-observation<br>Therapist observation | Identify assets<br>Identify deficits<br>Define problem behaviours<br>Determine reinforcement patterns<br>Determine motivation to change | Develop therapeutic alliance<br>Identify responses of other members to his/her problem behaviours<br>Identify responses to problem behaviours of other members<br>Determine motivation to change his/her responses to problem behaviours of others |
| 2. Family group | Family interview<br>Questionnaires<br>Self-observation<br>Structured family interaction tasks<br>Role playing<br>Naturalistic observation (e.g. at home) | Identify group assets<br>Identify group deficits<br>Define individual roles in group<br>Define communication and problem-solving patterns | Develop cohesive, problem-solving milieu<br>Determine mutual reinforcement patterns |
| 3. Specific problem behaviours | All of above | Pinpoint discrete problem behaviours that induce a negative effect on the family as a whole, and/or on individual family members | Determine whether family therapy vs. individual therapy vs. both indicated |

| | | | |
|---|---|---|---|
| 4. Functional analysis of specific problem behaviours | All of above | Identify all contingencies surrounding each specific problem:<br><br>– antecedents } short and long term<br>– consequences }<br><br>– modifying factors | What triggers problem behaviours; what maintains them; how people cope with them<br><br>Determine problems most readily modified<br><br>Determine probability of obtaining maximum benefit from potential interventions on family system |
| 5. Treatment goals | Family interviews | Choose one or more problem behaviours likely to produce maximum benefits for family system if effectively resolved<br><br>Define a treatment plan that details specific goals, specific interventions, specific duration of interventions, specific assessment procedures | Define sub-goals and sub-steps<br><br>Define therapist assets and deficits in conducting desired intervention procedures |
| 6. Review | Therapy observations<br><br>Family members' reports<br><br>Structured assessments | Define progress towards specific goals<br><br>Identify further problem behaviours<br><br>Continue functional analysis<br><br>Prepare future specific goals and intervention | Provide feedback to family and therapist |

## PROCEDURES

The assessment is conducted in a series of interviews with household members and in meetings with the family group. The focus of these interviews is problem-oriented, with problem issues presented by household members being subjected to a fine-grained analysis that seeks to pinpoint the precise dysfunction that may contribute to their lack of resolution. The presence of unresolved problems and continued high levels of ambient stress are the result of the household unit's best problem-solving efforts. The assessment is directed to confirm this assumption, and to define the specific deficits that might need to be countered to enhance problem resolution and consequent goal achievement. Thus, the assessor is interested in finding out the effective strategies that the family employs as well as any deficiencies.

### Assessment of individual members of the household

The initial step of assessment entails an interview with each household member. The suggested format is provided in Appendix B (page 204). Several issues are discussed with the individual in a semi-structured way. These include:

#### Background information

Relevant information is obtained about the person's medical and social background, in particular, to define that person's vulnerability to major health problems and psychosocial disability. The major concerns are associated with the person's past history of episodes of major mental or physical disorders, evidence of similar episodes in close relatives, general coping capacity as reflected by education, social, and vocational attainment. For example, 54-year-old May was the main carer of David, a 24-year-old who had had three episodes of a schizophrenic disorder. She had experienced a depressive disorder after the birth of her daughter, Janie. She worked as a school teacher, a job she found very stressful at times, particularly when her partner, Tony, was abroad. She had begun experiencing the menopause, and had found herself having brief periods of depressed mood. This background assessment suggested that May might be vulnerable to further major depressive episodes that might be prevented by biomedical and psychosocial stress management.

### Understanding of index person's disorder

Where one or more household members have experienced episodes of a major psychosocial or biomedical disorder, an assessment of each household member's (including the index person's) understanding of the key aspects about the nature and clinical management of those disorders is conducted. This includes the type of disorder, its suspected causes, factors that make it better and worse, the benefits and unwanted effects of the main treatment strategies that the person has received, and understanding of the expected outcome. This part of the assessment enables the assessor to determine the need for family education to correct deficits in understanding that may contribute to enhanced clinical management of the condition.

In the previous example, both May and David had experienced episodes of serious disorders. The assessor enquired about each household member's understanding of each episode. It was clear that May's vulnerability to hormonal changes was well understood by Tony, but he was unaware of any connection between environmental stress factors and worsening of her condition. All household members, including David, had minimal understanding about the nature and clinical management of his disorder, and reported that this lack of understanding was a major source of stress in the household, even during times when David's disorder was in remission.

### Impact of the disorder on the household

Specific examples of problems associated with the index person's disorder experienced by each household member are discussed. The manner in which each person copes with these problems is pinpointed. This includes discussion of both effective and ineffective coping strategies. An overall assessment of the burden that carers experience, perceived as being associated with the disorder, is made.

May reported that she often worried about David, particularly when she heard him playing music during the night. She associated this with the time when he had his first episode, when he spent long periods sleeping during the day and playing music throughout the night. Her usual way of coping with this behaviour was to ignore it, tell herself that he would be all right while he continued to take his medicine. But she tried to keep a close watch on him, and frequently asked him how he was feeling. This irritated him and reminded him of his disorder. She felt somewhat reassured when he told her he was OK. She said she was frightened that something dreadful would happen and she would blame herself for not having done something to prevent it, but she did not know what she should be doing.

Household members suffering from major disorders have a more extensive interview that seeks to target one or two key problems experienced as a result of the disorder. This *problem analysis* examines the strengths and weaknesses of individual and family problem-solving efforts. An attempt is made to define the manner in which the problems contribute to enduring disabilities and handicaps, and to pinpoint potential blocks to effective problem resolution.

David reported having difficulties getting off to sleep. He felt restless when he went to bed, and thoughts about how his disorder had disrupted his life's plans went round and round in his mind. He found that listening to music, looking at magazines, and taking an extra side-effects tablet seemed to help. Any setbacks during the day, discussions with Tony about his future, or days when he accomplished very little tended to make his restlessness worse. He also noted that it was at its worst for two or three days after his fortnightly injection of medication. He had not discussed this with his doctor or members of his household, but had read a book that said that restlessness could be a side effect of several drugs used for mental disorders. He noted that he would be more alert during the day if this problem was resolved, but on the other hand would spend less time listening to music – his favourite pastime.

This simple detective work suggested to the assessor that David might be experiencing difficulties associated with his drug therapy, and that consultation with his doctor might remedy this. However, he also noted that David did not communicate his distress to either his informal or his professional carers, and had not come to terms with his disabilities. The assessor helped David to set himself new goals that he could gain satisfaction from, despite all the setbacks he had encountered. It was also evident that David was not devoid of coping strategies, and was able to find methods to enable him to manage stresses that might have overwhelmed other people faced with his predicament.

The behavioural therapist tries to maintain an objective attitude throughout the assessment. No special emphasis is placed upon any particular aspect of the responses that people make to their life stresses. A person's thoughts, feelings, and emotions are all considered highly relevant aspects of problem solving. The assessor avoids being drawn into immediate demands for problem resolution during the assessment phase, unless it is clear that the problem represents a major crisis necessitating urgent resolution. This enables the assessor to maintain an open mind about the precise mechanisms that lead to persisting or recurrent problems and the specific strengths and weaknesses of family problem solving.

### Reinforcement survey

Patterns of human behaviour are never random, although at times they may seem haphazard and unplanned. It is assumed that the patterns of people's lives are determined by the rewards they experience from the variety of activities they engage in, and that those activities performed most frequently represent the most rewarding for them at any particular time. In contrast, those activities performed least are those that are less rewarding, and on occasions may be aversive in nature to that person. The reinforcement survey is a relatively simple way to assess the quality of a person's life that contrasts actual patterns of everyday activity with those the person desires. Each household member is invited to list his or her most frequent activities, as well as the people and places that he or she spends most time with. When they have completed these lists they are asked to list those activities, people, and places that they would like to spend more time with in an ideal world, where current problems and constraints were removed. The discrepancies between *current* everyday lifestyles and *desired* lifestyles are noted. High levels of discrepancy may reflect levels of dissatisfaction and frustration. They may also provide drive to define and subsequently achieve changes that will enable that person to reduce the gap between current and desired lifestyles. Such changes may be targeted as that person's specific goals in the intervention programme.

Tony completed the following reinforcement survey:

| Activities | Current | Desired |
|---|---|---|
| | work | holidays with family |
| | travel abroad | going to theatre |
| | playing golf | having friends over |
| | gardening | playing piano |
| Locations | office | home – patio |
| | hotels | resorts |
| | bedroom | friends' homes |
| | golf course | |
| People | work associates | May, David, Janie |
| | friend Roger | old friends |
| | golfing friends | |

**Supportive persons:** May, Roger

**Aversive situations:** flying, ill-mannered people, talking with or about David to anyone

It was evident that Tony was leading a kind of lifestyle that he was eager to change. He mentioned that he had been on a temporary assignment abroad when David was first unwell. He found it difficult to deal with his disappointment at that time, and had tended to avoid involvement with the family since then. His eagerness to work abroad was a direct response to this, and although he found little satisfaction from this, he preferred it to being at home. However, he was eager to change this situation and to become re-engaged with his family and old friends again.

*Goal setting*

Each household member is invited to choose two goals that he or she believes could be readily achieved during the contracted period of treatment (usually three to six months in the first instance). When achieved, these goals are expected to produce significant and lasting benefits in the everyday quality of life of that household member (and, preferably, other household members as well).

It is assumed that the current problems preventing attainment of these goals can be overcome as a result of enhanced household problem solving and stress management. Where individuals are suffering from persisting impairments and disabilities associated with health problems it is assumed that some progress towards recovery may be made, but goals should be set within

34

the constraints of current disability. This may mean breaking a goal down into a series of small steps, or choosing a simpler everyday goal in the short term. For example, David was eager to return to his university studies, and stated this as his goal. However, at the time he was unable to concentrate on reading for more than five minutes, and tended to lose track of programmes he watched on television. The assessor suggested that he consider taking the first step or two towards returning to his studies in the next three months. David agreed, and decided to finish studying an interesting book on ecology that was one of the basic texts for his biology course.

*Table 3.2* Principles of setting goals

---
- Choose readily attainable targets
- Prioritize goals that will enhance quality of life most easily
- Choose everyday goals – avoid the trip to paradise!
- The therapist may prompt participants by reminding them of activities they stated they wished to increase during the reinforcement survey or during other parts of the assessment
- Break ambitious goals down into attainable steps
- State goal in terms that describe the activity exactly: specify all behaviours, when, where, with whom, how often, for how long, etc.
- Avoid pressure – allow participants time to contemplate their goals; spread goal setting over more than one interview if necessary
---

Goals are chosen that will most easily achieve major improvements in each person's quality of life. These are usually everyday goals, rather than the sort of once-in-a-lifetime event, such as a special holiday or present. It may be difficult for some people to conceive of goals in such mundane terms, rather than as lifetime achievements. Spending more time in the garden or having friends over once a month may not seem exciting goals, but to the people concerned they may reflect the first steps to major changes in their lifestyles.

Each goal is described in detail, so that everyone can understand the precise activity that is being aimed for, and can readily agree when the goal has been achieved. For example, Janie stated that she would like to improve her social life. The assessor asked her what aspect of her social life she would particularly like to improve. She said that she would like to have a regular activity that she attended with a friend. Step by step she was able to pinpoint this goal, until it finally became:

Going to a sports club with a girlfriend once a week for at least one hour to participate in some sporting activity.

She was unable to be more specific about the precise activity they would engage in or the friend she would involve. However, the sporting nature of the activity, the frequency and duration of the event are clear.

It is evident that where people are setting goals involving activities that are novel for them they may find it difficult to be precise. In such cases, the initial step in setting a goal may involve seeking information to clarify community resources. Thus, goal setting may be extended over several weeks, as the person explores various possible activities. The assessor avoids putting pressure on the individual, and allows sufficient time for contemplation and choice of the goals likely to prove most rewarding for that person.

It should be noted that the goals are always the personal goals of each household member which involve changes in his or her own behaviour. While they may involve the collaboration of others, as in the case of Janie seeking a friend to go with her to a sports activity, they should not primarily target another person's behaviour. Thus, goals to change the behaviour patterns of other people are not employed. For example, May suggested that one of her goals would be to have Tony spend more time at home with her. The assessor suggested that she might consider a goal that involved increasing an activity that both she and Tony enjoyed doing together. She decided to make her goal:

Going out for a casual meal at a restaurant with Tony at the weekend once a month.

Some people, particularly those who have been under persistent stress, have difficultly considering positive goals. They suggest ideas such as having more time, being less distressed, and resolving major stresses. However, we encourage all participants to set at least one small goal for themselves. In such cases the reinforcement survey usually reveals many areas of dissatisfaction with everyday life, with activities that the person wishes to increase. Small steps towards restoring such rewarding activities may be tailored into constructive goals for those people. Faced with daily stresses of major proportions, such people may consider the goals as trivial. However, the ability to focus on small, yet constructive, steps towards a better quality of life may have profound consequences for many people who are coping with highly stressed lives.

In addition to setting the goals, we invite household members to describe any steps they may have already taken to achieve their stated goals, as well as any problems that they anticipate they may have to overcome in order to achieve each goal. Finally, they are asked to define the responses they expect from other household members in the pursuit of each goal. Expected support and conflict are highlighted briefly. On occasions people ask the assessor if they can keep their personal goals confidential, and not share them with other household members. Although there may be exceptional circumstances when the assessor may agree to keeping secrets, on most occasions the assessor suggests that the person sets goals that can be discussed within the household unit. However, in all instances the household member, not the assessor, is the person who decides whether he or she wishes to disclose his or her goals to others. When people report that he or she may find this disclosure difficult to perform, the assessor may assist and prompt such disclosure. For example, one young woman found it difficult to tell her mother that she wanted to move out of her home and share a house with two girlfriends, one of whom her mother had expressed disapproval of. Her assessor helped her to rehearse this disclosure in a series of practice role plays, until she felt confident to discuss this goal with her mother. When she finally managed to do so her mother was upset, as expected, but accepted her daughter's wishes and agreed to help her with her plans.

Of course, most people have more than two goals that they are working to achieve at any time. These goals may be highly explicit, such as targets set in the workplace, or less clearly defined relationship or leisure goals. The focus on merely one or two specific goals in behavioural family therapy does not preclude continuing to work on any other goals.

*Other problems*

The individual assessment concludes with a review of any other major problems that have not been disclosed during the remainder of the interview. These may include marital conflict, sexual dysfunction, lack of friendship, social skills deficits, lack of hobbies and leisure interests, substance misuse, financial stress, housing problems, work-related problems, cultural conflicts, etc. Whenever a problem is described the person is invited to give clear examples of the problem and the way in which it limits current everyday functioning, and how they cope with the problem. Where a problem is associated with major disability for the individual, a more detailed problem analysis may be conducted.

## Problem solving and goal achievement functions

Once each household member or intimate associate has been interviewed and personal assets, problems, and goals defined, a meeting of all participants is convened to assess the manner in which they collaborate in solving mutual problems and achieving mutual goals. This is divided into two main parts: (a) *reported*; and (b) *observed* problem-solving assessment.

### *Reported problem solving/goal achievement*

The aim of this part of the assessment is to establish the context for problem solving within the household. The household group is invited to describe several recent examples of their day-to-day problem solving/goal achievement functions. The precise manner in which they handled these everyday problems, such as planning an outing, paying a bill, or dealing with a minor crisis, is explored. A detailed description of exactly *how* they went about solving the problem is sought. This includes:

(a) *What was the setting of problem solving?* The place(s) where discussions between household members occurred is noted. For example, in the kitchen while washing the dishes; between mother and father in bed; while driving father to the station, etc.
(b) *Who was involved?* All those household members who were involved in parts of the discussion are noted. People and agencies outside the household who were coopted into the problem-solving process are recorded. These may include close friends, work associates, doctors, priests, therapists, etc.

(c) *How was communication structured?* The manner in which the discussion was structured is noted. This includes details of issues such as whether people were seated, without distractions, with one person clearly chairing the discussion, others communicating openly and directly, yet calmly, actively listening to each other's views, and clarifying problems, goals, and misunderstandings. Alternatively, was communication hostile, destructive, with distractions, interruptions, disjointed and without structure?

(d) *How was problem solving structured?* Did the discussion follow a structure that included evidence of clear problem/goal definition, brainstorming of potential solutions, evaluation of all suggested alternatives, consensus on the 'best' solution and detailed planning of implementation? Alternatively, was the problem solving disorganized, lacking clear definition of the problem or goal, selecting from a narrow range of possible options, with little consensus and inadequate planning?

It is the *structure* of the communication and problem solving that is the target of this part of the assessment rather than the content of the issues addressed. It is assumed that, where people provide a clear structure for their problem-solving functions, this will be associated with highly efficient stress management as well as facilitating the achievement of the personal goals of all household members.

### Family meetings

Households vary enormously in the amount of time and effort they expend on collaborative problem solving and goal achievement functions. Some households organize regular times to discuss important issues relating to the quality of life of all members; others provide minimal structure, but allow members to arrange discussions whenever needed; and still others appear to avoid planning household management in a collaborative manner, leaving such issues to individual problem-solving efforts.

In this part of the assessment the assessor attempts to delineate the specific times when households meet to conduct collaborative problem-solving and goal achievement discussions. This may be a well-defined regular meeting time when most

**Communication training**

1 Able to receive and process verbal communication.
2 Able to express specific positive feelings for specific positive behaviour change in a constructive way.

3 Able to request specific behaviour change in a constructive way.

4 Able to express specific negative feelings for specific behaviour.
5 Able to listen actively

- non-verbal attentiveness

- clarifying questions/check content, feelings.

**Problem-solving training**

1 *Family unit* is able to pinpoint a specific problem issue.

2 *Family unit* is able to generate five or more alternative solutions.

3 *Family unit* is able to acknowledge all suggested alternatives (i.e. make note of each).

4 *Family unit* is able to evaluate pros and cons of each alternative.

5 *Family unit* is able to agree on 'best' solution.

6 *Family unit* is able to plan strategies for implementing 'best' solution.

7 *Family unit* is able to implement plans.

8 *Family unit* is able to review outcome of 'problem' in constructive manner.

* FM = Family Member. Note each by initial of first name at top of column.
Criterion A – Spontaneous evidence in session/reported interaction at home.
Criterion B – Prompted by therapist within session.
Numbers represent dates on which the behaviour was observed or reported. O = observed before start of treatment sessions.

*Figure 3.1* Communication and problem-solving checklist

household members are likely to congregate; for example, a specific meal time, a time devoted to attending a religious service, or a gathering to watch a favourite television programme. In less cohesive households it may be more difficult to define such regular meeting points. These families are invited to define a regular time each week when they could all meet together for 20–30 minutes to discuss household issues. The assessor requests that they begin to meet at these times immediately so that they can discuss any issues that arise during subsequent sessions.

| | **Criterion A** | | | | | | | | **Criterion B** | | | | | |
|------|------|------|------|------|---|---|---|------|------|------|------|------|---|---|
| * FM | MrX | MrsX | JX | PX | | | | FM | MrX | MrsX | JX | PX | | |
| O | O | O | O | | | | | | | | | | |
| 14/1 | 21/1 | 14/1 | 14/1 | | | | | 7/1 | 7/1 | 7/1 | 7/1 | | |
| 28/1 | 28/1 | 21/1 | 28/1 | | | | | 14/1 | 14/1 | 14/1 | 21/1 | | |
| | 5/2 | 12/2 | 19/2 | | | | | | 28/1 | 28/1 | 28/1 | | |
| O | O | 19/2 | 26/2 | | | | | 12/2 | 12/2 | 12/2 | 19/2 | | |
| 19/2 | 19/2 | 19/2 | 26/2 | | | | | 12/2 | 12/2 | 12/2 | 12/2 | | |

| Criterion A | | Criterion B |
|:---:|:---:|:---:|
| 13/3 | | 26/3 |
| O | | 26/2 |
| | | 13/3 |
| 13/3 | | 26/2 |
| 13/3 | | 6/3 |
| 27/3 | | 6/3 |
| 27/3 | | 6/3 |
| | | 13/3 |

*Observed problem solving and goal achievement*

Upon completion of the assessment of reported problem solving, the assessor presents the family group with a current 'hot issue' to discuss, and asks them to attempt to define a resolution plan within 15–20 minutes. The issue is chosen by the assessor, either from the various issues raised during the earlier interviews with each household member, or by inviting the group to suggest another unresolved issue at this stage. Care should be taken to check that the issue is not likely to prove explosive and precipitate a major crisis. Ideally the issue should be of everyday importance, and be of family-wide concern, rather than one that focuses extensively on one particular member.

## Therapist instructions for observed problem solving/goal achievement

The assessor instructs the family group in the following manner:

'I would like you to spend the next 15–20 minutes discussing the issue of . . . (*give a brief description of the selected issue*).'

'I would like you to try to decide exactly what the problem or goal is and then try to develop a plan of how you might deal with this issue as a group. There are no right or wrong ways to deal with this issue.'

'I would like to record this discussion so that I can review it later. I am going to leave the room so that you can discuss this issue among yourselves.'

'Do you understand what I'm asking you to do? Do you have any questions about it?'

'I'll switch the tape recorder on now and you can begin your discussion about the issue of . . . (*repeat a brief description of the issue*) . . . and I will come back in 20 minutes.'

The assessor then retreats to a nearby room, but remains within earshot of the discussion. If there is evidence of a major argument developing the assessor is advised to terminate the discussion prematurely. After calming down the group a second less distressing issue may be chosen and the procedure repeated.

If the discussion lasts less than ten minutes, the assessor may re-enter the room and prompt further discussion, with instructions such as

'I would like you to go over the issue again to check that you have worked out a good plan.'

After 20 minutes the assessor re-enters and switches off the tape recorder. He or she then invites a spokesperson to summarize the problem-solving efforts. Generous praise is given to each participant for these efforts.

*Review of observed problem solving and goal achievement behaviour*

After the problem-solving assessment session the assessor reviews the reported and observed problem-solving skills that each household member has demonstrated during the assessment. Competent performance of a list of specific communication and problem-solving skills is noted on a checklist (see Figure 3.1).

The communication and problem-solving checklist (CPC) provides a simple record of the specific acquisition of skills as each household member progresses through behavioural family therapy. The assessor considers two sets of criteria of competent performance:

---

**Criterion A: spontaneous competent performance of skills**

*Criterion A* is met when a participant demonstrates on *at least one occasion* that he or she can perform a skill competently during '*spontaneous*' interaction. '*Spontaneous*' interaction refers to any of the following contexts:

(a) during the baseline observed problem-solving test;
(b) unprompted performance during any session;
(c) when the *precise behaviour* is reported by another household member during the reported problem solving during the baseline assessments, and subsequent reports of interaction between participants at home. This includes reports of between-session assignments. In such instances it is preferable that the report is corroborated by a re-enactment of the skill performance that the therapist can observe.

It can be seen that '*spontaneous*' performance of a skill implies that there is no direct prompting of the behaviour by the therapist, although there may be prompting by other household members, or indirect prompting associated with the assignment of between-session practice of specific skills.

**Criterion B: coached performance of skills**

*Criterion B* is met when a participant demonstrates competent performance, on *at least one occasion*, of a specific communication or problem-solving skill under the active coaching of the therapist. This provides evidence that the household member has the capability to perform this skill, but as yet may not display this competence in less contrived and more everyday contexts.

---

It should be noted that the CPC merely records the *first occasion* when each skill is performed competently. The frequency with which these skills are performed is not recorded on the checklist. A major aim of BFT is to increase the frequency with which effective problem solving and goal achievement skills are applied to everyday stresses. Where the therapist identifies the need to monitor the frequency of performance of a particular behaviour, other assessment tools may be added. Several of these methods are described in a later section of this chapter.

The assessment of specific components of problem solving involves the integrated efforts of all participants. The relative contributions of individual members may vary considerably according to the nature of the problems or goals addressed, the structure of the discussion, as well as the competence of each participant in the discussion. For this reason problem-solving competence is assessed in terms of the combined efforts rather than individual contributions. Once again, where individuals have difficulties participating appropriately in these discussions, specific assessment of their contributions may be targeted by the therapist and measured separately.

### Additional assessment strategies

In addition to the assessment strategies outlined here, behavioural family therapy may employ a range of adjunct assessments. These include the following.

### Diary records

A daily diary record of specific behaviours offers a ready source of information for the assessor. Such self-monitoring may enable a person to observe the context as well as the thoughts and feelings that they associate with their responses. Daily recording of this kind forms the basis for monitoring practice of specific communication and problem-solving skills throughout therapy. It may also be used to assess the frequency of specific problem issues, such as bed-wetting, temper tantrums, marital rows, or goals such as frequency of sexual behaviours or pleasurable events. Changes in the frequency of events may be highlighted by using simple display charts.

## Family and marital inventories

Several standardized checklists have been developed to assess the quality of family life. These list a large range of items that may occur in everyday family or marital interaction, both pleasing or displeasing. Participants are invited to complete these lists every evening for one week in order to examine the quality of interaction. The Spouse Observation Checklist (SOC) (Weiss *et al.* 1973) and the briefer Marital Activities Inventory are two examples.

## Family interviews

A number of standardized family interview schedules have been developed, mainly for research purposes. Perhaps the best known of these is the Camberwell Family Interview (CFI) developed initially by Brown and Rutter (1966) and subsequently modified by Vaughn and Leff (1976b). This interview has been employed extensively in recent family research, particularly that associated with delineating ambient stress factors that may be predictive of the course of major mental disorders. This semi-structured interview is conducted with individual household members in order to define their attitudes towards the index person and his or her disorder. Tape recordings of these interviews are subsequently analysed to determine among other things the number of positive and negative remarks made about the index person by each household member. An index of negative responses, predominantly criticism, is derived for each household. High ratings on the index are termed '*high expressed emotion*', and have been good predictors of a high probability of recurrent exacerbations of disorders (Leff and Vaughn 1985).

This assessment takes considerable time and expertise to complete, and extensive training to provide reliable ratings. For these reasons it is not useful in clinical practice. Furthermore, similar levels of prediction can be derived from prognostic indices that are much more readily assessed, such as sex of the index person, marital status, and recent employment record. However, perhaps the greatest limitation of this excellent research instrument is the tendency for clinicians to consider that only households rated as '*high*' on the index are likely to benefit from a family approach to stress management.

The individual interview schedule that we employ has been derived from the CFI approach, but seeks merely to gather information about aspects of family life, without making any specific ratings of the quality of that environment.

## Direct observation procedures

Similarly, several research procedures to measure the quality of observed problem solving of families have been developed. Several employ standardized ratings of communication and problem-solving behaviour to recordings of problem-solving discussions, similar to the observed problem-solving test we have outlined (Robin et al. 1977; Doane 1978; Doane et al. 1986; Goldstein et al. 1968; Weiss et al. 1973).

A more elaborate form of direct observation involves sampling real-life interaction in the home. This approach was pioneered by Gerald Patterson and his colleagues in Oregon, and refined by Christensen (1979). The development of modern technology now allows tape recorders, placed in people's homes, to be activated at random intervals to observe interpersonal interactions unobtrusively. This provides the assessor with a sample of real-life observations for either research or clinical purposes.

## Formulation of family functioning

At the end of the assessment process, the assessor completes a succinct summary of the specific strengths and weaknesses of the household as a problem-solving unit. The focus is on observed and reported problem-solving behaviour, rather than opinions about suspected attitudes and conflicts. Any major deficits in the interpersonal skills of individual members and clearly identified unresolved stresses may be noted. The use of a genogram to identify family relationships may be particularly useful when it is noted that more than one household member may suffer from vulnerability to stress-related disorders. Patterns of inheritance of such vulnerabilities may be displayed where similar deficits were present in past generations of the family.

A list of the personal goals of each participant is compiled using the family goal achievement record (see Figure 3.2).

ASSESSMENT OF THE FAMILY UNIT

Family Name __BRAMLEY__

*Dates*

*Expected/Achieved*

FM __JENNY__

| | | |
|---|---|---|
| 1 To go to social club weekly | 1/11 | 2/12 |
| 2 To phone one old friend each month | 1/11 | |

FM __SAM__

| | | |
|---|---|---|
| 1 To paint living room windows | 1/11 | 1/10 |
| 2 To go to football home matches | 2/1 | |

FM __WILLIAM__

| | | |
|---|---|---|
| 1 To work around house and garden for 20 hours a week | 1/11 | 1/10 |
| 2 To meet one friend to go out with socially every week | 2/12 | 1/11 |

FM __DIANA__

| | | |
|---|---|---|
| 1 To go to four interviews for a new job | 1/11 | 11/12 |
| 2 To attend evening classes in car maintenance (×5) | 2/1 | 3/10 |

FM _____

| | | |
|---|---|---|
| 1 | | |
| 2 | | |

FM _____

| | | |
|---|---|---|
| 1 | | |
| 2 | | |

*Figure 3.2* Family goal achievement record

47

## Continued assessment of problem solving and goal achievement

Behavioural approaches to psychotherapy view assessment as a continuous process. The aim is to evaluate the effects of the intervention upon the efficiency of household problem solving and goal achievement functions as applied to everyday stress management. Assessment methods have been developed that enable progress to be measured on a day-to-day and session-to-session basis, as well as at regular review sessions.

### *Assessment conducted at every session*

The behavioural therapist is continually guided by assessments of progress towards clearly specified goals. Every session is structured to provide a brief assessment of all areas covered during the baseline assessment. In addition, the session itself provides an opportunity to observe evidence of understanding of the index patient's disorder, specific communication and problem-solving skills, and progress towards each participant's personal goals. This review is conducted in the following manner:

1 *Progress towards personal goals.* Each session begins with the therapist inviting the participants to give a brief update on their progress towards their goals. All reported *efforts* are rewarded with praise. Difficulties encountered are analysed in a manner similar to that employed in the initial problem analysis. In particular, attention is paid to the problem-solving approach employed to attempt to resolve these difficulties. However, lengthy discussion is postponed till later in the session. The problem issue may form the basis for problem-solving training later in the session. Alternatively, participants may be invited to place the problem on the agenda of their next family meeting at home. For example, if a person reported difficulty in expressing annoyance at the boss for insisting that he or she stayed late on an evening when he or she had promised to be home early, this may be used as a topic for that person to practise expression of unpleasant feelings later during the training phase of the session.

2 *Review of index patient's mental health status.* The therapist checks the index person's *target problems*, particularly where that

person is experiencing continued evidence of a mental disorder. When the index person's disorder is in remission, evidence of the emergence of key signs that represent the earliest warning of an impending episode are checked at each session. These checks are brief screening procedures that should not take more than a minute or two. Clearly, when signs suggesting an episode are detected, a detailed mental status review is triggered.

3 *Review of between-session work assignments.* Throughout the therapy every participant is expected to complete between-session practice of specific skills. These assignments are reviewed next. Once again *all efforts* are reinforced with praise, especially when competent performance has not resulted in any obvious benefits.

Key aspects of the practice are selected for re-enactment. These may include examples of both competent and incompetent performances. They are recreated in scenarios as close to the real-life situation as feasible.

Specific strategies are employed to develop and maintain compliance with between-session practice assignments. Further details about this crucial aspect of the approach are described on page 91.

4 *Review of earlier sessions.* When there is evidence that one or more participants seem to have forgotten important aspects of earlier sessions, the therapist may choose to revise all or part of those skills during the present session.

5 *Review of family meetings.* The family provides a weekly brief report of the problem solving and goal achievement functions carried out during the family meeting. Once problem-solving training is introduced, the structure as well as the content of problems and goals are reviewed. This is aided by perusal of any problem-solving assignment sheets completed by the household since the previous session. As well as this *reported problem solving* the therapist may invite the group to re-enact one or more elements of their problem-solving discussions so that he or she can conduct abbreviated *observed problem solving.* The elements chosen are areas where the therapist suspects there are significant deficits that may require further training during the present session.

Where no family meeting has been convened, or no problem solving or goal achievement functions practised during

Name _____ **MAVIS**

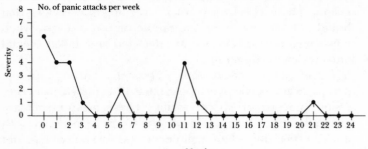

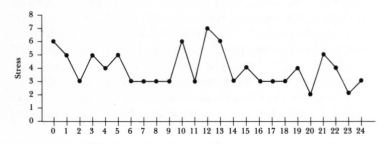

*Figure 3.3* Life chart

the meeting, the therapist may request that they identify an unresolved issue and conduct a 10–15 minute discussion immediately. The therapist removes himself from the discussion and observes their problem-solving functions without interrupting. In other words, the observed problem-solving test is repeated. New evidence of competent performance of communication and problem-solving skills by participants is noted on the CPC checklist.

6 *Throughout the session.* The therapist makes specific notes of the use of effective skills and evidence of the acquisition of understanding of educational material while each session is in progress. Progress is rewarded with specific praise and major deficits noted for further training, either during the present or subsequent sessions.

7 *Recording progress.* Wherever possible progress is recorded on simple charts, rather than in unstructured notes. Such records facilitate clear communication and improve objectivity. The key elements of these records are included in the charts provided in Appendix B. These include:

(a) Family goal achievement record. Each participant's goal(s) is summarized with the dates by which it is expected to achieve it noted. When the goal is achieved the therapist records the date in the designated space. The entire record is reviewed every three months, when new goals may be planned and unachieved goals modified.

(b) Life chart. This chart (see Figure 3.3) provides a graphical record of progress on the individual's target problems, social functioning, and environmental stress. Each participant who is vulnerable to a specific disorder is provided with a life chart on which, with the assistance of the therapist, he or she makes a monthly record of the severity of one or two key features of the disorder, current levels of social disability, and current levels of environmental stress.

Several standardized scales have been devised to measure these parameters (Falloon and Fadden 1993). However, such standardization is only necessary when comparisons are being made between different cases, or contrasting intervention strategies. For individual assessment, a standard scale can be devised for each person ranging from

0 = absence of problem/dysfunction/stress, to 8 = maximum severity of problem/dysfunction/stress, with 4 = moderate severity, and the other scale points representing intermediate ratings. Participants and therapists can negotiate the manner in which the scales are used and devise more specific criteria for each point on the scale to fit each person's unique context. For example, Mavis (see Figure 3.3) experienced five or six panic attacks each week when initially assessed. She and her therapist agreed to use the target problem rating scale to record the number of panic attacks she had experienced during the week before the monthly rating. At one stage she had been housebound and unable to manage basic household and childcare activities. This level of disability was agreed as scoring '8' on the social functioning scale, with '0' representing no impairment in her ability to perform all the roles she expected to perform in the community. The maximum level of social functioning during the month was agreed for the monthly record. Her stress scale was agreed to be rated from '0', indicating no stress at all, to '8', indicating extreme stress. The maximum level of stress during the month was recorded.

Name    BELINDA G.

| Date | Drugs | Dosage | % taken | Comments |
|---|---|---|---|---|
| 2/1/90 | Imipramine | 100mg nocte | 90% | Sl. dry mouth. Ham RSD |
| 10/1/90 | Imipramine | 150mg nocte | 100% | Sleeping better |
| 20/1/90 | Imipramine | 150mg nocte | 80% | Much improved mood. Dizziness – postural |
| 30/1/90 | Imipramine | 100mg nocte | 90% | Mood etc normal |
| 12/2/90 | Imipramine | 50mg nocte | 100% | Well |
| 26/2/90 | Imipramine | 50mg nocte | 100% | Well |
| 24/3/90 | Imipramine | 25mg nocte | 100% | Well. Hamilton RSD |
| 27/4/90 | Imipramine | discontinued | – | Early Warning Signs Card done, etc. |

*Figure 3.4*   Medication record

## ASSESSMENT OF THE FAMILY UNIT

| Date | Session No.* | Comments |
|------|------------|----------|
| 25/3/91 | 0 | Assessed Clare, Mr J.       Clare to develop goals for next week. |
| 2/4/91 | 0 | Assessed Mrs J.       Clare's goals completed. |
| 5/4/91 | 0 | Problem-solving assessment.<br>Household tensions high. Mr & Mrs arguing ++. |
| 10/4/91 | 1 | Education about bulimia. All attentive.<br>Clare explained her feelings of loneliness well. |
| 17/4/91 | 2 | Further education about nutrition, etc. Family meeting went well. Clare didn't binge at all this week. |
| 25/4/91 | 3 | Expressing pleasant feelings. M √ Clare √ father found it difficult. Tends to be critical. Further work needed. Missed F. meeting. |
| 1/5/91 | 4 | Good real-life practice, incl. F. Progress on goals.<br>Making requests – all satis.       F. meeting went well.<br>Work on Clare. Getting file. |
| 8/5/91 | 5 | Real-life p. satis. F. moaning – dealing with telephone bill. Expressing unpleasant feelings. All found it difficult. |
| 13/5/91 | 6 | High tension. F had argument with Clare about boyfriend. Rehearse use of –ve feeling shifts. Further practice. F. M. – not held. |
| 20/5/91 | 7 | Real-life p. satis. F. meeting re: F's job.<br>Introduced Problem Solving – planning family outing at weekend. |
| 27/5/91 | 8 | Excellent work on P.S. in F meeting. No binging etc – Clare. Active Listening – all did well. |
| 30/5/91 | E | F. called. Clare moved out with new boyfriend.<br>Emergency P.S. session. Plan: Clare to return home. |
| 3/6/91 | 9 | Things sorted. Clare moving to apartment in 6 weeks.<br>Planning trained. |
| 9/6/91 | 10 | F. meeting satis. Able to manage P.S. well. Clare well.<br>For review 2/52. |
| 24/6/91 | 11 | Review of progress. F. M. √ Clare √ Goals – good progress. P.S. satis. Communication good – F. still needs support re: feelings. |
| 30/6/91 | 12 | F. M. √ Clare √ Early warning signs completed and rehearsed. P.S. good. – p monthly sessions. |
| 28/7/91 | 13 | Progress maintained. Weekly F. meeting, continue.<br>Clare well. Further R.S. observed. See 1/12. |

\* Include *additional* emergency sessions; number as 'E'.

*Figure 3.5*   Family intervention summary

(c) Medication record. This provides a simple record of changes in a person's medication, and includes an estimate of the level of adherence to the recommended regimen (see Figure 3.4). The latter may be obtained from the person's reports, counts of residual tablets, or charts kept by household members to monitor tablet taking. The aim of this record is to assist the individual to self-monitor his or her behaviour so that the benefits of drug interventions are maximized, not to encourage coercive measures where adherence is not optimal.

(d) Family intervention summary. This chart (see Figure 3.5) enables therapists to keep a simple record of the sessions conducted. Key issues are recorded briefly in the 'Comments' section for the therapist's reference. Additional personal notes may be kept by the therapist in his or her own interest, but are not deemed necessary where all charts are completed in an optimal manner. All records are shared with all participants in an open and honest manner throughout the period of therapeutic contact. This minimizes problems associated with confidentiality, family secrets, and poorly substantiated therapist opinions.

(e) Updating the communication and problem-solving checklist. The CPC is completed at the end of the baseline assessment and updated after every session. Baseline competence in each skill area is noted by placing a zero in the box indicating the specific skills that each participant has been observed to perform in a competent manner *on any occasion before treatment sessions are started.* Every participant has his or her initials placed at the top of a column of boxes concerned with specific communication skills.

Once the training phase of BFT has begun, the therapist updates the CPC *after each training session* to reflect evidence of increasing competence in the performance of these specified skills. Criterion B reflects competent performance under the direct guidance of the therapist, and Criterion A reflects unprompted or 'spontaneous' performance. Evidence of the skill having been performed on at least one occasion is noted by placing the date on which this performance first occurred in the appropriate box, i.e. 2/12 = 2 December; 6/3 = 6 March. Evidence may be obtained both from observations made during sessions, *and from clear reports and re-enactments of performance between sessions.*

The aim of the therapist is to complete all the boxes in criterion A (i.e. 'spontaneous' competent performance) for all participants. The varied skills of individual participants enable the therapist to target relevant deficits of certain participants and to use the strengths of others, thereby tailoring the intervention to meet the needs of the group efficiently.

---

Examine the partially completed CPC on pages 40–1. What does that denote in terms of:

   (a) the initial skills performed competently by Mr X at baseline?
   (b) the skills Mrs X was able to perform after one month of training, when prompted by the therapist?
   (c) the deficiencies in the families' 'spontaneous' performance of problem solving after three months' training?

---

*Figure 3.1* CPC completed: Example

## Three-month review

In addition to this session-by-session assessment, every tenth session (or 13th week, where sessions are held less frequently) is devoted to a review of progress.

This review covers the same ground as the initial assessment, although more clearly targeted to issues relevant to each participant. Each person's personal goals are reviewed and revised as needed; their understanding of the disorders to which participants are vulnerable and the manner in which they cope with associated disabilities and handicaps are reviewed; changes in the quality of their lives as reflected by discrepancies between current behaviour patterns and desired patterns are highlighted on their reinforcement surveys. Progress in improving the effectiveness of their problem solving and goal achievement functions is noted on the CPC.

The observed problem-solving test may be repeated, although where the therapist has been conducting sessions and reviewing them in the manner outlined in later chapters, this will seldom be necessary. Indeed, where the therapist has completed session-by-session reviews in the manner outlined above, these three-month reviews will require very little further interviewing of active participants. Most of the information will already be recorded, so the review session will merely provide the therapist and participants with the opportunity to reflect on progress, provide praise for all efforts, define any specific blocks to progress, and set goals for the next three-month period.

## CONCLUSIONS

This chapter outlines the comprehensive procedures that form the basis for behavioural family therapy intervention programmes. The strengths and weaknesses, personal goals and problems of each member of the household are pinpointed, as well as the ability of the combined efforts of the household group to assist each other to achieve goals and resolve relevant problems. This assessment is conducted before the start of any treatment programme. It is then continued throughout the entire course in order to assess progress and provide a guide to modifications in the therapy from session to session.

# 4

# EDUCATING PEOPLE WITH DISORDERS AND CARERS ABOUT MENTAL HEALTH

Where one or more members of a household are highly vulnerable to a stress-related health problem, a key component of the stress management approach is comprehensive education about these disorders. This enables the vulnerable individuals, who may have experienced previous episodes of the disorder, to make sense of their experiences and to develop strategies for reducing the risk of further episodes. This may include psychosocial strategies to manage stress more efficiently, as well as taking prophylactic medication, changing dietary and exercise patterns, learning to recognize the early signs of an impending episode, and seeking professional assistance with minimal delay. Household members and close friends who may be involved with such persons in an informal caregiving capacity may also benefit from acquiring a better understanding of the nature of the disorder and its clinical management, so that they can become valuable assistants to the professional care team.

In the past there had often been a reluctance on the part of health professionals to provide detailed information to patients and their carers about the nature of mental (and physical) disorders, and discussions about symptoms, diagnosis, and prognosis were avoided. Practical information about what to expect, what is likely to make the situation better or worse, or what to do in a crisis was not given. In many services, this situation persists, and household members are rarely even seen by professionals. The reasons given for this by professionals generally vary from an uncertainty about diagnosis and a consequent wish not to confuse family members, a concern that providing a diagnosis may lead to stigmatization, worry that people may be distressed by knowing what is wrong, and their own inexperience as professionals in imparting information about various disorders and their management.

However, when patients and their informal carers are asked what they want, they consistently say that they want information from professionals and advice on how to handle the situations they face (Creer and Wing 1974; Hatfield 1990; Holden and Lewine 1982). They do not expect total certainty from professionals or expect them to have all the answers, but they want to be kept up to date with what the individual therapist or team thinks is wrong or what is likely to help (Fadden *et al* 1987). When provided with information they may not like all that they hear, but prefer this to uncertainty and not knowing what they are dealing with (Anderson *et al.* 1986). People have a preference for practical, concrete advice, with the focus on issues specifically relevant to them (Cozolino and Goldstein 1986; Fadden *et al.* 1987). There is no evidence that providing information to relatives increases the likelihood of stigmatization, or that family members are distressed by what they hear. On the contrary they value and welcome detailed information and the opportunity to discuss practical solutions to the situations they face (McGill *et al.* 1983; Leff *et al.* 1982).

## PURPOSE OF EDUCATION

The educational component of behavioural family therapy serves the following functions and is an essential prerequisite for the other elements of treatment.

1 *Establishes a working relationship between professionals and all household members.* Providing information establishes a good basis for communication and dialogue, and professionals are starting by offering something to families. This differs from the more traditional approaches where patients and their carers were seen to obtain information from them about what had been happening.

2 *Leads to increased understanding.* By being provided with information, participants gain a better understanding of the disorder, of what is helpful and what makes the situation worse. Equally, professionals learn about the pressures and strains in the particular household, and become aware of what issues will need to be addressed. An overall aim is to ensure

that all participants have a realistic view about the nature of the disorder, including its possible causes, various features, and likely outcome, as well as any specific strategies that they can use to deal with the disorder, or to prevent its recurrence in the future. It also provides an opportunity to correct any misconceptions that people may have about the nature or causes of the disorder.

3 *Provides a rationale for treatment.* If participants are expected to take part in clinical management plans and assist with various treatments, they need to understand why various approaches are being suggested and how each particular strategy will contribute to the overall aim of helping the vulnerable people to recover and remain well.

4 *Provides an opportunity for assessment of knowledge and coping skills.* Any discussions with the household group allow the therapist to gain detailed information about their communication and problem-solving skills, situations they find easy to cope with and those that prove more difficult. This approach to education is an ongoing process, and all discussions with the family about the disorder may uncover misconceptions or aspects which the participants are unclear about.

5 *Enhances self-management.* In the educational process, each person who has suffered from a particular disorder is viewed as an 'expert' in that disorder, capable of educating those who have not experienced the disorder at first hand. Other household members likewise have expert knowledge on what they have noticed helps and what makes the situation worse. Thus it is clear from early on that all participants have a major role to play in the mutual education process that is the cornerstone for managing the disorder and in helping vulnerable members recover and remain well.

Recently the management of mental disorders has increasingly included an educational component, and this chapter will describe the practicalities of how to do this, what issues arise in doing so, and what to do about difficulties encountered.

## PROVIDING INFORMATION – HOW TO DO IT

It is important from the outset to create an atmosphere which is relaxed and conducive to learning, and a working relationship between professionals and family members which is a partnership in dealing with the disorder. Attention should be paid to the setting in which meetings take place and the messages which may be implicit in meeting people in particular contexts. If meetings with the family take place in hospital or 'clinic' settings, it is easy for the family to think they are going to 'experts' for advice and it may be harder to convey the idea that they are the experts in their own experience of the disorder and that their contributions are valued. They may also find it difficult to relax in what can often be strange and confusing settings with lots of activity and distractions. On the other hand if meetings take place in their own home or other familiar surroundings, they are likely to feel more at ease, less distracted by outside events, more in charge, and that they have something to contribute.

In general, treatment models which have a strong educational component are more easily accepted by relatives than other approaches because, as Hatfield (1990) points out, they do not presume 'pathology' or 'dysfunction' in the family unit. Nevertheless, it is important that great care is taken in the early educational meetings in introducing the idea that everyone involved – the person with the disorder, family members or close friends and professionals – all have knowledge of particular areas and that together the best systems of management and solutions can be worked out. Mental health professionals may know about mental disorders in general, but the person with the disorder knows more about the experiences of that disorder than anyone else, and other family members know in detail how it affects this particular household. Therapists who wish to work with families using a behavioural family therapy approach must genuinely believe this and acknowledge each participant's expertise and their own lack of knowledge in some situations.

In sessions devoted mainly to education, an open relaxed atmosphere must be created so that all participants will share their concerns, ideas, and beliefs, will ask the questions that are troubling them, and will describe what is actually happening rather than what they think the therapist wishes to hear.

## TIMING OF THE EDUCATIONAL SESSIONS

Education is a process which should continue through all stages of contact with the family, and often the same topics and material have to be repeated as participants' ongoing experiences enable them to gain a deeper understanding of the disorder they are coping with. The question arises as to what point in this experience of a major health problem the educational process should begin. Traditionally there was a reluctance on the part of the professionals to tell people anything during their first experience of a disorder until they were sure themselves about diagnosis and could comment on prognosis. For several reasons we advocate that education should begin during the first major episode at the time the initial contact is made with mental health services. First, the patient and family are dealing with an unfamiliar, stressful and sometimes frightening situation, and need help in understanding what is happening. It would be difficult for anyone to justify not giving people information which alleviates their concerns and makes the situation more manageable and predictable. If the diagnosis is not clear it is important to say so, and then focus on the practical difficulties the family are trying to deal with.[1]

Professionals often seem to hold a misguided view that if nothing is said to family members they will continue to think in a vacuum, dealing with the situation without questioning what is wrong or why their relative is acting in a different manner. However, this is not the case, and people always try to make sense of the situations in which they find themselves. If professionals do not tell them what is wrong, they work out for themselves what they think has contributed to their relative acting out of character. Sometimes this is done through discussions with friends, through reading, or by making links between events they feel may be connected with what has happened. There is ample evidence from studies on general medicine that people's beliefs about causes and cures of illness are very strong and hard to shift once formed (Ley 1988). This has also been found in relation to mental health problems. Barrowclough *et al.* (1987) found that relatives of people with more long-term disorders were less influenced by an educational programme than those where the disorder had a relatively short-term history. It seems therefore to be essential to begin the educational process at the earliest opportunity before people begin to develop their own explanations for their experiences. Of course, one of the most important reasons for beginning education early is to minimize the chances of further relapses by increasing understanding of the disorder, and helping them to learn more effective methods of coping with the situations which contribute to its development.

The second point in relation to timing is at what point during an episode of a disorder the main educational component should be provided. Some education obviously takes place during the assessment stage in that people have queries or raise issues that have to be addressed. The bulk of the education, however, is probably best provided after the family member has recovered from a major episode, and is able to participate in sessions and contribute to discussions. It is also likely that at this time other family members will feel less stressed and anxious and therefore will be more likely to process information and see the situation in perspective. Overall therefore it is best to begin education as soon as it is feasible. If it is difficult to find the ideal time to begin, either because the person with the disorder is unable to concentrate or other family members are highly anxious, it is better to begin educational sessions in a brief, simple manner. Sessions can be kept short, focusing on one or two key points each time and concentrating initially on the more important relevant issues for the family unit.

## SKILLS EMPLOYED IN THE EDUCATION PROCESS

### Preparation

Previous chapters have dealt with the assessments carried out before any educational session or other interventions take place. Therapists need to be familiar with this background information and summarize for themselves what they know about the strengths and weaknesses of each participant's understanding of the disorder and what additional information would be helpful before beginning education sessions. The educational component of BFT is an ongoing process as is the assessment. Detailed discussions about the participants' experiences with the disorder, the problems that have arisen, and how they have coped enable the therapist to define those issues which need most time spent on them, and those that can be dealt with less extensively.

It is also essential that therapists are familiar and up to date with the topic they are discussing and that they know the facts so that they feel comfortable imparting this information to others. Many therapists may never have had to explain to a group the main symptoms of schizophrenia or how common depression is in the general population. During education sessions therapists will be faced with all sorts of questions, such as:

- 'Can you explain how I can hear a voice speaking to me unless there's some telepathy going on or some kind of supernatural thing out there?'
- 'I thought that only young women and women going through the menopause became depressed, so why am I depressed now – I have a good wife, lovely children, and a great job?'
- 'I heard that girls develop anorexia because they don't get on with their mothers.'
- 'So if schizophrenia runs in families the baby my sister's about to have might get it.'

Unless therapists are up to date with the facts and familiar with the current theories of disorders, they will not be able to deal with such questions and consequently will lose credibility with families. Or worse, they may provide inaccurate information, thereby perpetuating misunderstandings about mental disorders. Therapists must therefore be well informed, trained and practised in using these approaches. Practising conducting an educational session with colleagues and getting feedback is helpful and, even if this is not possible, using an audiotape and listening to a playback will help therapists to realize gaps in existing knowledge and topics on which they tend to falter. Unless therapists give time to adequate preparation, their anxieties about what they might be asked in sessions will distract from their ability to concentrate on family members and on what is happening in the session. Of course, no one has expertise in all areas, and if therapists are unfamiliar with some particular issues, they should admit lack of knowledge but agree to find out the answers from someone who knows. Sometimes all that is required is to check up facts but at other times it may be useful to bring someone with expertise along to a family meeting. For example, if someone is on a complex drug regime and the therapist does not have medical training, it is probably helpful to invite along a medical colleague to discuss the effects of the drugs and their interactions. Similar situations may arise where the particular contribution of a social worker, nurse therapist, or psychologist may be appropriate.

A final point on preparation is that therapists should prepare in advance what will be covered in a particular session, and have available handouts and any audiovisual or other aids that may be used. Well-recognized teaching skills, such as the use of a chalk-board or flip chart to highlight key points, or diagrams and graphics to simplify complex issues, or the value of frequent repetition of the main principles, need careful planning and rehearsal. It is particularly important when working with a co-therapist that a preparatory meeting is held each time, so that the approach is coordinated.

### Conveying the facts

The ongoing nature of the educational process was referred to earlier. The second important point about providing information is that the attainment of knowledge results from a two-way interactional process with time given for assimilation of material and processing of what was heard. Smith (1984) draws attention to the fact that often little attention is paid to the way in which material is presented 'seemingly based on the unwritten assumption that information is information irrespective of how it is given'. Once again the work of Ley (1988) leaves no doubt as to how little information is retained if presented in a didactic manner. Berkowitz et al. (1984) describing an educational approach in which information was presented in a lecture format reported that people remembered only a fraction of what they had been told. On the other hand when material is presented in an active interactional manner with practice and rehearsal between sessions, retention does not seem to be such a problem (McGill et al. 1983; Smith and Birchwood 1987).

There is evidence that family members have their own models of dysfunction and explanations for unusual behaviour (Tarrier and Barrowclough 1986) and that if these views are entrenched they can be difficult to shift (Falloon et al. 1981). At the first educational session the first step is to elicit from all participants their understanding of the disorder under discussion. The therapist may make an opening statement such as:

'As you know I have met with Julie and you all on a number of occasions and we have had lots of time to talk. It is clear to me that over the past six weeks, Julie has been experiencing severe depression. I wonder what each of you understand by the term "depression". John, can you tell me what you understand by someone being depressed?'

When any term such as autism, schizophrenia, anxiety, panic, or bulimia is mentioned to people initially, it is likely to trigger them into thinking about their own understanding of that term or their own experience of the issue in question. If you give them further facts at this point you are unlikely to get their full concentration as they will be pondering over their own experiences, and you will also miss the opportunity of gaining fast access to their experiences and also their concerns about the topic being discussed. Each person may have many misconceptions about the nature of disorders or what causes them, and if the therapist does not find out what these are it is not possible to correct them. These misconceptions frequently result in emotional reactions which can get in the way of progress if they are not rectified. To give some examples: many people think that someone with schizophrenia has a split personality and therefore feel frightened when told that one of their household members has experienced a schizophrenic episode; a husband may think that depression is something you can 'snap out of' if you make the effort, and blame his wife for not trying hard enough and feel angry towards her; a mother may feel that her son's learning difficulty resulted from something that happened while she was pregnant, and therefore feel guilty. If these misconceptions and consequent feelings are not addressed, they will hinder progress being made towards dealing with the problem.

Repeated checking of what has been understood and questioning on the particular topic being discussed are essential if education is to be effective. The therapist must maintain an open, non-blaming, non-critical approach so that family members will disclose their views, theories, and concerns, even when they are aware that some may seem foolish. Another skill which therapists need to practise is being able to convey the facts about the relationship between stressful events, which can frequently include situations in the household, and vulnerability to episodes of mental disorders, without those individuals who were involved feeling blamed or responsible for what has happened. Again it is useful for therapists to practise doing this with colleagues or audiotaping themselves before a session.

The language used by the therapist should be simple, non-technical, and as jargon-free as possible. Information provided should be detailed enough to ensure that the family understands what they are dealing with. There appears to be a misconception among some professionals that education is the same as 'labelling' and it is of concern that some writers on this topic, e.g. Berkowitz *et al.* (1984) seem to use the terms interchangeably. In a behavioural family therapy model, *education does not in any way equate with labelling*. The purpose of the educational component is that all participants should have a realistic understanding of a particular disorder, what caused it, and the most effective management of it. One of the best ways of increasing the family's understanding, and to make it more likely that sessions remain comprehensible and jargon-free, is to use the participants' own experiences and expertise. The person with the disorder is in the role of 'expert' and is used as a co-presenter. No one knows more about the experience of the disorder than the person who has just experienced the phenomena being described. The knowledge of what it actually felt like to feel so down you wanted to die, to hear people talking when there was nobody there, to be unable to resist doing something that you knew was stupid, is the best aide to helping other household members understand exactly what is meant by 'suicidal thoughts', 'auditory hallucinations' or 'compulsive actions'. Equally other household members have expert knowledge about what makes the person feel worse, what situations are difficult to cope with, and the signs that their relative is becoming unwell.

## When people have difficulty accepting facts

The technique of using participants' own experiences can be helpful when family members find it difficult to accept the facts being presented. They usually find it easier when reminded of their own experiences and the descriptions given by those who are close to them.

Where people have difficulty accepting facts which have been presented and which are not in doubt, the therapist should avoid confrontational situations and should not try to persuade the participant verbally to come round to her way of thinking. It is easy for therapists to forget that what is familiar to them after years of working with people with disorders is new to the family experiencing the particular problem for the first time, or to the family who have coped without professional help for years. A useful exercise for therapists is to imagine how they would react if someone tried to persuade them that something they believed firmly to be the case was not true. This usually makes it easier to see things from the family's point of view, and to feel less irritated with the family's refusal to accept particular facts as true. It is important not to get bogged down in one particular session, and to bear in mind that people need time to process and assimilate new information. Sometimes what people find hard to accept in one session, they have come to understand by the next because they have had time to think about it and adjust to its implications in their own time.

Another useful strategy is to help the family members involved set up experiments or think about what would prove to them whether what they believed was in fact the case. This experimental style of learning is usually much more effective, and more rapid than ongoing theoretical discussions.

In summarizing how to convey information to household members, the most important points to remember are that 'telling' is not 'educating' and that 'hearing' does not mean 'understanding'. The process of educating families is lengthy and requires constant checking of understanding, repetition as people gain understanding at different levels, and an avoidance of the assumption that what was once understood will be retained.

## CONTENT OF EDUCATIONAL SESSIONS – WHAT TO INCLUDE

While the content of what is presented will vary from disorder to disorder, and the emphasis will vary from group to group, there are a number of general areas that need to be covered. Educational sessions should always cover what the disorder is, and what kind of behaviour and thinking to expect. The last two points are very important, as actions and thoughts are often attributed to personality or to the person not trying hard enough, rather than to the disorder in question. It is easy for family members to attribute their relative staying in bed and being inactive to laziness rather than a schizophrenic disorder; or somebody who finds it difficult to make decisions may be thought to be avoiding responsibility or not doing his or her fair share rather than experiencing symptoms of depression. Causes of the disorders should be covered carefully and thoroughly, and this is often something about which there are misconceptions and a lack of understanding. Factors which makes the situation worse and what is likely to protect against further episodes need to be addressed, as well as rehearsing what to do in crises. It is worth spending time preparing people realistically for the possibility of future episodes, what to do if they occur, and also discussing the fact that there are always 'bad days' when someone is recovering from an episode of a disorder. This reduces the likelihood of the family overreacting or becoming dispirited when progress is not steady.

Counselling people about the implications of genetic factors associated with serious disorders is an area that requires special attention. Whereas some disorders, such as Huntington's disease, have a major genetic aetiology, and counselling potential carriers of the defective gene may have a profound impact on its prevalence, most mental disorders and learning disabilities are not inherited in such a dramatic and direct manner. For example, there is a ten-fold increase in the risk of developing schizophrenia if a parent or sibling has the disorder. This compares with a 300–fold increase in the risk of lung cancer for a cigarette smoker. However, if an individual's identical twin has schizophrenia, or if both his or her parents had the disorder, the risk becomes around 40 – 50 times higher than that of other people in the general population. But even then the story is more complex. It is unlikely that a disorder like schizophrenia is actually inherited. More likely, it is the metabolic weakness that is inherited, and the disorder only develops under certain conditions; for example, when that person is under high stress, or takes stimulating drugs, or suffers some brain injury or epilepsy, etc. A comprehensive understanding of these points is crucial to effective education so that people can be presented with a clear understanding of the risks, and can make rational choices about vital life decisions, such as marriage and childbearing. Inadequate presentation of these issues may be frightening, stressful, and potentially harmful.

The rationale for any treatment regimes, whether they be social, psychological, or pharmacological, should be presented in detail with plenty of checking back on each participant's understanding as mentioned earlier. Much of what professionals describe as 'non-compliance' results from people not having been given a sufficiently detailed explanation of how the strategies being described will help them, and why it is important that they are adhered to in a particular way. It is not unreasonable for people to think that they should take anti-depressant medication only when they feel particularly depressed, or that they should use relaxation exercises only when they feel anxious if it has not been explained to them why regular adherence to such regimes is essential. A final topic which must be covered is how to detect the warning signs that someone is developing an episode of a disorder and rehearsal of strategies for dealing with this.

The amount of time spent on different aspects of the topics mentioned above will be determined by the needs of each specific household. There is much to cover, and it is easy to be side-tracked from essentials because of the family's need for detailed discussion of one particular issue. It is helpful for the therapist to have a checklist to ensure that important topics are not forgotten.

## CONDUCT OF SESSIONS

The educational sessions are conducted in the same way as the other therapeutic sessions. At the beginning the therapist should decide with the family on the plan for the use of time during that session and as far as possible adhere to it. Therapists should remember to deal with any issues carried forward from the previous session. Time spent on discussion of issues of relevance to this particular family should be maximized and general discussions of less relevant material kept to a minimum.

If people are to get the most benefit from educational sessions, the 'emotional climate' needs to be kept under control as family members are less likely to be able to attend to what is being said or remember discussion if the atmosphere is heated

69

or emotionally charged. A focus on factual information presented in a calm, neutral manner is more likely to result in an atmosphere conducive to learning. Therapists should avoid taking sides but instead stick to empirically proven facts. Lengthy discussions about hypothetical situations or treatment approaches may be interesting but are unlikely to result in improved management of the disorder or enhanced coping skills on the part of the family, who are more likely to leave or will not attend further sessions.

Sessions should generally last no longer than an hour with factual information being presented in four- to five-minute segments followed by family members discussing the points raised, their own concerns, experiences, or queries. The difficulties that family members may experience in taking in new, unfamiliar information should be recognized. Therapists should be constantly alert to whether or not attention is being maintained and create a break by changing the format or mode of presentation to maintain concentration. Some disorders have resultant cognitive dysfunctions, most affect concentration at times, and some pharmacological treatments can also have adverse effects on people's ability to attend for anything other than short periods of time. In these situations, sessions can be shorter and more frequent; planned breaks during sessions can ensure that all family members participate as much as possible. Motivation, which is an important component in learning, is generally not a problem when conducting educational sessions with families as they are usually only too eager to have the opportunity to discuss topics which are extremely relevant to them. Interruptions during sessions, e.g. TV, phone calls, people calling to the house, need to be addressed in a problem-solving way with the family and should be dealt with at the start of contact with the family. If not dealt with early on, established patterns are harder to break and there is a risk that therapeutic interventions are seen as less valued or important.

Audiovisual aids such as handouts, tapes, etc. can be helpful in overcoming problems of retention because family members can go over the material at their own pace. Handouts should be directly related to the particular topic being discussed at each session, easy to read, and jargon-free. They may need to be simplified depending on the literacy level of the family involved. Sometimes people find graphs, diagrams, or information presented visually, rather than verbally, more effective. For people with severe literacy problems, tapes can be a useful substitute for handouts. Some families like to tape their sessions with the therapist and then arrange a time among themselves to listen and discuss it again between sessions.

The main thing to remember is that educational sessions should be conducted in a way that can be understood by, and is acceptable to, the particular family. Content should be relevant, and the particular needs/deficits of particular family members should be recognized and accommodated.

### Home study and family meetings

Participants are given handouts or booklets to read between sessions. They are asked to talk together in family meetings about what has been discussed in sessions, and prepare any questions for clarification at the beginning of the next session. In this way facts are rehearsed and material is repeated frequently so it is more likely to be retained. Therapists too should ensure that they obtain information on points about which they were unclear or check up on issues as agreed with the family. Each new session begins with a question and answer discussion, clarifying points from the previous discussion and revising the key points.

## DETECTING EARLY WARNING SIGNS

A key component of the educational module of BFT is identifying, monitoring, and responding to the earliest signs of major episodes of mental and physical disorders. The outcome of most major health problems is usually better better where episodes are treated optimally at the earliest opportunity. The ability to recognize the earliest signs of an impending episode is vital to effective management. Sufferers and their carers may then initiate crisis management with minimal delay.

The early signs of many disorders are similar. Most involve excessive stress that threatens to overwhelm the person's coping capacity. Sleep and appetite disturbances, muscle tension pains, irritability, and social avoidance are among the common prodromal features of depressive, manic, anxiety, and schizophrenic disorders. However, each person tends to have his or

71

her own pattern of signs that warn of an impending episode of the disorder to which he or she is most vulnerable. These patterns tend to remain constant before each episode. John M. always noted that he became restless and could never fully relax before the onset of his episodes of acute anxiety.

Some people may find the early signs of an episode of a specific disorder difficult to distinguish from stress responses. After a clearly recognized stressful event, some people may be able to recognize the features associated with excessive levels of stress that often occur before the onset of their more specific early warning signs. Such stress may be recognized in terms of thoughts of potential negative consequences, dysphoric mood, and physiological changes such as increased heart rate, blood pressure, or muscle tension. Again, these stress responses tend to be specific to each individual, with one person experiencing a rapid heart rate, another muscle tension in a specific muscle group, another an apprehensive mood.

In some disorders the effects of overwhelming stress act as triggers to an acute episode. This is characteristic of schizophrenic and manic episodes, where overwhelming stress may result in an episode within a few days. Episodes of other disorders, such as depression and anxiety, tend to develop over longer periods of exposure to high stress levels, usually weeks or months.

Discrete life events, such as bereavement, loss of job, relationship breakup, accident, are superimposed upon background stress in the environment. High levels of everyday stress are often associated with unemployment, poverty, hunger, family tension, or substance misuse. In such instances relatively small increases in stress levels may overwhelm a person's coping capacity and place him or her at high risk of an episode of the disorder. In such cases the early warning signs may be difficult to recognize, and the onset of an episode may occur with minimal delay.

The therapist assists the family in their efforts to pinpoint the clearest, and earliest, signs of an impending episode. This work may extend over several sessions, and may be facilitated through the use of checklists of common early warning signs (e.g. Fava and Kellner 1991; Herz and Melville 1980; Birchwood et al. 1989). At times household members may have noted subtle changes before the person developing the episode became aware of them.

Once one or two key signs have been agreed upon, the therapist and family problem solve the specific strategies that they may employ to prevent a major episode developing. These will usually be a combination of stress management to deal with any stress factors that may have precipitated the episode, and in the case of disorders such as schizophrenia, specific medical strategies, such as drug treatments or special diets that counter the physiological responses. Such early interventions must be clearly planned, and triggered immediately the early signs have been detected. Where the family have been trained in BFT communication and problem-solving skills, they will form the basis of the stress management approach, and can be initiated as soon as possible. It is crucial that similar efficiency can be provided by the professional care team, and that assessment and specific treatments can be provided with minimal delays. Where BFT is provided within the context of a mental health team, and all members of that multidisciplinary team are trained in these methods, little difficulty arises.

Records of the early signs as well as the specific strategies to implement when they appear are provided for patient, carers, family practitioners, and mental health services. Patients are given small cards to carry in their wallets, and sheets, such as the one illustrated in Figure 4.1, are displayed prominently within the household to ensure that all key people are prompted to recognize the early signs and to act in an effective manner should they arise.

Occasionally people express concern that they might over-react and report signs that are of little consequence. It is crucial that the therapist and colleagues accept that many calls will prove negative, but take care to respond to such contacts in a positive way that encourages future early intervention, when the signs may indeed be those of an impending episode.

Once the participants have compiled their early warnings cards and prompt sheets the therapist rehearses with them a scenario where one or more signs seem to emerge. Patients and family members practise their responses, including role playing how to contact professional services. Potential hitches are rehearsed, such as dealing with busy family doctors, who are not aware of the procedures, or therapists who are deputizing when their key therapist is away.

People experiencing the disorder and their household members are invited to review the early warning cards at their

---

**Early warning signs**

Name: JOY ALLEN

I have a risk of developing episodes of a SCHIZOPHRENIC disorder.

My early warning signs are:

1. REDUCTION IN MY SLEEP OF 2 HOURS FOR 3 NIGHTS IN A ROW

2. NOT ABLE TO READ FOR MORE THAN 5 MINUTES AT A TIME

3. SPENDING MORE THAN 4 HOURS ALONE IN MY ROOM FOR 3 DAYS RUNNING

Whenever I experience *any* of these signs I will respond by:

a) INFORM MY DOCTOR BY PHONE IMMEDIATELY

b) INFORM MY THERAPIST (JAMES MCDOWELL) BY PHONE IMMEDIATELY

c) PINPOINT ANY STRESSES & ARRANGE EMERGENCY PROBLEM-SOLVING DISCUSSION

My doctor is: DR FRASER        Phone: 819 468

My home contact is: JAMES MCDOWELL        Phone: 829 641

If I have any concerns about my disorder I will contact JAMES MCD. immediately.

---

*Figure 4.1*  Early warning signs

weekly family meetings. An additional review is conducted by the therapist at the beginning of each session. Any problems or misunderstandings concerning any aspect of the disorder are dealt with in the most effective manner. At times it may be necessary to devote an entire session to revision of educational aspects, where continued evidence of major misunderstandings is evident, particularly when these appear to be contributing to continuing stress in the household.

## CONCLUSIONS

Evidence suggests that education alone is not sufficient to bring about marked changes in coping behaviour or in how patients and their carers manage the difficulties they face (Berkowitz *et al.* 1984; Smith and Birchwood 1987). However, it is an essential prerequisite in order that all subsequent interventions are effective. Education provides a basis and a rationale for treatment strategies and results in greater adherence to drug, social, and psychological interventions. In addition to this there is evidence that education results in reduced anxiety and stress levels in family members, and also more hopeful attitudes towards the future (Anderson *et al.* 1986; Smith and Birchwood 1987). Household members and key friends are more likely to show increased tolerance towards those persons with high vulnerability to potentially disabling disorders and, perhaps more important, may be able to assist directly in promoting lasting recoveries from these disorders.

The process of providing education is not simple or quick. It requires preparation by and training for therapists who have to devote time to work with people for as long as is necessary to ensure a comprehensive understanding of the disorder and its clinical management. It also requires that therapists are willing to see patients and their carers as partners, as fully fledged members of the therapy team, and as people who often have greater expertise in dealing with the unique difficulties that arise in their particular household. This requires a shift in thinking that may prove difficult for therapists trained in other models.

However, working with people in this way proves satisfying and rewarding, and the sharing of knowledge and expertise involved results in the most effective management for all participants.

## NOTE

1 Issues of confidentiality are often cited as reasons for avoiding contact with a person's relatives or supportive friends when they experience a mental disorder. Of course, certain intimate details of an individual's personal life that might be divulged to an interviewer during an assessment should not be discussed with third parties without that person's full consent, and then only when such revelations are deemed beneficial to the patient, or in certain cases where a patient makes serious threats of harm to others and the therapist has an obligation to warn those targeted. However, where someone with a serious disorder is living in a household, it is crucial that all household members are provided with a basic understanding of the disorder and any ways that they may contribute to the recovery

process. In the same way that a doctor advises the family on the appropriate diet for a member who has diabetes, a peptic ulcer, or kidney failure, it is important to advise on the appropriate measures to take to alleviate a panic attack, to cope with paranoid ideas, to respond to a depressed person's profound hopelessness, or an obsessional's handwashing ritual. Failure to address such issues adequately is clearly negligent.

# 5

# COMMUNICATION
# TRAINING

## INTRODUCTION

Good interpersonal communication skills help all families to
cope with everyday stresses and problems. A lack of skill in
expressing one's thoughts and feelings in a clear manner to
other people in the household may contribute to situations
where families deal with problems by arguing with raised voices
and expressing feelings in a hostile manner; or where people
get so upset that they do not talk to each other at all, and may
resort to inappropriate actions, such as suicide attempts or
aggressive behaviour to cope with overwhelming stressors. This
makes for a very stressful environment at home. When household members are vulnerable to stress-related disorders, these
unresolved tensions may lead to more frequent episodes of
those disorders (Leff and Vaughn 1985).

All family therapy approaches consider interpersonal communication between family members as a key aspect of the
interventions employed (Hoffman 1981). Working with the
living group, rather than merely with the individual with presenting health or psychological problems, provides the opportunity to enhance patterns of communication among the group
that may help to reduce stress and thereby contribute to fewer
stress-induced episodes of disorder. In behavioural family
therapy special attention is given to examining the way in which
household members communicate their thoughts and feelings
to each other, particularly at times when they are attempting to
resolve a stressful problem or assist one another in achieving
personal goals (Falloon 1988). A careful analysis of the specific
interpersonal communication styles of each participant is conducted while they are interacting in a problem-focused discussion.

The manner in which each person expresses pleasant as well as unpleasant feelings and ideas, listens to others, and makes requests for changes in others' actions are all examined in terms of their verbal and non-verbal components. Intervention strategies are then targeted to each household's specific strengths and weaknesses.

The main aim of communication training in behavioural family therapy is to enable the household group to meet together on a weekly basis and to hold a constructive discussion about issues of major concern to one or more of the participants. It is preferable that this meeting is comfortable and amiable, that all participants feel able to express their specific needs and contribute to the support of others, and, above all, that major stressors are addressed in a manner that leads to efficient resolution. At times discussions may become heated and stressful. However, it is hoped that such animosity is relatively shortlived, and that the discussion is concluded with a clear plan of action directed to resolving the key stressors. Interpersonal communication is an extremely complex process. Behavioural family therapy does not attempt to focus on every aspect of this process; instead, four basic interpersonal communication skills are addressed initially, with more complex issues targeted for subsequent specialized intervention. These four skills have been observed to be most lacking in families under stress (Leff and Vaughn 1985) and may be expected to contribute to substantial improvements in the efficiency of problem resolution and goal achievement. The core curriculum of communication skills includes:

- expressing pleasant feelings;
- making constructive requests;
- expressing unpleasant feelings;
- active listening.

Each of these skills will be described in detail and examples given later in this chapter. It may be noted that these basic skills include the expression of positive as well as negative emotions. Behavioural methods attend not merely to problem issues but provide interventions that aim to enhance the quality of life of all participants. This is often achieved through helping participants to perceive the frequent performance of pleasant responses, not merely to focus on the infrequent occurrence of unpleasant events. It has been noted that in non-distressed families the frequency that pleasing events are acknowledged by household members is about one out of every ten such events; whereas the frequency of noting (and commenting on) negative events approaches nine out of ten. When households are distressed this ratio is even more extreme, with acknowledgement of negative events approaching 99 per cent, and comments on positive responses being made on less than 1 per cent of occasions when pleasing behaviours are performed (Stuart, personal communication, 1977). Thus it is considered crucial to attempt to rectify this almost exclusive focus on unpleasant issues, not merely by attempting to suppress such responses or their negative consequences, but also by promoting increased attention to the small pleasing behaviours that people perform, even at times of high stress.

## THE TECHNIQUES USED IN COMMUNICATION TRAINING

The strategies used in behavioural family therapy for training interpersonal communication skills have been derived from the skill training methods developed in behavioural group therapy (Liberman *et al.* 1975; Falloon 1978). These methods make extensive use of repeated rehearsal of responses as a format for training more effective response patterns. They are based on a teaching model and use the theories of learning of social responses and self-efficacy (Bandura 1977). The therapist is seen as the teacher, helping families to learn new skills. The focus is on rehearsing new responses, not merely on insight or understanding. The therapist emphasizes positive reinforcement of specific desirable behaviours; hostile criticism or coercion is avoided. One of the important roles of the therapist is to teach family members to increase their positive reinforcement to each other for desired behaviours, both during the therapy meetings and, most crucially, in their everyday lives.

It is important to keep in mind that changes in communication style do not occur overnight. It takes time, patience, and repeated practice. The therapist must be prepared to teach and review the skills many times in the course of teaching families alternative ways of coping and expressing themselves. All families have had years of practising communicating in their own style in the past; regardless of how ineffective or stressful, these styles of communication are often firmly established. A small change in communication can be a major accomplishment for family and therapist.

The specific techniques used in teaching communication skills are:

• assessment of participants' interpersonal communication skills;
  ↓
• providing a rationale;
  ↓
• outlining steps of skill;
  ↓
• rehearsal of skill;
  ↓
• constructive feedback;
  ↓
• repeated rehearsal with coaching;
  ↓
• real-life practice and review.

### Assessment of interpersonal communication skills

The initial behavioural assessment provides the therapist with an initial assessment of the way in which participants communicate when they are engaged in a family discussion about a problem issue. As well as noting the overall patterns of communication among the group, the therapist notes the specific strengths and weaknesses of each individual in the four basic skills outlined on page 78. In addition he may note the use of these skills in a variety of other less formal contexts, such as during education sessions and individual interviews. Any observation of competent performance of these skills is noted on the CPC form (see pages 40–1), which serves as a rapid reference. Substantial discrepancies between an individual's performance in problem-solving discussions with other household members and performance in non-family settings may be noted.

Further assessment is provided by re-enactment of brief scenarios during the sessions, including performances of skills practised in assignments between sessions.

## Providing a rationale

In the initial step of the training process all participants are provided with a clear understanding of the potential advantages of using each specific communication. Participants are invited to suggest potential benefits from employing the particular communication skill when attempting to resolve problems or work on achieving personal goals. The therapist then summarizes the benefits identified and adds any other major benefits not elicited from the group.

For example, the therapist asked the participants to suggest ways in which expressing unpleasant feelings in a clear and direct way might help to resolve problems and achieve personal goals. They suggested that such expression might reduce tension by 'getting things off their chest', and help inform people what they thought needed to be changed. Simon commented that merely expressing negative feelings might lead to increased nagging and arguments. The therapist summarized these points and added that Simon had made an important observation. He attempted to differentiate from nagging, which he said occurred when one person blamed another for doing things that made them feel upset, and tried to coerce them to change their ways. He pointed out that coercion and making others feel guilty was less effective in encouraging people to commit themselves to lasting behaviour changes than making positive requests. Furthermore, he suggested that it may be best to target no more than one or two displeasing issues to work on at any time, rather than pick on every little fault that irritates you about every other person sharing the home.

### Review of current skill levels

Once the rationale for a specific communication skill has been established, the therapist reviews the current performance of that specific skill among participants. He reports on his observations during initial and ongoing assessments giving specific examples of occasions when he has observed a participant employ the specific skill being considered.

For example, the therapist noted that Jessica had, on several occasions during the previous week's education session about her daughter's depressive disorder, remarked how pleased she was with the efforts Celia had made to continue her work. The therapist had also noted that during the observed problem-solving discussion Jessica had made two similar positive comments to Celia and Joseph, her husband. In his review of current skills he gave her the following feedback:

'Jessica, I have noticed that on several occasions you have made comments about how things people have done have pleased you. I remember that when I asked you to discuss a problem during my assessment you told Joseph that you liked the way he helped you care for Celia when she was very depressed. I also recall you telling Celia in our session last week how her efforts to continue working when she was feeling pretty low pleased you. I suspect that you make many similar positive comments to other people on a day-to-day basis. Is that right?' (*addressing Celia*)

Celia:   'Yes. Jessica's very good at finding positive things to say, and gives me tons of encouragement.'

At this stage the therapist gives feedback to participants on skills that they appear to perform with some degree of competence. He does not mention any deficiencies. If there is no evidence of competent performance of the specific skill, this step is omitted.

### Outlining the steps of the skill

The skill is then broken down into its main component verbal and non-verbal steps. The steps are clearly explained and presented in written form, preferably as handouts but also as flipcharts or on a blackboard (see Figure 5.1). The steps always focus positively on what participants need to do rather than on what they should *not* do. The therapist gives an explicit example of the skill. Wherever possible this example involves expressing a genuine feeling to one or more of the participants. For example, the therapist was very pleased that Simon had managed to leave work early so that he could attend the meeting at 5 p.m. He addressed the participants thus:

'I would like to show you an example of what I mean by the steps of expressing a pleasant feeling by telling Simon about something he did that pleased me. I would like you all to see which steps I use when I communicate my pleasant feelings to him . . . Simon, I was very pleased that you were able to arrange to leave work half an hour early today so that you could make our meeting on time . . . Now what steps did I use?

Jessica:   You looked at Simon and smiled at him.

Joseph:   You said what he had done that pleased you.

Simon:   I didn't hear you say exactly how you felt.

Therapist:   Did anyone else hear me say how I felt?

Joseph:   I thought you said you were pleased or something, didn't you?

Therapist:   I said I was pleased, that's all. It was not a great deal, so I did not make a fuss over it, I just said I was pleased, because that was exactly the way I felt, not overjoyed or ecstatic, just pleased. Did I come across as if I was pleased, Simon?

Simon:   Yes, sure. You seemed really quite pleased with my efforts and that made me feel good.

Therapist:   Do you think that my saying that to you will help in any way in future?

Simon:   Well, not really. I suppose it might encourage me to do the same next week. Yes, your appreciation certainly helps. I guess I'm likely to try to do the same next week.

---

- Look at the person and speak in a warm tone
- Tell him or her exactly what he or she did that pleased you
- Tell him or her how it made you feel

---

*Figure 5.1*   Expressing pleasant feelings

## SKILLS TRAINING: REHEARSAL, FEEDBACK, COACHING, AND MODELLING

During this part of the session the therapist aims to coach participants who have deficiencies in performing each specific skill in the manner outlined. This is achieved through guided practice of the skill in a realistic context. The behavioural family therapist employs training strategies that have been demonstrated to be most effective in enhancing interpersonal communication in controlled experiments (Brady 1984; Curran and Monti 1982; Trower *et al.* 1978). These strategies will be outlined briefly here.

### Initial rehearsal

The therapist invites the participants to give examples of when they used the specific skill recently within the household. Often participants may recognize that their performance was sub-optimal, not following the explicit steps that have been outlined. They may also have difficulty recalling the precise manner in which they expressed themselves. For these reasons the response to the therapist's request may be hesitant and the therapist may need to be persistent in eliciting examples. It is helpful to emphasize to the family that the example does not have to be a major event; it can be a small, everyday thing that someone in the family does. In teaching the expression of positive feelings, questions such as 'Who made dinner tonight?' or 'Who got you up this morning?' or 'How did you get to the meeting?' or 'Did someone set the table for you?' can encourage families to think of their own examples. Further-more, participants may be able to identify occasions when they might have employed a particular skill but did not.

The therapist chooses the participant whom he has observed as having the highest level of competence in the specific com-munication skill to re-enact the first example. This enables participants who are less skilled to observe and pick up specific points prior to their attempts.

Once an example is given, the therapist then elicits as many details as possible to help participants reconstruct the situation in a realistic manner. He may ask:

'Where were you when this happened?'
'What time of day was it?'
'What exactly did you say?'

Once a situation has been established, the therapist asks the relevant participants to *show* everyone what happened. This often involves asking them to go to the place in the home where the interaction took place: 'OK, so you were standing in the doorway and Jessica was sitting on the living room sofa.' People not involved in the scene are asked to observe the re-enactment closely, keeping in mind the specific steps of the skills being taught.

> The therapist might say, 'I would like the rest of you to watch closely, and notice if Joseph is able to look at Jessica, and say exactly what it is she does that he likes, and tell Jessica how he feels when she does that. And I'll ask you afterwards to tell Joseph the particular things you like about the way he follows the steps on the guide sheets.'

84

In some instances it may be helpful to ask each family member to concentrate on observing a separate step, such as 'looking at the person'. Sequences are kept brief. The responses given to expressions of feelings or requests are not considered at this point. The therapist may need to interject with 'Let's stop here' as soon as the target person has rehearsed his or her expression. The nature of the response is not considered important, merely the manner in which the feeling or request is expressed. Clearly training in active listening skills is an exception to this, with the *responses* being the target of training. It is the *structure* of communication that is trained in behavioural family therapy, not the *content* of that expression. It is assumed that when expressions are made in the manner recommended the responses are more likely to prove mutually beneficial, though not invariably so. This assumption is supported by extensive interaction research, such as that of Kurt Hahlweg (Hahlweg *et al.* 1984).

Where expressions of feelings, particularly those involving unpleasant feelings, highlight unresolved conflicts, participants may be invited to attempt to resolve these issues in their own family meetings. Where such issues are particularly explosive, or the capacity of the household to handle them is thought to be inadequate, the therapist may counsel participants to avoid further discussion until they have gained additional problem-solving skills in the course of therapy. On occasions, such expressions may lead to an immediate crisis, and the therapist may have to chair a crisis-oriented problem-solving discussion before continuing the communication training. Careful behavioural assessment will usually enable the skilled therapist to target potentially explosive issues, and enable her to steer clear of such issues at this stage. It is important to note here that the crisis approach employed by the therapist will be identical to the problem-solving approach that will be employed during subsequent training sessions. The skilled therapist will, therefore, take advantage of such a crisis to introduce the structured problem-solving approach.

## Eliciting constructive feedback

As soon as a participant has completed his or her re-enactment of the communication the therapist requests other participants

85

to give constructive feedback to the target individual about the specific steps of the skill. They are initially requested to tell the person what they liked about the performance, and subsequently for suggestions about major improvements. This feedback includes comments on the performance from the individuals to whom the communication was directed. The therapist may summarize, or add specific comments where these have not been covered by the other participants. For example:

Celia has just completed a re-enactment of requesting that Jessica give her a ride to the city centre. She is standing next to her while she is reading the newspaper at the breakfast table.

Therapist: What did you like about the way Celia made her request, Simon?
Simon: I liked the way she said exactly what it was she wanted . . .
Therapist (interrupting): I would like you to tell Celia, not me.
Simon: Oh, I'm sorry. I liked the way you told Jessica exactly what you wanted her to do. And you asked her in a nice way.
Therapist: What did she do that made it come across as particularly nice to you?
Simon: Well, I think she spoke softly and didn't sound as if she was putting her under any sort of obligation.
Therapist: What did you like about it, Jessica?
Jessica: I liked the way you said you would appreciate it if I gave you a ride.
Therapist: So we agree that Celia used each of the steps on the guide sheet. Does anyone have any suggestions about how she might have made any major improvements to the way she expressed that?
Joseph: No . . . Not really . . .
Therapist: What about her non-verbal expression and use of body language?
Celia: I could have sat down next to Jessica at the table. Would that have been better than standing?
Therapist: It might have been. What do you think, Joseph?
Joseph: I wondered if you might have waited until Jessica had finished reading the paper, or perhaps if you had said something like 'Excuse me, Jessica, I'd like to ask you something.'

Celia:     Yes. I like that idea.
Therapist:    I would like you to see whether it seems better to sit down next to Jessica and get her attention before you make your request.
Celia:    O.K. I'll try it again.

At times a performance may appear grossly incompetent, and it may be difficult to find any aspects to provide positive feedback about. At these times the therapist looks hard for something positive to feed back, and tries to prompt similar positive statements from the other participants. This may be some small aspect of non-verbal communication that was competent, such as the participant's eye contact, posture, or voice volume. For instance, he might ask, '*What did you like* about *the way Celia looked at* Jessica?'

If one family member starts to criticize another, it is important to interrupt, 'For now I'd like you to focus on what you *liked* about what Simon did.' The therapist, as always, models effective communication skills himself. Suggestions for change are never given until all positive aspects have been reviewed. Furthermore, they are always expressed in terms of suggestions for change that the person may choose to incorporate into subsequent performances or not. Participants are constantly reminded that there are no right or wrong methods of interpersonal communication and the sessions are merely workshops that allow people to try out alternatives that may suit them better, and may be more likely to produce the mutual benefits they seek.

Although some skills training may be assisted by videotaped feedback procedures, it has been our experience that such feedback often distracts people from the key communication issues to matters of their appearance, tone of voice, etc. The added benefits seem outweighed by these matters, as well as by the time expended in setting up the equipment and dealing with technical hitches.

## Repeated rehearsal and coaching

Once the target person has been given constructive feedback, the therapist requests that he or she rehearses the communication sequence again. The therapist identifies one major source of improvement from the various suggestions made during the feedback phase and prompts the target person to change this specific aspect of his or her performance. For example, Joseph had expressed his frustration about his difficulty in getting a suitable job to Jessica, but had been looking downcast with his gaze directed towards the floor. The therapist requested the following:

> 'Joseph, I would like you to show us how you expressed your frustration to Jessica again. Only this time *I would like you to look* at Jessica while you are talking to her, just as Celia suggested.'

It is important to focus on improving one step at a time, and to focus only on major deficits. Where performance has several major deficits, no more than two are dealt with during one session, and coaching may extend over several sessions.

Coaching usually consists of making verbal suggestions for change. The therapist adheres to effective communication principles by making these suggestions in the form of 'positive requests'. Immediately following the repeated rehearsal further feedback is provided from other participants. Once again the therapist ensures that this feedback emphasizes positive features of the performance, before focusing on any major improvements that might be suggested. The target person is praised for any effort he or she makes, even when the performance is viewed as highly deficient and still in need of major improvement.

At times the target person may be assisted by prompts from other participants. These may include hand signals to prompt increase in voice volume or to encourage eye contact. On occasions verbal prompts may prove useful to help someone express himself using unfamiliar verbal expressions. For example, Joseph (in the example above) had difficulty verbalizing his feelings of frustration. The therapist had him practise saying 'I feel really frustrated' on several occasions until he could express himself in a manner that he felt was consistent with his feelings. However, he became tongue-tied when he attempted to express these feelings to Jessica. The therapist stood behind him and whispered the words he had used during the repeat rehearsals, until Joseph felt comfortable expressing himself without such prompting. A more technical version of this prompting method is called 'the bug-in-the-ear' device. A small radio transmitter, similar to a hearing aid, is placed in the target person's ear, while the coaching therapist gives verbal prompts during the rehearsed performance. However, the highly artificial nature of such technical aids, and the difficulties associated with ensuring that they work correctly, appear to detract from their value in most training settings. The value of simple interpersonal prompting is that it is readily employed in the natural setting, where a simple hand or facial gesture may help to remind a person to speak more loudly, more slowly, make better eye contact, or use a specific verbal expression that has been practised, in a relatively unobtrusive manner. Of course, the use of such prompts outside sessions should be clearly agreed by all concerned.

## Modelling alternative performance

Another strategy used frequently in communication training is the overt demonstration of an alternative performance by the therapist or another participant. This approach is called 'modelling'. This is used either when a participant has difficulty understanding the suggestions that others have made for alternative behaviours, or when the instructions are difficult to put into simple instructions. At such times simply showing the target person what he or she might do may prove helpful.

The methods we use have been derived from an extensive body of social psychology experimentation that suggests that modelling is most effective in promoting the specific desired changes in performance when it adheres to the following guidelines:

- The person acting as the model is viewed positively by the target individual.
- The performance of the model should not be vastly superior to that of the target individual, so it can be imitated effectively.
- The target person attends to the specific elements of the performance being demonstrated.
- The responses of other participants to the specific elements of the modelled performance are positive.
- The target individual has an opportunity to imitate the modelled performance immediately after it has been demonstrated, and is rewarded for his or her efforts.

These conditions for imitating the performances of others may be promoted by the overall structure employed in the sessions. However, they are highlighted when modelling is used to demonstrate a specific skill to a target person. The therapist employs the following steps:

1 Selects a person who has demonstrated competence in the performance of a specific element to demonstrate that element of performance. The therapist may choose himself as a model if no other participant is known to be competent, or other participants express their discomfort in demonstrating their competence in this manner.
2 Invites the target person to switch places with the person who is planning to model the specific behaviour.
3 Sets the scene for the modelled performance so that it is clear that the setting is identical to the one rehearsed earlier by the target person, and the model is performing the role of the target person in that setting. He may say: 'Joseph, I would like you and Celia to change places. I would like Celia to imagine she is playing your role and to express the frustration you experienced in a similar manner.'
4 Provides the target person with clear instructions about the specific element of the model's performance to attend to. For example: 'Joseph, I would like you to note the way that Celia speaks in a firm tone of voice when she tells Jessica how frustrated she feels about the job situation.'
5 As soon as the modelled performance is completed the therapist invites the targeted person to provide feedback on what he or she liked about the *specific elements* of the modelled performance. He invites the target person to consider whether the model's performance of the *specific elements* had any specific advantages that he or she might incorporate into his or her own subsequent performance. Discussion of other topics, particularly any other aspects of the model's performance that were more competent, is avoided.
6 The therapist instructs the target person to resume his or her role, by changing back to his or her original position, and to repeat a rehearsal of the brief sequence, while attempting to imitate that *specific element* of communication that was modelled. He or she is reminded to incorporate the modelling into his or her own style of communicating in a manner

that feels comfortable, not merely to repeat the model's performance 'parrot-fashion'.

7 All efforts to incorporate some specific elements of the modelling are praised by participants immediately after the repeated rehearsal.

8 It may be necessary to repeat modelling on several occasions before the target person can acquire the specific elements that are being demonstrated.

Of course, in most households individuals will have a range of strengths and weaknesses in their interpersonal skills. The therapist must use good judgement in choosing appropriate models for other participants. In particular, it is important to avoid excessive use of one participant, and to rotate the choice of models. Where one household member has gross deficits in all aspects of their communication skills specific plans may need to be formulated to provide additional coaching for that person. Devoting small periods of each session may be preferable to lengthy attempts to remedy skills deficits, which may reinforce the person's sense of inadequacy. Specific strategies that may be employed to assist such individuals are described in Chapter 7, pages 144–59.

### Real-life practice

The goal of communication training is to enhance participants' abilities to communicate about mutual problems and goals with each other in the household environment, particularly at times of stress. No matter how well participants perform during practice in sessions with the therapist, there is little likelihood that they will incorporate these communication skills into their lifestyles unless they practise using the same skills in the everyday environment. Thus, after each participant has been given the opportunity to practise a specific interpersonal communication skill during the session and has received coaching until competent performance of that skill has been demonstrated, 'homework' or 'practice outside the sessions' is organized. The manner in which this real-life practice is organized is of vital importance to the success of behavioural family therapy.

Real-life practice is structured in the following manner:

1 *Rationale*. It is crucial that all participants share an appreciation of the purpose of real-life practice. The value of practising skills in everyday life situations until they become
second nature is explained. The therapist checks out any
queries that participants may have about work outside
the sessions. In particular, issues about feelings that being
expected to complete assignments to do with everyday skills
may seem infantilizing, like school, or that 'good' communication of feelings is always 'spontaneous' may be addressed at
this stage. It is important that all participants realize that their
efforts between sessions are the most important aspects of this
approach, and whereas excuses may be accepted for being
unable to attend the occasional session, the therapist will not
accept any excuse for non-completion of assigned practice.
An unequivocal stand of this nature at the beginning of
therapy may save considerable effort during later sessions.

2 *Outline of the task*. Once all participants have completed
their practice during each session, the therapist outlines the
steps to be followed for practising the specific communication skill in the everyday environment. Each participant is
handed a worksheet specific to the communication skill that
is being trained (see Figure 5.2). The therapist explains that
each day of the week participants are expected to record
one example of an attempt to employ the specific skill in
the effective manner rehearsed during the session. The
diary-style worksheet is used to record notes about specific
elements of the real-life performance for review at the
beginning of the next session. A brief rationale for
employing such a diary chart is provided, with special
emphasis on the efficiency of making such notes for
subsequent rapid and accurate review of the specific
performances recorded.

3 *Checking out participants' understanding of task*. A major reason
why people find it difficult to complete their work assignments is that they have failed to process the instructions.
Although the worksheets are relatively straightforward and
the instructions given to participants quite simple, it is
surprising how few people are able to recall them once the
session ends. Such information processing appears unrelated
to intelligence, social or educational background, etc. We have
found that it is essential to check out with *every participant* his

● Say exactly what displeased you ● Tell the person how it made you feel ● Suggest how this could be avoided in future

| Day | Person who displeased you | What exactly did he or she do that displeased you? | How did you feel? (angry, sad, etc.) | What did you ask him or her to do in future? |
|---|---|---|---|---|
| Mon | | | | |
| Tues | Joe | Forgot to tell me he was going out | Angry | To tell me |
| Wed | | | | |
| Thurs | | | | |
| Fri | Sandy | Said she would help, but didn't | Disappointed | To do things promised |
| Sat | Joe | Shouted at me | Upset | Not to do it again |
| Sun | | | | |

**Examples:**

I feel angry that you shouted at me, Tom. I'd like it better if you spoke more quietly next time.

I'm very sad that you did not get that job. I'd like to sit down and discuss some other possibilities with you after dinner.

I feel very anxious when you tell me I should get a job. It would help me a lot if you didn't nag me about it.

*Figure 5.2* Expressing unpleasant feelings

or her precise understanding of the instructions given, and to correct any misunderstandings. Better still, we have found that requesting each participant to complete the worksheeet for the current day has enabled any deficits to be remedied before the session ends. Participants are invited to: 'Try to recall an occasion during the session when you have attempted to make a positive request (or whatever skill module that has been trained during the session). I would like you to complete the entry for today on the worksheet using that example. I will be happy to help anyone who has any difficulties or questions about that.'

4 *Display of promptsheets and worksheets.* The therapist helps the participants to choose strategic places about the household to display sheets outlining the steps of the skill being trained. These sheets serve as prompts for household members to practise the specific skills during their everyday lives. Finding the best locations may prove highly amusing, and often assists in breaking down the tension sometimes experienced with families who experience this approach as overly structured, and merely validating the current good communication practised throughout the household.

In addition to displaying promptsheets individuals may find it helpful to place their worksheets in prominent places so that they are unlikely to forget to complete them on a daily basis.

The session is concluded when all participants have agreed to complete the real-life practice and to record their efforts on the worksheets.

The therapist reminds the household that they are also expected to conduct a household meeting during the course of each week and ensures that a specific time and place have been agreed for the meeting. Participants may ask if they can use the meeting to practice further their communication skills. The therapist may encourage such practice, but should remind participants that the household meeting is convened to deal with their problems and goals, and that although this provides an ideal opportunity to employ effective communication skills, they are expected to try to use these skills every day of the week, not only during discussions at the household meeting.

Real-life practice is expected to involve interpersonal

communication between household members. However, the same skills may be applied in a wide range of work and social contexts. Examples noted on the worksheets should focus on other household members.

5 *Review of real-life practice.* At the beginning of the next session the real-life practice efforts of each participant are reviewed in detail. Each participant is asked: 'I would like you to tell us about your efforts at real-life practice of expressing pleasant feelings (or whatever skill they have been practising) over the past week.' (*Avoid* introductions such as 'How did you get on with your practice?' or 'Did you get a chance to do any practice during the week?' which allow participants to make lame excuses for lack of practice.)

Each participant then reviews each example noted on his or her worksheet. The focus is on the structure of the communication skill, not the content, or the responses engendered. The therapist praises *all efforts*, even when they are relatively meagre, or fail to induce successful responses. Any major deficits in the way in which the steps of the skill were performed are noted.

The therapist selects one reported example and constructs a re-enactment in the manner described above. Participants provide feedback on the steps followed and make constructive suggestions about any major deficits. Further training may be needed where participants show continuing deficits. This may form the main part of the remainder of the current session as well as subsequent sessions; where residual deficits are minor, or when only one participant has deficits in the particular skill, continued training may be provided as part of one or more sessions, while the group moves on to more difficult communication skills modules.

Where there is a lack of clear evidence that the specific elements of a communication skill have been incorporated in the everyday lifestyle of the household, further training is provided and real-life practice assigned until such generalization has been established. This evidence is gleaned mainly from reports and observed re-enactments, but may also be noted during unrehearsed interactions during sessions. For example, Joseph continued to have difficulty expressing his negative feelings to his household members. However, at the beginning of one session when he was reviewing progress on his goals, he responded to a question by Simon in the following manner: 'Simon, I just get so anxious when I have to sit in a room with all those other people that after a while I just have to get out of there.'

The therapist noted that Joseph had expressed an unpleasant feeling to Simon. He responded by praising Joseph immediately, and invited the other participants to note the steps that Joseph had followed. Jessica noted that Joseph had made a clear statement of his feelings as well as describing the exact setting in which those feelings had arisen. He had not invited any problem solving of his predicament in a direct manner, but as a result of highlighting his difficulty the other participants were able to assist him with several suggestions that led to more effective anxiety management on future occasions, and consequently to his regular attendance at a local job club programme.

Difficulties encountered during real-life practice are rare. On occasions expression of unpleasant feelings may open emotional wounds in families. Where the therapist suspects that such 'hot' issues may be readily inflamed, he or she may delay training in expression of unpleasant feelings until participants have acquired some competence at problem solving, and even then may attempt to steer them away from stressful confrontations and on to everyday issues.

Other households may make jokes about the communication skills. At times this hilarity may prove disconcerting to the therapist. However, providing the participants are following the specific steps when performing the specific skills, such humour should not be discouraged, and may facilitate the training process. Sarcasm and put-downs are discouraged, as they seldom follow the guidelines for effective communication of feelings.

However, the greatest difficulty encountered by inexperienced behavioural family therapists is to get participants to complete their real-life practice assignments. The most common cause for this appears to be a failure to follow the procedures outlined above. It is crucial to allow sufficient time at the end of each session to organise real-life practice in a comprehensive and unhurried manner. At least ten minutes is required, particularly in early sessions. Nevertheless, some problems are more complex, and further strategies for dealing with such problems are described in Chapter 8, pages 160–73.

# CONTINUING ASSESSMENT OF INTERPERSONAL COMMUNICATION SKILLS

The training process is completed by the therapist's continued assessment of the interpersonal skills acquired during the period of training. At the end of each session the therapist updates the communication and problem-solving checklist (CPC) (see pages 40–1) with evidence of either:

(a) spontaneous competent performance of expressing any of the core curriculum of communication skills (Criterion A); or

(b) competent performance of any skills after coaching and prompting by the therapist (Criterion B).

Communication skills training is completed once every participant has demonstrated ability to employ each of the core skills in a 'spontaneous' way, i.e. under conditions other than those directly structured by the therapist. Continued coaching of deficient participants continues throughout the course of BFT. Performance of the skill on one occasion is sufficient evidence of the acquisition of training. However, the habitual use of effective communication skills is the aim of therapy, and the therapist may prompt and reward efforts to employ such skills throughout therapy sessions as well as in reports of household discussions.

Of particular importance is the transfer of effective communication skills to problem-solving discussions, where their value in the stress management process is maximal. This transfer of skills is assessed at the beginning of each session when the therapist reviews the household meetings and each participant's personal goals. Enquiries are made about the specific nature of any interpersonal communication involved in these settings. Efforts to employ the core skills are praised and difficulties may be incorporated into rehearsals during the later parts of the session.

# CORE CURRICULUM OF COMMUNICATION SKILLS

A core curriculum of basic interpersonal communication skills forms the basis for communication skills training. Expression of pleasant and unpleasant feelings, making requests and listening in an active, empathic way have been targeted. These skills have been chosen from a series of studies in social psychology that have associated deficits in these aspects of interpersonal communication with a wide range of stress-related problems. In addition to these issues of content of communication, a range of deficits in the more discrete elements of interpersonal communication, such as attentiveness and accuracy of perception of interpersonal cues, appropriate non-verbal and verbal expression, is targeted for training where major deficits are evident. It has been noted that all these aspects of communication tend to become less effective when people are placed in stressful situations, and that many of these deficits tend to compound stresses, delaying their resolution.

## Communication of pleasant feelings

Almost every adult can express positive feelings competently. However, in almost no household group have we observed a high frequency of this behaviour, particularly when members are under stress.

Research indicates that the expression of positive feelings about specific behaviour is one of the most powerful motivators for behavioural change and skill learning (social reinforcement). Thus, an increase in positive exchanges within a household not only feels good and increases morale under stress, but it may provide the basis for operant strategies to increase mutually desirable behaviour patterns (see page 166). When people have encountered a series of difficulties they tend to focus on the problems around them and forget to notice the good things that people do. Telling people about the little things they do that please helps to encourage them to keep trying when things are difficult, improves morale in the household, and creates an atmosphere in which people are more able to work together to solve problems. In addition, and crucially, it provides participants with a readily attainable first step towards enhancing their mutual collaboration towards specific, everyday problem solving and goal achievement.

The key elements of expressing a pleasant feeling to another person include:

- Looking at the person in a friendly manner – perhaps smiling – and speaking in a warm tone of voice. (Other non-verbal gestures such as close proximity, hugs, kisses, etc. may be appropriate in certain situations.)
- Telling the person exactly which actions that he or she performed pleased you.
- Telling the person exactly how it made you feel when he or she performed those pleasing actions.

Examples of this skill include a mother, who was pleased that her teenage daughter returned home from a date at the time she had agreed, hugging her when she came into her bedroom and saying: 'I am very pleased that you came home at the time we agreed.'

A flatmate who had just finished his dinner looked across the table to his friend and said (smiling): 'That was a wonderful peach pie, Nick, I really enjoyed that.'

A woman, who had arrived home after a busy day at the office sat down and relaxed for half an hour before her sister initiated a discussion about difficulties with the household finances. She noted the considerate response and said: 'I'm grateful that you waited until I had relaxed before you hit me with this bad news. I've had a bad day at the office and I would have probably shouted at you had you brought this up when I walked in.'

It is important to note that all these examples involve everyday events and simple expressions of pleasant feelings. It is the straightforward, frequent use of expressions of positive feelings that is more important to stress management than the efforts made to reward special events and infrequent achievements.

It should also be noted that expressions are brief and, with the exception of the last example, unelaborated. Some people have difficulty expressing their simple feelings without adding some explanation or rider. For example, Simon frequently expressed his pleasure to the other members of his household, but accompanied the pleasant expression with a request for improvements in some other aspects of their behaviour. He would say: 'I am so pleased that you have cleaned your bedroom, but I wish you would do your bathroom as well.' Such complex expressions often convey a stronger negative message to the recipient, who may interpret repeated communications of this sort as 'I can never please him.'

Many household members devalue the significance of every-day expressions of praise, compliments, encouragement, or appreciation. They argue that household members should go about their chores and duties without expecting any rewards. They may say, 'He knows I love him, isn't that enough?' Or 'What about all the things he doesn't do? If I start praising him he will think that he's doing enough already.' The therapist avoids discussions about the relative 'goodness' or 'badness' of participants and merely encourages participants to attempt to focus on those small aspects that please them, and to evaluate for themselves the benefits of expressing those fleeting feelings of pleasure to each other. Surprisingly, even small changes in this behaviour induce notable changes in the ways in which people view one another.

Another common difficulty is the person who makes general expressions of positive feelings but has difficulty finding specific examples. 'I love her cooking and I always thank her after meals.' The therapist helps such people to break down situations into more specific components. For example:

Therapist:   What particular aspects of her cooking do you like best?

Joseph:   Well, it's all good, first class.

Therapist:   Are there any dishes that are your special favourites?

Joseph:   Well, I suppose my favourite is roast beef and Yorkshire pudding.

Therapist:   Great. That's my favourite too! How do you like it cooked?

Joseph:   I prefer it quite well done. You know some people like it half raw, but I think the taste is better when it's good and brown.

Therapist:   Does your Celia know that?

Joseph:   I don't know really. Do you, dear?

Celia:   No, I didn't know that, but I always cook it well and you never complain.

Therapist:   I would like you to tell your Celia *exactly* what you like about the way she cooks roast beef.

Joseph:   I love the way you cook roast beef, with it nice and brown. I also love the soggy Yorkshire pudding covered in thick brown gravy.

Therapist: What did you like about the way your Joseph expressed his feelings about your cooking that time? Was it clear exactly what he liked?

Celia: Yes, you made it a lot clearer. I already knew you liked roast beef, but I didn't know that you preferred my Yorkshire to the fluffy stuff you get at restaurants. That's new to me.

Therapist: So you can learn more about exactly what you each like if you are more specific in expressing your pleasant feelings. Is that clear now?

Training participants to express mutually pleasing feelings towards one another in training sessions is relatively easy, and seldom raises any problems, even where relationships appear tense and conflict-ridden. More difficult is the ability to increase the frequency that participants perceive pleasing events and to express that pleasure in their everyday interactions. The real-life practice assignment is entitled 'Catch a Person Pleasing You' and aims to cue participants to recognize opportunities for expressing pleasure at everyday efforts that others make.

In addition to this practice the approach to giving feedback for performances throughout the sessions provides further opportunity for participants to practise providing specific expression of pleasure at their mutual efforts. All opportunities to promote expression of pleasant feelings among participants are exploited by the behavioural family therapist. Care is taken to ensure that the feelings expressed are always genuine and that insincerity is avoided. For therapists trained in techniques that focus mainly on deficits, the emphasis on detecting and reinforcing small elements of positive behaviour may be uncomfortable for a period. However, as with the participants, this positive emphasis is soon appreciated for its benefits.

## Making positive requests

The ability to make a request for another person to make some change in behaviour in a pleasant, non-coercive manner is a useful interpersonal skill. It is clear that people living in the same household are likely to engage in a range of actions that bother other individuals, while at the same time not engaging in the patterns of behaviour considered most desirable by others. There are many ways of expressing our mutual desires and needs, but all too often requests for behaviour change are communicated in the form of nagging, demanding, or guilt-inducing remarks. For example, 'Why don't you help Jessica in the garden?' or 'Go and wash the dishes immediately!' Such expressions tend to increase stress and tension in households, and are complied with reluctantly. This often leads to escalating coercion as threats are needed to overcome increasing resentment.

A positive request avoids the use of coercion by simply stating the desired behaviour, and expressing the expected feelings when that behaviour is performed. For example, when Jessica feels annoyed with Celia's frequent lateness for the evening meal she might request: 'Celia, I'd like you to come home for dinner at 6 o'clock.' Simon, who wishes that Joseph would help Jessica in the garden, may request: 'Joseph, I'd feel very pleased if you would go and help Jessica in the garden.' It may be seen that these requests are made up of the following elements of communication:

- Looking at the person to whom the request is directed, and using appropriate non-verbal expression, such as speaking in a firm yet friendly tone.
- Describing exactly what you would like the person to do.
- Telling that person how you expect to feel when he or she performs that behaviour.

The way in which the request is made does not need to follow these steps in sequence, and more commonly starts with the expression of feelings. Expressions commonly used include:

> 'I'd like you to . . .'
> 'I'd be most grateful if you would . . .'
> 'I'd be pleased if you . . .'

In many households this form of request has been shortened to merely saying 'please' when asking for something. Unfortunately such abbreviations do not convey the same personal expression of feelings, and are usually less effective. However, the same may be said of expressions such as 'I'd appreciate your doing (something) . . .' which is a more impersonal way of expressing one's feelings. Once again the non-verbal element of communication is extremely important. The same positive verbal expression may be negated by a demanding or threatening quality to the voice tone and gestures used when it is communicated.

It is important to note that these expressions are brief and straightforward, and that elaborate reasons to justify the request are not employed. It is sufficient that the request is reasonable and will result in pleasing the person who makes it. Of course, this is no guarantee that the target person will comply with the request, no matter how reasonable it is or how well it is expressed. Many problems or goals are complicated and are unlikely to be resolved simply through the use of positive requests. Nevertheless, requests made in a firm, specific and constructive manner help to create a collaborative problem-solving atmosphere. Above all, less stress tends to result than where attempts to modify the behaviour of others are made in a demanding, coercive, or threatening manner.

Throughout the course of every session the therapist will need to make numerous requests for participants to perform various actions. It is crucial that the therapist employs the same approach to making requests that he or she is endeavouring to promote with the participants. Rather than saying 'Now I want you to do this . . .' the behavioural family therapist may say 'Now I would like you to do this . . .' Such a difference in expression may appear trivial, but when participants are reluctant to attempt rehearsals or to complete real-life assignments, this small difference in the quality of interpersonal communication may have substantial benefits. Once again the benefits are only derived from repeated practice, and it is crucial that participants attempt to use this skill in their everyday lives and then report back on its effectiveness.

### Expressing unpleasant feelings

The clear, direct expression of unpleasant feelings, such as unhappiness, frustration, anxiety, anger, is the initial step in identifying problems. In stressful circumstances there is an increased tendency for people to express such feelings inappropriately by blaming others for their distress, becoming hostile, aggressive, violent, or withdrawing into a shell. Thus, the problem of excessive criticism and hostility among household members is the most commonly cited sign of distress in family and marital households. While it may be argued that frequent expressions of minor unpleasant feelings may be counter-productive, the responsible targeting of specific major concerns clearly and concisely may lead to effective problem resolution.

In a minority of households the direct expression of unpleasant feelings, especially anger, is discouraged. Such emotions are considered bad and household members are encouraged to bottle them up. However, repression is seldom possible and strong emotions are released either in dramatic outbursts, through indirect expression, such as nagging or withdrawal of affection, or possibly in pathophysiological disorders, such as stress-related illnesses. Although there is limited evidence that expression of negative feelings in a cathartic manner (getting it off your chest) is beneficial, we suggest that clear, direct expression, leading to resolution of the problems that trigger those feelings, is more likely to lead to lasting benefits. Whereas there is evidence to suggest that expression of pleasant feelings has maximum benefits in shaping the behaviour of its recipients, when its expression closely follows the behaviour that has triggered it, no such benefits accrue from rapid expression of unpleasant feelings, and it may be better to delay such expression until it can be communicated calmly and clearly.

Effective communication of unpleasant feelings contains the following elements:

- Look at the person. Adopt a relaxed posture, preferably seated. Speak calmly and firmly. Maintain a facial expression appropriate to the unpleasant emotion – avoid smiling if unhappy, anxious, or angry.
- Tell the other person exactly what triggered off your unpleasant feeling.
- Tell the person how that made you feel.
- Offer a suggestion as to how this unpleasant feeling may be resolved, either by making a positive request for that person to do something to help you or by arranging a problem-solving discussion.

Examples of expressions of unpleasant feelings include:

'I feel very unhappy when you say you are going to help me clean the house and then you make excuses for not being able to do the job. I would like to talk to you about this to see if we can make some better arrangements.'

'I am very anxious about the interview I have for a job tomorrow. I would be most grateful if you could spend a few minutes going over the kind of answers that I might give to the questions that could be asked.'

'If you do not phone when you are going to be later than you say, I feel very worried. I would like you to phone whenever you are going to be late.'

'I have been feeling very frustrated about the way we seem to be arguing about lots of things lately. I would like to arrange to go out for dinner so that we can talk about this without interruptions from the children.'

It is important that the last element is included wherever possible. A person's feelings are considered their own responsibility. Although there is a tendency to blame others or external events for our unhappiness and discontent, these events are merely triggers for our own emotional responses, and the first step in resolving these unpleasant responses is to recognize that they can be controlled primarily through our own actions which, of course, include actions to seek the help and advice of others. Although some major events tend to trigger off similar responses in most people, for example, the death of a close and loved associate usually triggers feelings of sadness, emotional responses tend to be highly individualized, with similar events triggering a wide range in the type and quantity of emotions. One person may find a habitual trait of a household member 'quaint' or 'fun', whereas another may be intensely irritated by the same behaviour. Behavioural family therapy does not usually concern itself with the complexities underlying such differential responsiveness, but recognizes that every person's response patterns are unique and above all *valid*. However, it is considered important to help people clarify that unpleasant emotions are *caused by their own psychobiological responses* not by the actions of others which are mere triggers. Changes in emotional responsiveness can be brought about by reducing the occurrence of those triggering behaviours, as well as by altering one's response to those events. In order to achieve efficient resolution, the cooperation of other people may prove vital.

105

Blaming them for one's unpleasant feelings, or coercing them to change, is seldom the most effective method of gaining their full collaboration.

It may be evident that adopting this approach to expression of unpleasant feelings tends to reduce personal attacks on others, and enables participants to focus on key issues where some resolution may be feasible. Where one household member is the trigger for many unpleasant feelings in others, for example, a chronically disabled or dying person, or a behaviourally disturbed person, this targeting of specific problems may help people to manage the stress associated with such cases. Sharing feelings of disappointment or frustration may help the target person to become more actively involved in the resolution of everyday problem issues, even when the basic afflictions cannot be resolved.

There are some instances where the therapist may consider it necessary to take a strong stand to eliminate the behaviour of another household member. This will usually concern serious abusive behaviour, such as personal violence, sexual abuse, or emotional blackmail. Where such behaviour violates the accepted societal rules and laws, the therapist should clearly express his or her personal feelings, and request immediate cessation of such behaviour accompanied by crisis problem solving to plan in detail the consequences of continuation. It may be necessary for the therapist to initiate welfare or legal proceedings immediately in such circumstances. However, even when such actions are necessary, where this can be conducted within the problem-solving framework, involving all participants, such problems may be more readily resolved.

There may be other occasions when the therapist may choose to express his or her own unpleasant feelings towards participants. These often concern poor compliance with vital aspects of the therapy, such as attendance at sessions or efforts to complete real-life practice assignments. The expression of anger, frustration, or disappointment towards one or more participants conducted in the suggested manner assists in providing a context for the collaborative resolution of such problems. Many therapists have difficulty with such a direct approach and resort to less effective nagging and coercion when faced with such issues. Once more it is important that the therapist communicates using the same methods advocated for participants.

Training participants to express unpleasant feelings may lead to explosive outbursts. Where the therapist suspects that such hostility may arise he or she should take care to steer participants away from issues that might lead to major confrontations. The initial and continuing review process provides cues to such issues. During initial training it is helpful to focus on small, but stressful, problem issues that engender unpleasant feelings. In some families where tension and hostility are high, training in expression of negative feelings may be delayed until they have acquired some competence in the structured problem-solving approach. Expression of unpleasant feelings can be introduced as a key component in defining problem issues. Real-life practice should emphasize the need to reduce the frequency of expression of unpleasant feelings in those households where such expression is excessive. Participants are prompted to prioritize issues, and to choose to express their feelings about those issues of prime importance in their everyday lives, where clear expression may lead to efficient resolution. The therapist may need to spend considerable time planning real-life assignments with such households.

However, hostile outbursts cannot always be avoided. When they do the therapist should *stop the heated discussion immediately*. She may be able to prompt the angry participants to restructure their communication in terms of the steps outlined in the training. Where such an approach does not lead to a reduction in tension he may need to abort further training and conduct a crisis problem-solving discussion (see Chapter 6, pages 111–43).

## Listening skills

Complex problems or goals cannot always be stated in a simple, clear way by the people concerned, even when they are competent at expressing their feelings about specific issues. Active listening is a skill that can play a crucial part in assisting a person to target a goal or a problem in a precise manner that will facilitate problem solving. The goal of this training is to help participants to attend in an empathic manner to what others are attempting to express and to use clarifying questions to understand exactly how that other person defines the problem or goal. The two major elements are enhancement of attentiveness and clarifying expression of the key issues. Components of these elements include:

- The listener should adopt a position that maximizes the ability not merely to hear what is being said, but also to pick up non-verbal messages from facial expressions and body language. Sitting comfortably on the same level and leaning slightly towards the speaker is recommended as the optimal posture for active listening. Ensure that distractions are minimized so that the participants can focus undivided attention on the subject under discussion.
- Simple verbal and non-verbal gestures (head nods, 'uh-huhs') provide the speaker with feedback that the listener is attending to and processing what he or she is saying.
- Clarifying questions help the speaker to define aspects of the situation more clearly. They may focus on both factual and emotive aspects of the issue. For example: 'How long have you worked at that job?' 'How did you feel when the boss told you that you were not working hard enough?'
- Checking out what the speaker is trying to communicate is achieved by summarizing your understanding and inviting him or her to correct any inaccuracies. For example:

Joseph:   You were so angry with your boss that you told him you were quitting the job. Is that right?
Celia:   No, I wasn't angry with the boss. I was angry with myself, that I couldn't get myself to work fast enough. I told him that I couldn't seem to do that particular job no matter how hard I tried.
Joseph:   I see, so you didn't actually say you were quitting.
Celia:   That's right. But when I went back the next day he told me I had said I wanted to quit.

Most participants have some basic listening skills. However, these skills are least apparent when they are under stress. Furthermore, people with mental disorders and learning disabilities may have specific problems in maintaining attention to the wide range of cues employed in interpersonal communication about problem issues. There is a tendency among family members and carers to avoid checking out the thoughts and feelings of such disabled people, and to make assumptions in an intrusive manner. For example, a carer of Dorothy, a chronically disabled young woman, repeatedly told her social worker that Dorothy preferred to stay at home with her rather than attend a nearby day centre, and that she had no interest in having contact with men. These conclusions had been based on the carer's interpretation of Dorothy's responses to one or two distressing incidents. However, during active listening training the carer checked out Dorothy's current feelings on these issues and was surprised to learn that she was eager to continue to socialize, particularly with mixed groups. Speaking for people who are close associates is a common source of family and marital stress, and it is always wise to check precise thoughts and feelings, rather than assume that we know their responses so well that we can read their minds.

It may be noted that the importance of attending to non-verbal expression is emphasized once more. People under stress may communicate more clearly through their facial expressions, voice tone, and gestures than through their attempts to put their thoughts and feelings into words. The skilled listener may be able to pick up discrepancies between verbal and non-verbal messages and help clarify the issues. Such skills may be difficult to train in the context of behavioural family therapy sessions, but may be important to address where participants have a habit of giving contradictory messages; for example, Joseph has difficulty asking for help with problems, and says when questioned about his worried expression, 'It's OK', but appears far from content.

Reducing attentional deficits may appear relatively simple in principle, but in practice may be hard to implement in many households. It is often difficult to get household members to turn off the television and take the telephone off the hook during weekly household meetings, avoid discussions about important issues when distracted by other tasks, such as cooking, gardening, or driving the car, and restructure living areas so that they can sit facing one another at the same level. The value of conducting sessions in the home environment, where such issues can be addressed directly, is clear.

Participants with attentional difficulties may require special strategies to assist them. These include keeping interactions brief, frequent summaries of the content of issues, repetition of key points, brief breaks in sessions after every five to ten minutes, including the disabled person in all aspects of the session, the use of promptsheets, and rewarding the person's continued efforts to attend with frequent praise. Less severe attentional problems manifest themselves in a variety of ways, including long-winded, repetitious, vague, and rambling comments. Active listening skills may be employed to help such people remain focused on one topic at a time, and to shape their expression into briefer, clearer statements. The therapist will usually have to demonstrate these skills repeatedly to participants in the initial phases of listening skills training. However, it is important that he or she follows the guidelines for such modelling outlined on pages 194–6, and ensures that participants have the opportunity to learn these skills through attempting to emulate the specific skills demonstrated. Where major deficits are present, training in listening skills may extend over several sessions, usually in the context of enhancing the skill of defining problems or goals precisely.

## CONCLUSIONS

It is concluded that effective communication of personal desires, concerns, and needs is a basis for efficient problem solving and goal achievement. The approach outlined here attempts to train participants to express their feelings clearly, to make requests in a non-coercive manner, and to enhance their listening skills. A structured approach is employed that uses skill training methods of rehearsal, constructive feedback, coaching, modelling, and real-life practice.

# 6

# SOLVING PROBLEMS AND ACHIEVING GOALS

## INTRODUCTION

The greater the efficiency of a household in resolving problems, the greater its capacity to manage environmental stressors and achieve personal goals. Where problem solving and goal achievement efforts can be coordinated in a mutually supportive manner the combined efforts of the group may exceed those of individual members of the household. Furthermore, conflicts that may arise when one person's goals or coping efforts are contrary to those of other members can be avoided if plans are devised in a cooperative way. Of course, one major source of environmental stress is the ambient tension in the household which, in addition to the stress associated with interpersonal conflicts, comprises stress from resolving the myriad practical difficulties encountered in everyday household management, as well as the shared stress experienced when one or more members of the household experiences a major life event or other persisting stress from difficulties outside the household. For example, when Jane broke up with her boyfriend of several years the stress she experienced was shared by her parents and brother. When her father was threatened with redundancy, all the other members of the family were concerned about the potential consequences of a loss in household income.

The impact of stress upon the health of individuals living together depends on their vulnerability. People who are highly vulnerable to major disorders are placed at risk of having further episodes of these disorders when they experience high levels of stress. The more severe the perceived stress, and the longer it remains unresolved, the greater the risk of major health problems (Brown and Harris 1978). Furthermore, when

111

a person's efforts are being extended by the need to cope with stress, they have less time and energy to devote to progress towards their personal goals.

Efforts to enhance the efficiency of family problem-solving functions is the cornerstone of behavioural family therapy. The therapeutic interventions employed to achieve this include: (a) training in a structured approach to collaborative problem solving that can be applied to any problem or goal; and (b) training in specific strategies to manage specific stresses and problems. This chapter will focus on efforts to enhance generic problem solving and goal achievement. Chapter 7 will describe methods to manage more specific stresses.

In the previous chapter we have seen how a range of interpersonal communication skills provides a foundation for efficient pinpointing of specific stresses and personal goals. The ability to express both pleasant feelings and concerns, to listen in an empathic manner that clarifies mutual problems or goals, and to make constructive suggestions for change are all crucial skills that facilitate cooperative problem-solving discussions (Hahlweg et al. 1984; 1988). Ideally, a family or household can sit down together, without major distractions, discuss openly and clearly a particular issue of concern to one or more of its members, and at the end of the discussion devise a plan of action that can be readily implemented.

In our experience few families in western societies structure their problem solving in this manner on a regular basis. Thus we have found that it has been necessary to train families to use a structured problem-solving approach to facilitate their efforts. The approach comprises six steps (see Table 6.1), and has been derived from the method described for use in individual and group interventions (D'Zurilla and Goldfried 1971; D'Zurilla 1986; Spivack et al. 1976). It is similar to that employed in specialized marital counselling (Hahlweg et al. 1984; Jacobson and Margolin 1979).

*Table 6.1* Problem solving and goal achievement

- Pinpoint the problem or goal
- List all possible solutions
- Highlight likely consequences
- Agree on 'best' strategy
- Plan and implement
- Review results

The first step is to discuss the problem or goal and to pinpoint an exact definition of the issue. Next, the participants apply the brainstorming approach to generate a list of all potential solutions. The third step entails a review of the advantages and disadvantages of each of the proposed solutions in turn. In the fourth step the participants reach a consensus on the solution that best fits their needs and resources. The fifth step involves making specific plans about how to implement the solution. The final step provides a constructive review of efforts to implement the plan that ensures that problem solving is maintained as an ongoing process.

To assist people to structure their problem-solving efforts, we provide them with a standard form listing the six steps with space to jot down notes while conducting the problem-solving session (see Figure 6.1). These notes provide a record of the plans agreed and facilitate subsequent review and revision. Families are encouraged to save these forms in a folder so that they have a convenient reference for problems and goals tackled and plans and strategies that have proved helpful.

This problem-solving method has several advantages. These include: defining problems and goals in an everyday way, encouraging all participants to seek a diversity of ideas, defining solutions in terms of current needs and resources, and careful consideration of practical constraints involved in planning for successful implementation. The approach can be applied to a comprehensive range of issues – those related to one participant or those of concern to the entire living group, everyday problems, and major life crises and decisions. The same approach can be employed to assist the therapist with problems that arise in the process of therapy, such as poor adherence to recommendations or exacerbations of a major disorder. Table 6.2 summarizes the range of problem areas addressed in therapist-led sessions during a study of behavioural family therapy with people vulnerable to schizophrenic disorders (Falloon et al. 1984).

Although the approach appears well structured and relatively straightforward, there are many issues that arise when families attempt to implement this approach in their own family meetings. The aim of the therapy sessions is to help families to incorporate efficient problem solving and goal achievement into their everyday lives, and differs from other approaches where

STEP 1: WHAT IS THE PROBLEM/GOAL?
Talk about the problem/goal, listen carefully, ask questions, get everybody's opinion. Then write down *exactly* what the problem/goal is.

To go out somewhere on Sunday afternoon, with all family, costing less than £10

STEP 2: LIST ALL POSSIBLE SOLUTIONS.
Put down *all* ideas, even bad ones. Get everybody to come up with at least one possible solution. List the solutions *without discussion* at this stage.

1) Zoo

2) Sanford Park

3) Lake

4) Walk through forest

5) Balloon flight

6) Stay home and have barbecue

STEP 3: DISCUSS EACH POSSIBLE SOLUTION.
*Quickly* go down the list of possible solutions and discuss the *main* advantages and disadvantages of each one.

STEP 4: CHOOSE THE 'BEST' SOLUTION.
Choose the solution that can be carried out most easily to solve the problem.

Walk in forest and picnic

STEP 5: PLAN HOW TO CARRY OUT THE BEST SOLUTION.
Resources needed. Major pitfalls to overcome. Practise difficult steps. Time for review.

Step (1) Pack picnic – get meats and salads, etc. (Jo).

Step (2) Take boots and jackets    Leave at mid-day sharp

Step (3) If raining, visit Aunt Jean.

Step (4) Review time – Family meeting 5pm Friday 15th.

STEP 6: REVIEW IMPLEMENTATION AND PRAISE *ALL* EFFORTS.
Focus on *achievement first. Review plan. Revise as necessary.*

*Figure 6.1* Solving problems and achieving goals

114

*Table 6.2* Content of problem solving and goal achievement in BFT
sessions*

| *Disorder focused* | | % of sessions |
|---|---|---|
| ● COPING WITH DISORDER<br>symptons, medication, weight gain,<br>substance abuse, grooming | | 17% |
| ● REHABILITATION<br>job seeking, training, education | | 12% |
| ● SOCIAL ACTIVITY<br>friendships, activities, dating, social skills,<br>neighbours, relatives | | 11% |
| ● INDEPENDENCE<br>leaving home, coping with intimacy,<br>marriage plans | | 12% |
| | Total | 52% |
| *Household focused* | | |
| ● FAMILY PROBLEMS<br>siblings, employment, marital conflict,<br>illness, bereavement | | 16% |
| ● FINANCIAL<br>budgeting, bills, purchases | | 9% |
| ● HOME MAINTENANCE<br>housing, repairs, chores, garden | | 9% |
| ● FAMILY MEETINGS<br>schedules, real-life practice | | 6% |
| ● LEISURE ACTIVITY<br>vacations, guests, weekends, parent<br>socialization | | 6% |
| ● TRANSPORTATION<br>cars, public transport | | 2% |
| | Total | 48% |

* during 442 BFT sessions with 18 households with members
highly vulnerable to schizophrenic episodes.

the therapist conducts problem solving with families in a
collaborative manner. Such collaboration is reserved for occasions when family coping resources are overwhelmed during
crises, when the therapist may then become an active participant

in planning effective strategies to resolve major stresses. However, in all other circumstances the therapist adopts the role of a teacher and coach, who assists the family group to achieve greater efficiency in their problem-solving discussions. The remainder of this chapter will describe this approach to training problem-solving skills.

## TECHNIQUES USED IN PROBLEM-SOLVING TRAINING

The role of the therapist continues to be that of a teacher or coach during problem-solving training. The structure and techniques remain similar to those employed in teaching communication skills. During the initial and continuing behavioural assessments the therapist defines the relative strengths and weaknesses of each participant's problem-solving skills, as well as the manner in which those skills are used during group problem-solving activities. Crucial deficits are pinpointed as targets for training. Then, after eliciting a rationale for embracing a structured problem-solving format, the therapist employs a range of skills training strategies to remedy the targeted deficits. Instructions are accompanied by guide sheets, demonstrations are provided by the therapist and competent participants, constructive feedback and prompting are employed during repeated rehearsals, and practice sessions are convened by household members between training sessions. The approach differs from other problem-oriented therapies in that the treatment sessions are considered, with few exceptions, to be training workshops, where participants learn strategies to enhance the efficiency of their problem-solving functions in their everyday lives. Only rarely does the therapist become actively involved in the actual problem solving or goal achievement process during sessions. Rather, he or she takes the role of a coach, who is explicitly removed from the field of play, but stops the action at key points in order to provide feedback and further coaching of major deficits. It is crucial that therapists accept this role from the initial phase of problem-solving training so that they avoid difficulties when they are absorbed into family problem-solving functioning, and the training sessions become the focus for problem resolution for the family, rather than workshops where the family learns skills that may facilitate their own problem-solving efforts on a day-to-day basis.

116

## Behavioural assessment

The baseline assessment of problem-solving skills *begins* with the initial behavioural assessment of family problem solving. Reports and observations of the individual and combined efforts of the household unit to solve problems and achieve goals will have been recorded during the initial assessment. However, throughout the educational and communication training sessions the therapist will have gathered further specific information about family discussions concerning problems and goals. For example, you will know whether the family has been able to organize weekly meetings, whether they have all attended sessions regularly and on time, how they have completed their homework. The therapist may have gleaned further specific information about their interactions during their weekly family meetings and in dealing with any crises that may have arisen.

Before initiating problem-solving training the therapist reviews all this information. Where specific problem-solving skills are clearly evident, check that this has been noted on the communication and problem-solving checklist (CPC) (see pages 40–1) which will serve as the guide during the training sessions.

It may be some time since the initial assessment and the therapist may have been unable to get a clear picture of family problem solving. In such cases the therapist may decide to repeat the reported and observed problem-solving assessment as an introduction to the problem-solving module. Indeed, it may be noted that the training sessions all involve repetitions of this assessment format as the therapist reviews reports of problem solving and goal achievement efforts between sessions, and then invites the family to perform problem-solving functions that he or she can observe during the session.

It is important that the therapist is aware of the current problems and goals of all participants. The therapist will need to guide the family to tackle straightforward issues that do not elicit intense emotions in their initial attempts at practising a more structured approach, and to steer them away from 'hot' issues that will detract from learning the structured steps which the therapist is teaching. In addition to the family goal records therapists may find it helpful to make a list of problems and steps towards goals mentioned during assessment or during previous treatment sessions.

An effective assessment provides the therapist with a preliminary guide to the strengths and weaknesses of the family unit's problem-solving functions. The skill training strategies are then applied to overcome any evident major deficits. Many households demonstrate competent skills when they merely follow the guidelines provided on the worksheets during the introductory session, and attempt to employ the six-step approach to resolve a straightforward problem. They may experience greater difficulty when dealing with more emotive or complex issues, or in applying the structured approach during their own family meetings in the absence of the therapist's supervision. Others may require several sessions before they can apply all six steps of the structured approach competently, and sessions devoted to coaching each specific step in turn may be essential.

### Initial problem-solving session(s): introduction to the six-step approach

The first session of problem-solving training is used to demonstrate the use of the structured six-step model. In order to achieve this the therapist helps the family to choose a straightforward everyday problem to resolve. This may be completion of a household chore, such as cleaning, gardening, food shopping or preparation, or planning a recreational activity. Ideally it should be an issue that involves all participants and is unlikely to generate any highly emotive responses. Subsequent sessions then focus on one or more specific steps of problem solving where the family have difficulties adhering to the guidelines for the structured approach.

In the introductory session the therapist helps the family to choose a straightforward issue that can be resolved within 15–20 minutes. The approach is then outlined in the following way.

#### *Rationale for structured problem solving*

A brief rationale is provided to explain how a more structured approach to problem solving may enhance efficiency of problem resolution and achievement of personal goals. Whenever possible the therapist elicits the rationale from participants by asking them why they think a discussion among household members may assist in solving problems and achieving goals, and how that discussion could be structured to maximize efficiency and minimize stress.

Some family members will report having been trained to use a structured problem-solving approach in their jobs. They may be invited to outline the approach and describe its advantages and disadvantages.

The therapist summarizes the points made by participants and may add his or her own perspective if necessary.

### Review current skill levels with family members

The therapist provides the family with a summary of the assessment of their competence at problem solving. Their collective strengths are emphasized, citing clear examples of competent use of components that the therapist has observed. *Major* deficits are highlighted.

### Define components of the skill

Each participant is then handed a problem solving and goal achievement worksheet (see Figure 6.1, page 114). This outlines the six steps of structured problem solving. The therapist outlines each of the steps briefly. It is useful to provide an example of how another family has solved an everyday household problem using the structured approach (see the following section for an example). Where attention is poor it may help to have participants take turns to read out the guidelines for each step as outlined on the worksheet. The therapist may then amplify the key points and answer questions.

### Build competent performance by repeated rehearsals, feedback, coaching and modelling

Once the therapist has reviewed all the steps and provided an example, the family is asked to practise, using the method in the session. This practice is set up like a family meeting (see page 20), with participants assuming their roles as chairperson, secretary, etc. The therapist may need to outline the specific functions of the chairperson and secretary in the application of the problem-solving approach.

119

The *chairperson* is responsible for moving the discussion through the specific steps, for keeping to the subject of the discussion, and adhering to the rules laid down for each step. The *secretary* makes brief notes of the discussion on the worksheet and helps the chairperson to prompt adherence to the six-step structure. The effect of this is clearly to hand over responsibility of leadership of the problem solving to the participants. The therapist coaches them through trouble spots and rewards competent use of each of the steps. Therapist involvement diminishes as they master the approach, allowing them to achieve full independence at the *earliest possible* time.

### Rehearsal using six-step method

Once the structure has been outlined the therapist requests that the participants address the specific straightforward problem or goal defined earlier in the session. He or she then hands over the session to the chairperson and tells the participants that he or she will withdraw from the discussion, observe their efforts, and provide feedback and coaching where necessary. The therapist then removes himself from the discussion by taking a seat *clearly outside* the discussion group.

### Feedback

Where possible the therapist waits until the family have attempted to complete the entire problem-solving format before re-entering the session to provide feedback and coaching. Initial feedback emphasizes the strengths of participants' performance. For example: 'I particularly liked the way all three of you stated your views on the problem. You all agreed that the home is a mess. I also liked the way you made sure that people kept to the point of the discussion, Judy, particularly when they wanted to start talking about Sam changing his job.'

Deficits are not highlighted during the introductory session, unless they are stalling progress through the steps or hostility threatens to induce major stress. In such conditions the therapist intervenes without delay, provides corrective feedback, and then returns immediately to the observer role.

## Modelling

At times the therapist may find it helpful to demonstrate one or more steps of the problem-solving approach to the family. Rather than join the family discussion and covertly model the designed performance, the behavioural family therapist stops the discussion, changes places with the chairperson, and leads the session for a few minutes covertly modelling the desired skills, before handing back to the family, who then repeat the performance attempting to replicate the skills modelled by the therapist. Modelling is particularly helpful in families with limited verbal skills, where each session may be devoted to training competence in one step of the method. In these families it is recommended that the therapist begins each session with a ten-minute problem-solving discussion, identical to that employed in the behavioural assessment. The body of the session is then used to coach the family in one or two steps where major deficits persist.

## Homework practice

It is important to remember that the sessions are workshops *to learn how to solve problems*, whereas the weekly family meetings are the venues for discussing plans for solving problems and achieving goals. The success of behavioural family therapy hinges around families incorporating more efficient problem-solving functions into their everyday lives. Lasting benefits depend on this lifestyle change. At all times the efforts should be adhered to achieving this goal with efficiency.

This rationale is provided at the end of each session after which the secretary is given a supply of problem solving and goal achievement worksheets. Participants are instructed to tackle a goal or problem issue at their family meeting, to employ the six-step method, and to bring the completed worksheet to the next session for review.

The therapist checks exactly how each participant has understood the outline of the homework task and corrects any misunderstandings.

The completed worksheet is reviewed at the start of the next session and participants are praised for all their efforts to employ the method.

**Continued behaviour**

Assessment of family problem-solving                           ach
session. This is achieved through:

1 Reports of discussions at weekly fa
2 Review of problem solving and goa                            ts.
3 Reports of problem solving/goal ach                          ld
  outside family meetings.
4 Check on progress towards each f......y member's personal
  goals at start of *every* session.
5 Observation of problem-solving discussions during each
  session.
6 Review sessions conducted at three, six, twelve months
  when reported and observed problem-solving assessment is
  repeated.

The therapist records all evidence of competent problem-solving
skills performed by the family as a whole on the communication
and problem-solving checklist (see pages 40–1) after *each*
session. Achievement of the personal goals of each participant
is noted on the family goal achievement record (see page 47).

## EXAMPLE OF TEACHING PROBLEM SOLVING/ GOAL ACHIEVEMENT

### Behavioural assessment

The therapist noted that at the baseline assessment the family
reported that they had successfully solved a problem of a leaking
roof. Three household members had discussed this problem
over breakfast, and a clear plan had been agreed.

The observed problem solving concerned the issue of cleaning
the house. Father tended to chair the discussion. No clear
definition of the problem was achieved, alternative solutions
were not listed, and the discussion concluded without reaching
agreement on any plan of action or clear solution to the
problem.

Despite repeated prompts, the family had not conducted any
family meetings between sessions. They had worked on their
personal goals, but tended to do this as individuals and did not
seek the collaboration of other family members. They had

completed most homework tasks in a marginally competent manner. No crises had arisen during the six weeks since the beginning of therapy.

The therapist had noted several issues that might be suitable for initial problem-solving training. They included: household chores, arranging the family meeting, planning a weekend visit to a family friend, and helping mother to find a part-time job. Issues to be avoided in the initial phase of problem-solving training included: Harold's drinking, household finances, Jenny's inactivity, concerns about suspected criminal activity of Brenda's boyfriend.

### Rationale

After reviewing the participants' goals, family meeting, and homework from the previous session, the therapist introduced problem-solving training in the following way.

'This session I would like to begin teaching you a structured problem-solving approach. I have noted that you do sit down and discuss problems or goals on occasions when there is a crisis, such as the time when the roof was leaking. At these times you told me that Father tends to lead the discussion and you get things sorted out quite quickly. However, at other times each of you seems to get on and sort out your problems on your own. You don't often sit down together to have a discussion about the problem or goal and what to do about it. Is that right?' (Several comments follow.)

The therapist continues: 'You have shown me that you can use the specific communication skills quite well. These skills can sometimes avoid problems, or help to reduce stress and arguments in the household. But in every family problems are bound to come up. Big problems or everyday ones. Sometimes they affect only one person, but often everyone in the home is affected. The quicker and better you can sort out these problems the less stress they cause and the easier it is for people to work on their goals.

'What ideas have you got about things you can do to help sort out problems in the most efficient way?' (Several suggestions are given, which are all rewarded by the therapist, who then summarizes.) 'We agree that what seems to work best is to work regularly on problems or goals together as a family, and to structure these discussions in a step-by-step fashion. These family meetings need practice before they work well. The more often families meet to discuss problems and goals, the better they get at sorting them out. We have found that holding your family meetings every week is essential to efficient family problem solving. There are no perfect solutions, but the family approach seems to lead to more effective plans for everyone's problems and goals.'

## Component steps

The therapist gives out the problem solving and goal achievement worksheet and continues.

'Here are some steps to follow when discussing problems and goals:

- Pinpoint the problem or goal.
- List all possible solutions.
- Evaluate each possible solution.
- Choose the optimal solution.
- Review the results of the efforts.

'Pinpointing the problem involves getting everyone's opinion, asking questions, and checking out exactly what the problem or goal is. The more exactly the problem or goal can be stated, the more likely that effective solutions can be devised.

'The second step involves "brainstorming". Does anyone know what I mean by "brainstorming"? Essentially everyone thinks of an idea off the top of their head; the ideas can be good or bad – all are listed, regardless. This leads to new, creative ideas, which may help when the issue has failed to be resolved by current problem-solving strategies.

'Once five or six solutions have been listed each one is evaluated *briefly*. The main advantages and disadvantages of each solution are highlighted. No solution is ideal. All have good and bad points.

'The next step is to decide which solution best fits the problem or goal using the current resources at the family's disposal. This is not usually the ideal solution, rather one that can be readily applied with minimal delay or special skill or money, etc.

'Once a solution has been chosen a careful plan of action is worked out. This may take some time to organize. The

124

chairperson must get each person to agree: to carry out each step of the plan, a time when it is best done, the resources that may be needed, and check that the steps are carried out according to the plan. A specific time to review implementation of the plan is an essential component of every action plan.

'The final step is to review the effectiveness of the plan in resolving the problem or achieving the goal. All efforts, even those that have been unsuccessful, are rewarded with praise from family members. Further problem solving may be needed to achieve the goal. This may necessitate a revision of some aspects of the plan, or at times a return to identifying the problem or goal itself and a full problem-solving discussion. Although this last step cannot usually be completed until some time after the initial discussion about the problem, each person's efforts at completing specific steps may be rewarded. Indeed, the efforts in developing the initial plan may be reviewed at the end of that discussion. The chairperson can invite each person to express his or her positive feelings about the contributions of others to the discussion, both during the discussion and after the plan has been agreed.

'Many people find this approach to solving problems helpful, but there is no magic in it. Most important problems and goals are only sorted out with a lot of sustained effort, often over months or even years. Problem solving is a continuous process, and difficult problems are solved only after many repeated efforts. I would like you to tell me about any problems or goals any member of your household has solved or achieved after a lot of hard work.'

Harold described how Brenda had sorted out a telephone bill that had been overcharged. He emphasized her persistence over several months and her refusal to be fobbed off. She commented that Harold's encouragement had helped her to sustain her efforts. The therapist pointed out the steps they had carried out throughout this process.

### Skill training

The therapist then requested that the family discuss a current everyday problem using the steps outlined. He asked them to suggest a straightforward, everyday issue. After a brief discussion they agreed to discuss the issue of keeping the house

125

tidy. The therapist handed over to the chairperson (Harold) and secretary (George) and reminded them of their respective roles. He went and sat on a chair in the corner to observe their performance, and make notes on specific communication and problem-solving skills they employed.

Brenda expressed her frustration (noted by the therapist) that the house was untidy despite her efforts to persuade people to keep it tidy. She had been making repeated positive requests (noted) to each household member with limited benefits, but had not sought the help of the family as a whole. Several clarifying questions were asked (noted) and it was agreed that they would narrow their initial problem-solving efforts to cleaning the kitchen – in particular, washing dirty dishes soon after they were used, rather than piling them up throughout the day (competent problem definition skills noted).

Each person participated in listing possible solutions (noted). These included:

1 Brenda to wash all dishes.
2 George and Brenda to take turns to wash.
3 Harold to wash all dishes.
4 Get a dishwasher.
5 Each person to be responsible for own dishes.
6 Pay a housekeeper.

At the end of this step the therapist requested permission to interrupt the proceedings to provide feedback on their efforts so far. He told the family how pleased he was that they had broken the problem down into a readily manageable issue and had come up with six solutions. He praised the specific examples of use of effective communication skills he had noted. He reminded them that the next step involved a brief highlighting of the advantages and disadvantages of each alternative, not a detailed discussion of their relative merits. He then handed back to the chairperson to continue the discussion.

Despite his reminder, the household group began to discuss details concerning the implementation of several possible solutions. The therapist again requested permission to interrupt and on this occasion swapped roles with the chairperson to demonstrate how to review quickly the advantages and dis-advantages of each proposed solution. He then handed back the chair once Harold had gained a clear idea of the need to structure that step actively.

The group agreed that the best solution was that each person should wash any dishes used between meals and that a rota should be devised for washing dishes after meals.

They planned to begin washing personal dishes that evening, within ten minutes of use, Jenny and George to work out a rota for meal time dish washing, Brenda to monitor the plan, and report back to the family meeting on Sunday at 2 p.m. for review. This clearly specified planning was carried out with several prompts from the therapist, who praised each participant for the specific efforts made towards their highly competent initial performance of the method. (Note. Most households can use the method very well when they follow the clear guidelines noted on the guide sheet, providing the therapist does not intervene excessively!) He indicated that the next session would be devoted to further practice of the planning.

He invited the participants to praise each other for any specific efforts that had pleased them during the problem-solving discussion. Each person was able to identify at least one contribution that each member had made and provide appropriate praise.

The worksheet completed during the session (see Figure 6.1) was placed on the household noticeboard in the kitchen to remind participants of the steps they had agreed to take. The session concluded after the therapist gave ten further work-sheets to the secretary and requested that they select another problem or goal to discuss at their family meeting. He suggested that Harold and George, in their roles as chairperson and secretary, might be responsible for ensuring that all family members attended the Sunday meeting.

The therapist reviewed the behavioural assessment at the end of the session and was able to check off the competent performance of:

- pinpointing specific problem/goal;
- generating five or more solutions;
- agreement on 'best' solution.

Because he had prompted each step with his detailed introduction he considered they had met criterion B at this stage.

He noted also that Brenda had begun an evening class in

pottery, which was her second goal. He noted the date this had been achieved on the family goal achievement record.

After reviewing each family member's goals at the start of the next session, the therapist reviewed the family meeting. He was disappointed that the meeting had not been held, but a brief discussion had occurred after George had reprimanded Brenda for not washing her dishes. Although there had been some improvement in washing dishes between meals, the rota for dish washing after meals had not been organized.

The therapist praised each person's specific efforts to implement the plan, and spent 15 minutes coaching the family on planning later in the session. Before that he expressed his disappointment that the family meeting had not been held and invited the family to assist him in achieving the goal of having a weekly family meeting between therapy sessions. This became one of the topics used in training planning skills during the session.

## TRAINING IN THE SPECIFIC STEPS

Once the family have attempted to carry out resolution of a straightforward problem issue in the initial problem solving/goal achievement session, the therapist will have made note of specific steps that may require further coaching during subsequent sessions. These sessions provide repeated practice of the deficient steps, until the family is able to apply each step competently.

### Step 1: Pinpointing problems and goals

The ability to define problems or goals in terms of realistic, clearly defined objectives is perhaps the most important step in problem resolution. Vague objectives, or unattainable goals not shared by the majority of participants, seldom lead to effective plans. To achieve problem definition in a highly efficient manner, participants must show competent communication skills, particularly those involving clear expression of their personal concerns or desires, and an ability to assist one another to pinpoint precise objectives through the use of active listening skills. An additional component of this step is the ability of the chairperson to structure the discussion, so that participants remain focused on the issue at hand, and to facilitate a consensus on the precise definition of the problem or goal efficiently. Where participants display high levels of competence in communication skills this step may be achieved with limited coaching. However, with less skilled participants considerable training may be necessary. After eliciting a rationale for clear problem/goal definition, the therapist invites the family to list a number of problem issues or goals that they would like to resolve during the next few weeks. After reviewing their communication skills, especially active listening, the chairperson is instructed to convene a discussion that aims to define the first of these issues. A time limit, usually five minutes, is set, after which the therapist elicits feedback and provides further coaching, with instructions or explicit modelling. The discussion is repeated until the problem or goal has been effectively defined. Two of the deficits encountered most commonly are defining problems or goals too broadly and agreeing on unrealistic short-term objectives.

*Enhancing specificity of problem/goal definition*

Goals such as 'getting more friends', 'finding a new job', 'becoming independent', or problems such as 'financial difficulties' or 'feeling anxious' are among those frequently cited by families experiencing stress. The goals may appear reasonably specific, and at least provide some clues to the general area of concern. However, attempts to employ the structured problem-solving approach will reveal the lack of specificity, and the subsequent difficulty in finding clear solutions to these issues. These broad definitions are contrasted with those pinpointed by participants who displayed competence in this step:

| | |
|---|---|
| Getting more friends | Having one male friend to go with to a leisure activity on one evening each week. |
| Finding a new job | Getting an interview for a hairdressing job within a ten-minute bus journey of home so that I can work from 9 a.m. to 3 p.m. weekdays. |
| Becoming independent | Making my own bed every day and cleaning my own room every week. |

129

| | |
|---|---|
| Financial difficulties | Saving £25.00 each month by stopping smoking cigarettes. |
| Feeling anxious | Having feelings of fear that I am going to die, with palpitations and sweating in crowded places. |

Here is an example of how the family are trained to use active listening to pinpoint specific problems and goals.

Therapist:  I have noticed that when you begin to discuss a problem issue you tend to spend very little time making it clear exactly what the problem or goal actually is. As a result, each person seems to have a different idea about what they are trying to find solutions for, and this seems to lead to misunderstandings, and sometimes to arguments. I would like you to practise this important first step of problem solving today. Jenny, I would like you to read the hints about this step listed on the problem solving/goal achievement worksheets.

George:  It says 'Talk about the problem or goal; listen carefully; ask questions; get everybody's opinions. Then write down exactly what the problem or goal is.'

Therapist:  Does everyone understand what those guidelines mean?

Harold:  I presume that we are supposed to ask the person who has the problem questions.

Therapist:  That's right. You ask questions to make it clear exactly what each person sees as the key problem or goal. What communication skill that you have been practising in recent weeks might help you here?

Harold:  Well, I suppose expressing your unpleasant feelings clearly would be the first step if we are trying to say exactly what our problems are.

Therapist:  That's right. I'm pleased that you thought of that point. Can anyone suggest what other communication skills might be useful?

Brenda:  Yes. Active listening might be helpful, especially being able to ask clarifying questions.

Therapist:  That's right. The more you can ask the person to tell you about his or her problems or goals, the more the person may be able to pinpoint the exact issue. What are some of the other aspects of active listening?

Brenda:  Looking interested and nodding your head.

130

Therapist: Yes, those are two other aspects. Well, what I would like you to do now is to discuss the issue that we talked about a little when I was checking on how you were getting on with your personal goals, and Harold said he wasn't sure what sort of job he wanted. I would like you to organize this as if you are having your family meeting with Harold as the chairperson and George as the secretary. But I would like you to spend five minutes asking Harold as many questions as you can think of about the kind of job he might like to consider. Ask any questions you can think of. I will count the number of questions each person asks and will stop you after five minutes. Is that clear?

Harold: Who do I ask questions to?

Therapist: Ah. You don't ask questions, unless you want the others to make it clearer what they are asking you. You just answer them. OK?

Harold: I've got it, I think. Shall we start now?

Therapist: Right.

Jenny: Do you want another office job, Harold?

Harold: No. I'd like a change.

Jenny: Like work outside? Gardening or something?

Harold: Yeah. I'd like an outside job.

Brenda: Would the salary be the same? We couldn't manage on less than you get now.

Harold: You're right, I'd like to earn a bit more, but that might be difficult.

Brenda: Well I don't think you should be thinking about something that is not possible. It doesn't make sense to me.

Harold: I agree.

George: We're supposed to be asking questions, aren't we? I want to know why you want to change your job, Harold?

Harold: I don't really know. I just feel I need a change of scenery.

(The discussion continues in this manner for another two minutes before the therapist interrupts.)

Therapist: Great! The five minutes is up and I heard plenty of clarifying questions about Harold's job ideas. Brenda asked three questions, George asked seven and Jenny top-scored with eight. I was very pleased with your efforts. George, I was also very pleased when you prompted everybody to stick to

131

the topic on two occasions. Harold, I'd like to ask you if the questions helped you to get a clearer idea of the sort of job you might consider?

Harold:   Yes, I think they did. They thought of things that I hadn't considered.

Therapist:   Well, I'd like you to continue asking questions for another couple of minutes and then I'd like you to come up with a clear statement of the exact goal you might consider.

(The family helped Harold to pinpoint a goal of 'getting a full-time, outdoor job, working 9–5 p.m. weekdays only, earning £1000 a month'. The therapist suggested that they complete the problem-solving steps during their next family meeting and moved on to practise further pinpointing with another issue concerning grocery shopping.)

George:   Asking questions.

Therapist:   That's right, George. I appreciate your mentioning the most important strategy for pinpointing problems and goals.

### Breaking down complex problems/goals to manageable steps

A second difficulty experienced by some families in defining problems and goals is the tendency to try to tackle a complex issue in one sitting. This difficulty is made worse when a therapist has been trained in theories of mental disorders that propose unitary causation and support the notion that once 'the problem' can be defined the disorder can then be miraculously cured. The behavioural approach disavows such simplistic notions and supports the idea that effective management of stress and high quality of community living necessitate incessant problem solving of issues, big and small. Problems and goals are broken down into a series of small steps to be tackled on a day-by-day basis within the personal resources readily accessible to the household group. For example, the goal of 'achieving independence' for one young man was broken down into learning the skills of cleaning, budgeting, banking, shopping, cooking, nutrition, personal hygiene, making telephone calls, dealing with social security benefits, using buses, entertaining friends, attending leisure clubs, assertive skills, handling emergencies, health and dental care, friendship skills, sexual skills, etc. 'Getting a new job' for a recently widowed woman comprised the following steps – attending evening classes, job searching, preparation of résumés, car purchase, arranging childcare, interview skills, and clothes shopping.

Training in these skills is facilitated by instructions, repeated prompting, and by therapists demonstrating the skills through explicit role-played modelling (see pages 194–6).

## Step 2: Brainstorming

The brainstorming approach to seeking alternative solutions to problems has the following aims:

- to maximize the scope for alternative solutions;
- to facilitate the participation of all household members;
- to maximize creativity;
- to reward all efforts in a non-judgemental way.

Participants are invited to list any possible solution that occurs to them without considering its relative merits. Every suggestion is written down until five or six alternatives have been noted. Rather than focusing on stereotyped or ideal solutions, participants are encouraged to relax and suggest any ideas that occur to them, regardless of how ridiculous or nonsensical the ideas may seem. Comment about each idea is withheld, apart from a simple acknowledgement of every suggestion, whether deemed good or bad.

Few households have difficulty with this step after it has been clearly outlined and demonstrated by the therapist. On occasions participants may appear to run out of ideas after two or three suggestions. Strategies to overcome this include instructing the chairperson to suggest 'doing nothing' as a possible solution. This somewhat paradoxical solution often disinhibits participants and allows brainstorming to flow again. In some families who are inhibited about appearing foolish, particularly in the presence of a professional therapist, it may help if the therapist role plays a household member and makes one or two outrageous suggestions. For example, one family could not list more than three alternatives to increase their household income. The therapist exchanged roles with Harold and proposed 'robbing a bank' and 'spending all their savings on lottery tickets'. These 'bad' ideas enabled the family to exhibit a more relaxed, playful approach that facilitated more creative problem solving during subsequent sessions.

The chairperson must ensure that this step is structured so that discussion about each proposed solution is minimal, with brief acknowledgement and listing of every idea.

### Step 3: Evaluating alternatives

In the next step the chairperson invites the participants to highlight the potential advantages and disadvantages of each idea suggested as a possible solution. No alternative is ideal, every good idea has drawbacks, such as the cost, time, or skill required for successful implementation. On the other hand, every apparently 'bad' idea has some good points. For example, robbing a bank to get money to pay the electricity bill may solve the problem, but has a high risk of creating more severe stresses in the long run!

It is crucial that participants are clearly oriented to the task of merely highlighting the *major* advantages and disadvantages of each alternative in quick succession, rather than debating the relative merits of each, or engaging in planning as to how they might implement the alternative if it was chosen as the best solution. This necessitates assertive chairmanship, so that participants move swiftly from alternative to alternative, with minimal discussion. To facilitate this efficiency we have purposely avoided taking notes on the worksheets. Instead, participants are expected to make mental notes of the points that are highlighted briefly. In addition, there is no expectation that each participant should comment on each alternative. Rather, participants may act as spokesmen for the group as a whole. It is useful to focus on the advantages of each alternative first before moving to their disadvantages. At this stage every alternative is considered a viable option, and no idea is dismissed or especially favoured until the following step is reached.

Very few chairpersons are able to structure this step effectively in the initial phases, so it is usually helpful for therapists to demonstrate the assertive manner in which participants are encouraged to move quickly from one idea to the next, merely listing the possible advantages and disadvantages of each.

## Step 4: Choosing the optimal solution

After all the proposed solutions have been reviewed, the chairperson leads the participants in a discussion that aims to choose the solution that is likely to produce maximum benefits, and can be readily implemented with the resources currently available to the household. This is not necessarily the 'ideal' solution, but one that can be initiated with minimal delays and without undue stress or complexity. This may not be expected to resolve the problem in its entirety; it is perhaps merely the first step towards resolution. Of course, where the problem has been broken down into manageable steps in the problem definition phase, there will be a higher probability that the solution will achieve full resolution.

At this stage it may be necessary to carry out more detailed reviews of the pros and cons of the choices favoured by participants. Reasoned debate, with the deployment of effective communication of positive and negative feelings and active listening skills, is favoured over angry bullying. The therapist must be prepared to interrupt the discussion whenever hostility arises and to rehearse appropriate communication skills. For example:

George:    I am not going to be able to get a job just by going to the Job Club for a week or two.

Harold:    Of course, you are. All you need to do is to make your mind up that you're going to work and you'll get a job tomorrow. When I was your age I walked into a factory and asked them to give me a job and they told me to start work immediately. You could do the same, but you are so damned lazy!

Therapist:    Stop! I'd like you to stop immediately. Jenny, I'd be grateful if you could tell us what you heard Harold trying to tell George about getting a job.

Jenny:    He was showing his frustration that George doesn't seem very keen to work.

Therapist:    That's exactly what I was hearing. Brenda, was he using the steps of expressing an unpleasant feeling?

Brenda:    No, I don't think so. At least not all of them.

Therapist:    Harold, how could you have told George how frustrated you are in a more constructive way that might have got him to cooperate with you more?

Harold:    I could have just told him how it makes me feel,

135

without getting into the issue of how I was when I was his age.

Therapist: Right. I would like you to try that, remembering to use the steps of expressing an unpleasant feeling. Here's a promptsheet to remind you.

Harold: George, I get pretty angry when you tell me how difficult it is to get work when you haven't even given it a try yet. I'd like you to go to the Job Club for a week, say, and then you'd be in a better position to judge your chances of getting work. OK?

Therapist: That's great. I really liked the way you put that. George, I would like you to reply to Harold now, and I'll let you carry on without my interruptions.

George: You've got a point there, Harold, but I still don't think I would choose the Job Club as my first step. I'd rather go to the rehabilitation counsellor and get her advice.

At times participants may have difficulty choosing between two solutions that appear to have equal benefits. In such cases the choice of the optimal solution may be determined on the basis of which one can be most readily implemented with minimal delays. Alternatively, participants may agree to try one first and then the other.

Wherever possible, it is preferable to avoid choosing complex combinations of solutions. Planning such solutions becomes unwieldy and confusing, and may contribute to increases in household stress. Instead, it may be helpful to settle for completing the initial steps before moving on to the next, possibly more complicated, stage.

### Step 5: Planning

Once the best solution has been chosen it is crucial to plan the exact steps everyone is going to take to implement that solution. Many well-conceived solutions are not implemented effectively because there are deficits in the planning phase. It is worth spending considerable time making detailed plans, particularly when the solution requires the cooperation of several participants to carry out several steps.

Planning entails consideration of a number of points. These are summarized in the planning checklist (see Figure 6.2). It is

| | Yes | No |
|---|:---:|:---:|
| 1. Are all resources (time, skills, materials, money) needed to carry out the solution available? | ✓ | |
| 2. Has person(s) agreed to arrange necessary resources (time, skills, materials, money)? | | ✓ |
| 3. Have all the steps in the plan been arranged so that everybody knows what they are doing and when they are doing it? | ✓ | |
| 4. Have the steps been checked to highlight specific likely hitches? | | ✓ |
| 5. Have specific plans been made to cope with likely hitches? | | ✓ |
| 6. Have people practised difficult parts of the plan (e.g. meetings, interviews, phone calls)? | | ✓ |
| 7. Has one person agreed to check that people do what they have agreed to do at the right time? | ✓ | |
| 8. Have a time and place been agreed when overall progress with the plan will be discussed? | ✓ | |

*Figure 6.2*   Planning checklist

not necessary to employ this detailed checklist to every planning session, but it may be useful for the therapist to instruct the chairperson to use it on at least one occasion, particularly when it is reported that planning deficits may have contributed to suboptimal implementation of a solution to a problem or goal that the family had been working on. Subsequent use of the checklist may be restricted to reminding participants to account for key steps in planning, or when a complex plan is needed.

### Review of resources

This step involves ensuring that participants have access to the full range of resources needed to implement the plan. In addition to material resources, such as equipment or ingredients, and money for any purchases, fares, etc., it is important to consider whether key participants are competent and confident in performing the skills needed and whether they have allocated sufficient time to carry out the plan. Skills may include interpersonal skills, such as the conversation skills needed for developing friendships or interviewing skills needed for a job interview, as well as instrumental skills needed to carry out a specific job task. Where crucial skills are lacking, or participants lack confidence in their performance, skills training may be an essential step in the plan. This may be feasible within the context of the sessions, or may require courses of specialized training or education.

In addition to possessing the resources needed, it is important that one or more participants agree to ensure that the resources are coordinated, to be readily available when needed. This may be a matter of getting a group of people to a particular place at a particular time, or buying ingredients for cooking, or materials for cleaning or gardening, etc. It may be helpful to designate one person as the overall coordinator for this plan.

### Coordinating steps of plan

An effective plan requires explicit planning of each step in sequence so that everybody knows exactly what they are expected to do and when they are expected to do it. So often vague agreements, such as 'I'll phone them and see what they can tell me', or 'I'll arrange something next week', contribute to failed implementation. Where such commitments are followed up by a more clearly specified action plan to be implemented at a specific time, the chances of success are enhanced. Notes of these agreements may need to be made in personal diaries, on calendars or noticeboards to serve as prompts. The coordinator may arrange to remind people of these agreements and further prompt their actions.

### Anticipation of consequences

In an earlier stage of problem solving, the pros and cons of each potential solution have been reviewed briefly. During planning a more detailed review of anticipated consequences is conducted. Any specific likely hitches are highlighted. These will include not merely negative consequences, but also potential problems that may arise from unexpected success. For example, with job seeking it may be important to know what to do if you are offered a job that you do not feel capable of doing, or with

138

dating it may be crucial to know how to handle unwanted sexual overtures assertively. One young man, who had prepared himself well for the expectation that he would be rejected as usual, was surprised when his date invited him back to her apartment for coffee, kissed him passionately, and asked him to make love with her. He was not prepared for this consequence, panicked and fled from the apartment, accompanied by a profound sense of failure and despair that he could ever learn to cope with women.

Although the focus of most participants tends to be on catastrophic consequences that might arise, the most common hitches are much more mundane. Failure to organize transport, failure to leave sufficient time for delays, not noting telephone numbers, having insufficient funds to cover expenses, not making lists of items to purchase, giving inadequate directions, are among the multitude of everyday failings that limit the effective implementation of optimal solutions.

A strategy to assist this aspect of planning involves rehearsing the plan step by step, and considering potential hitches at each step. For a complex plan where participants have not had much previous practice, it may be helpful to carry out a comprehensive rehearsal, in the same way that a football team may rehearse a specific move. For example, a woman who had been recently widowed rehearsed joining a social club by arranging for a friend to accompany her to the club, where she was able to meet the organizers and several members who told her about the functioning of the club. She met a member who lived in her neighbourhood who offered to accompany her on the bus journey, which she found anxiety-provoking.

However, with some plans it is difficult to rehearse in a real-life setting; moreover, it is difficult to rehearse coping with hitches in this way. Role-played rehearsal may be used to practise coping with hitches, such as handling difficult questions in an interview, coping with interpersonal crises or emergencies. Where participants are preoccupied with concerns over negative consequences, a strategy we have called the 'cognitive safety-net' may prove useful. Participants think through each step and the adverse consequences they foresee but, rather than stopping at the point where catastrophic thoughts overwhelm them, they proceed to think through alternative strategies that could be used to cope with that catastrophic situation. These strategies may encompass behavioural responses, such as leaving the situation or engaging in some distracting behaviour, affective responses, such as expressing negative feelings in an appropriate manner, or cognitive responses, such as thinking through possible alternatives, leaving the situation, and accepting that the efforts had provided a valuable learning experience, and revising strategies to enhance the effectiveness of future efforts. It is helpful to make a list of the strategies discussed so that they can be used in the catastrophic situations, should the need arise. Once a safety net has been constructed that seems sufficiently robust to contain the participants' anticipated worst fears, the participants are usually able to implement key elements of the plan with greater confidence. Of course, there are many people who suffer from disabling effects of persistent fears of negative consequences, who may benefit from more extensive cognitive restructuring strategies (Beck *et al.* 1979).

Here is a list of the strategies that a person with learning difficulties, who was afraid of being left at home alone, made:

- Parents to leave forwarding number.
- Parents to phone at prearranged times.
- Lock herself in bathroom.
- Watch favourite video to take mind off fears.
- Leave lights on in main rooms.
- Phone the police if intruder enters house; number left on the telephone.
- Run next door to a friendly neighbour.
- Family dog likely to scare off intruder.

Once this plan had been discussed, she found staying at home much less frightening, and her parents were able to re-establish their social life.

*Setting time for review*

The final step in all plans is to agree on a specific time and place for a review of progress in the implementation process. This time is noted on the plan and will usually be arranged within the context of the weekly family meeting.

## REVIEW OF IMPLEMENTATION EFFORTS

The final step in problem solving and goal achievement is to review the results of participants' efforts to implement the agreed plan. Achieving problem resolution and goals is seldom completed after one attempt and is usually an ongoing process. It is important for families to understand that, despite their best efforts at applying this more structured approach to their problem solving, total success is usually only achieved with persistence and commitment over a considerable period, particularly when the problems are complex and the goals substantial. Although initial training is aimed at everyday issues where rapid success may be experienced, as families move on to more difficult issues, they must be cautioned against the expectation that this approach can provide any miraculous solutions to longstanding problems necessitating major lifestyle changes.

A comprehensive and constructive review of participants' efforts to implement the plan is a vital step in the ongoing problem-solving process. The chairperson structures a review of each step of the plan on the worksheet. Steps are discussed in terms of:

- Was the step carried out as planned?
- How successful was the outcome? Partial or complete success?
- What hitches were encountered?
- What modifications were made to cope with these hitches?
- How successful was the modified implementation? Partial or complete success?
- What has been learned with regard to continuing efforts?
- Praise for all efforts made, no matter how significant or how successful.
- Arrangements for further problem-solving efforts where problems/goals unresolved.

A crucial part of this review is the importance of reinforcing the *efforts* that participants have made, without regard to their *achievements*. The natural tendency to dismiss unsuccessful efforts as 'a waste of time' is countered. This approach may prove extremely difficult for achievement-oriented families and repeated therapist modelling and prompting may be needed before this approach is adopted. A constructive review of this kind helps to motivate participants to persist with their efforts in resolving difficult problems, even when progress appears slow. The emphasis on team work assists in providing mutual support and effective stress management.

An example of this was Brenda's attempt to enhance the cleaning activities in her household. This was initially defined as a problem by Brenda. A plan was devised that gave each household member responsibility for one tidying or cleaning activity. At the first review a week later, only Brenda had completed her task as agreed. She expressed frustration that the other members had not attempted to perform their tasks. The review revealed that Brenda had done the tidying and cleaning assigned to the other members before they could do the jobs themselves. She said she had done this because she could not bear seeing the house in such a state for the entire week. Further planning resulted in each member agreeing to do their chores on a specific day. Brenda was to remind them on the day the task was to be completed, and to express her gratitude to them when the task was completed. At the following review this plan appeared to have worked well, although Brenda complained that the tasks were not performed as well as she would have done them. She agreed to carry out some coaching of the other household members until they were competent, but to avoid taking over and doing the jobs herself. After six weeks the family were all helping Brenda in a manner that satisfied her, and she was able to express her unreserved praise for their efforts.

Another common deficit in the review process is the cursory review of successfully implemented plans. The therapist is encouraged to point out to participants that they may be able to recognize why some plans appear to be implemented more readily than others, and to pinpoint the ingredients that may lead to consistent levels of success so that they can be incorporated more often into plans.

The initial review may need to be modelled by the therapist taking the chairperson's role. However, as with all steps in this problem-solving approach, it is essential that the therapist does not adopt this review function, but trains the chairperson to structure the review discussion for the group. Of course, the therapist employs the same style of review at the start of each session when he or she reviews progress achieved between training sessions.

## CONCLUSIONS

Enhancing the efficiency of the problem-solving functions of all members of a household is the key to this family-based approach to stress management. The therapist coaches the participants to structure weekly meetings where they use a straightforward method to discuss their stresses in dealing with their problems and in achieving their personal goals in an organized way. The same skill training approach employed in enhancing the quality of interpersonal communication is used, with instructions, guide sheets, prompts and explicit demonstration of specific skills. The therapist hands over control of the discussion and its contents to the participants, much in the same way that a football coach observes the game from the sidelines. This enables participants to practise their ability to structure their own probelm-solving discussions, so that they can convene similar meetings in the absence of the therapist. The therapist continues to promote the use of effective communication skills throughout these discussions so that hostility and destructive communication patterns are minimized.

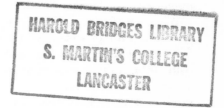

# 7

# CRISIS INTERVENTION

During behavioural family therapy crises will often arise in the household. For the most part, these crises occur as a result of ineffective problem solving by the household members, both individually and collectively. A potentially stressful event or situation has not been dealt with in an optimal manner and the stress has built up to the point where it threatens to overwhelm the coping resources of the household unit. Some stresses tend to be more specific to family living. These include life events such as marriage, childbirth, leaving home, unemployment, homelessnesss, serious illnesses, divorce, and bereavement.

When faced with a major crisis the response of most therapists is to jump in and assist the household to reduce the stress. The behavioural family therapist is encouraged to approach the issue differently, at least in the initial stage. The crisis is viewed as an ideal opportunity for the household to employ the problem-solving functions acquired during treatment. These may include employing principles outlined in the education sessions, specific communication skills, or structured problem-solving strategies. Only when these strategies have been employed, or where the therapist considers the risk too great to permit such a trial of self-management, does the therapist intervene directly.

The main elements of crisis intervention in behavioural family therapy include:

1 Early detection and crisis prevention.
2 Pinpointing the problems underlying the crisis.
3 Assessment and promotion of the household's problem-solving efforts.

144

4 Expert consultation and advice, particularly where the crisis involves health problems, or other special needs.
5 Continuing support and availability.
6 Review of successful strategies for application during future crises.

## EARLY DETECTION AND CRISIS PREVENTION

Most crises develop over a period of days or weeks before coming to a head. Where household members have acquired the skills of recognizing the early warning signs of an impending crisis, the opportunity to avert the crisis by early problem solving may be feasible. In households where the problems that lead to therapeutic intervention are emotional, behavioural, or health crises, the behavioural assessment will encompass aspects of these disorders, including precipitants, exacerbating features, and prodromal signs. In the case of mental and physical illnesses continuous monitoring of early signs of future episodes may be initiated systematically (see pages 71–4).

The enhancement of household stress management through improved efficiency of interpersonal communication and problem solving may be expected to result in fewer and less severe crises as the coping capacity of the household increases. However, in the early stages of training such benefits may be relatively small.

The approach we advocate for crisis management is one that views a crisis as an opportunity to learn to cope more effectively with subsequent crises, preferably to avoid them, or avert them through early problem-solving efforts.

For example, Sid and Polly noted that they had major rows, often leading to violence and separations, when they went to friends' parties and drank excessively. They problem solved this issue before the next party they attended and decided to limit themselves to two drinks apiece. Unfortunately, their host persuaded Polly to drink the fruit punch, which he assured her contained minimal quantities of alcohol. She became drunk and Sid took her home, expressing his anger at her behaviour. The following morning she explained what had happened and Sid accepted her explanation. They subsequently planned to take their own non-alcohol drinks to parties and rehearsed refusing drinks from persistent hosts. In passing, Sid commented that he doubted that they would row the way they had in the past, because they were dealing with stresses on a day-to-day basis and the tension did not build up in the way it had previously.

## PINPOINTING THE PROBLEMS UNDERLYING THE CRISIS

The most difficult step in problem solving is the initial one of defining the precise issue that is the key problem. Most households find this difficult, even when dealing with relatively straightforward issues. Thus, it is not surprising that this skill is likely to be least effective during a crisis. When a wife storms out of the home to stay with a friend, a son or daughter threatens suicide, anger boils over into violence, or an eviction notice arrives, there is a tendency to panic and focus on responding to the immediate issue at hand. Although an immediate response may be needed to resolve the emergency, it is important that problem-solving efforts are directed rapidly towards underlying problems that may have led to the emergency.

An example of this was the case of Gerry, a 25-year-old single man, who was extremely shy. His major goal was to develop a friendship with a girl he fancied. After several weeks of attempting to arrange a date through a variety of dating agencies he finally enjoyed some success. He spent a very enjoyable evening with an attractive young woman at the movies. After he drove her home she invited him in and began to make sexual advances to him. His lack of experience, coupled with this unexpected behaviour, caused Gerry to panic. He escaped from the woman's clutches and sped home. When his father greeted him he appeared distraught, telling his father that it was finished, and that he planned to kill himself immediately. His father and mother also panicked and phoned their family doctor for emergency advice. They also phoned a member of the therapy team, who advised them to convene an emergency household meeting and attempt to develop a plan to cope with the crisis. They did this, and by the time the family doctor arrived they had redefined the problem from 'suicide prevention' to 'getting experience of sex'. Although Gerry still appeared very upset, the crisis was well on the way to being resolved. The therapist reviewed the plan the next day, suggesting some minor modifications.

The response in this example may be contrasted with the more typical responses of mental health services, where responses to crisis seldom consider the underlying precipitants. In many cases the issues are not straightforward and, in households where problem-solving skills are more limited, therapists may need to chair the emergency problem-solving sessions to help participants to define the key issues. The value of working with a team of therapists who respond in a consistent way is also illustrated. Services to families and similar living groups must provide 24-hour contact to assist with crises, which may occur outside office hours. Contact by telephone is usually sufficient for most crises, but the ability to make visits to the home or to see people at the clinic out of hours is essential, even if it is a rare necessity. The confidence that such provisions engender in informal caregivers is substantial, and facilitates their ability to deal with issues in a calm, reasoned manner, knowing that they can call for expert assistance if they become overwhelmed by the situation.

## ASSESSMENT AND PROMOTION OF THE HOUSEHOLD'S PROBLEM-SOLVING EFFORTS

It is clear that the therapist's response to a crisis will depend partly on the nature of the crisis, and partly on the coping capacity of the household to deal with that specific crisis. Where the therapist concerned has had considerable contact with a household such assessments are relatively straightforward. However, when a crisis occurs early in the course of therapy, or a therapist is deputizing for a colleague, the following issues may need to be evaluated:

• Are participants being provided with effective support in terms of need for lodgings, food, hygiene, healthcare, etc?
• Is the household capable of monitoring participants' disturbed behaviour patterns?
• To what extent are the coping efforts of household members contributing to reduction in household stress and alleviation of precipitating problems?
• To what extent are the coping efforts of household members contributing to exacerbations in household stress and maintenance of precipitating problems?

147

- To what extent will the household benefit from or be harmed by expert consultation and intervention to alleviate problems and/or stress?

These issues are of particular concern when the crisis is associated with current or impending major health disorders. It may seem surprising that we consider the potential for expert consultation to cause harm to the household but this may occasionally be the case when experts' efforts tend to undermine participants' coping efforts. A common example is the prescription of tranquillizing medication to reduce distress, rather than assisting people to resolve the problems that precipitated the distress. Removal of people from the household to hospital or other residential settings may create similar harmful effects, where this is not problem solved with all members of the household, particularly the target individual.

The behavioural family therapist assesses the current problem-solving efforts of each household member as well as the combined efforts of the living group. It may be necessary to complete a further behavioural analysis, at least in part, to gain a clear impression of the overall quality of problem solving. However, where the problem issues appear reasonably discrete, observing the participants conducting a problem-solving discussion about these issues may provide sufficient information to make an adequate assessment. It is important to recall one of the basic assumptions that underpin the behavioural approach: at all times each participant is doing his or her best to cope with the situation, with the skills at his or her disposal, subject to the specific constraints present at that time. In other words, each person will be behaving in the crisis in the best way possible for that person, even though his or her coping efforts may actually be contributing to increased stress to self and others. Nevertheless, the assessment of a crisis from this perspective helps the therapist to acknowledge all forms of coping efforts as being positively motivated and, rather than discourage these efforts, restructure them into a coordinated effort that maximizes mutual benefits to all participants.

For example, the Barry family had completed two sessions of problem-solving training when their 17-year-old daughter, Helen, failed to return home after attending a friend's party. Despite many phone calls to her friends' homes, they had been unable to trace her whereabouts. She phoned the next evening to tell them that she had decided to move out of the home and stay in the flat of a 20-year-old man she had met at the party. Her father demanded that she return home immediately, while her mother pleaded with her to consider the potential problems associated with this arrangement. Her younger sister, Samantha, attempted to calm her parents by reminding them that the last time Helen behaved in this way she returned home within a few days and was pleased to be home. Father considered phoning the police, but his wife told him that it was unlikely they would do anything. Both parents spent a sleepless night before they phoned the therapist the next morning.

The therapist listened to Mr Barry's report of the situation, clarifying specific aspects, particularly the way in which the family had attempted to resolve the crisis. He told Mr Barry that he was pleased that the issue had been discussed by all three, and that they had agreed the goal of having Helen return home. He also noted that they had discussed several possible options and had evaluated the potential advantages and disadvantages of each. However, they had not employed the six-step problem-solving method in any formal sense, and the discussions were lengthy and often heated. The therapist suggested that they waited until Samantha returned from school and then convened a household meeting to discuss the crisis using the structured approach. He requested that they report their plans back to him the next morning so that he could review them.

Once he has completed his assessment of their efforts to cope with the crisis, the therapist provides feedback to each member of the household. He or she praises their efforts, highlighting specific behaviours that appear to have contributed most to crisis resolution. In some cases these contributions may seem trivial, but nevertheless they are clearly pinpointed and acknowledged by the skilled therapist. For example, a therapist responded to a young man who sat through a problem-solving discussion saying very little: 'Billy, I was pleased to see that you were involved in the problem-solving discussions, and that you listened throughout to what was being said even though the issue did not involve you in any direct way.'

Although it is preferable that participants express their unpleasant feelings in the most effective manner described earlier, there may be times when voices are raised and shouting matches ensue. Whereas the therapist may be tempted to stop the action and prompt less hostile exchanges, the main concern during a crisis discussion is whether the communication is clearly contributing to resolving the problem. Thus, such heated discussion may be ignored, until a point where it ceases to further the problem-solving process or becomes abusive in nature. Of course, the therapist will note that further efforts will be needed in future sessions to help participants communicate their strong feelings in a less hostile manner in such stressful circumstances.

## EXPERT CONSULTATION ON CRISIS RESOLUTION

As ever, behavioural family therapy aims to facilitate the ability of the family or other household groups to devise their own solutions to their own perceived problems. The therapist acts as a coach, seated on the sideline, supporting the structure of interpersonal problem solving, rather than becoming immersed in the problem-solving process itself. Although the experienced therapist may have strong personal views on how he or she would resolve various problems if he or she could change places with the participants, this is only possible where he or she is indeed a member of that household. Such situations pertain where behavioural family therapy is applied within residential care, where professionals function as residential house parents.

However, we have noted that therapists are expected to intervene in situations when significant abuse is evident or threatened. The other context where therapists may offer specific advice on problem resolution strategies is where the crisis involves physical or mental health problems. In these cases the therapist is expected to offer personal advice, including suggestions for seeking expert consultation with health profes-sionals or agencies. Behavioural family therapists from a social work background may also offer personal advice on specific issues where they have particular expertise, such as emergency housing, financial, legal, childcare, and other social welfare facilities. Examples of specific strategies frequently incorporated in behavioural family therapy are described in Chapter 8.

Wherever the therapist offers advice and actively participates in the problem-solving process, he or she must adhere strictly to the guidelines taught to the family. This includes occasions when a crisis arises before the structured problem-solving approach has been introduced to participants. On such occasions the therapist may take the chairperson role in the discussion, employ the problem solving and goal achievement worksheet, and follow the six-step model. When participants are familiar with the structured approach, the therapist adds his or her expert advice as one or more of the alternative solutions, or helps the family in the planning stages by refining their chosen solutions. His or her proposals are subjected to the same scrutiny as those of any other participant, and do not take precedence unless they are deemed the optimal choice by the household group. Often people will look to the therapist to provide simple answers to their problems, and many therapists are eager to take over responsibility for crisis resolution. However, as with all problem solving there are never any perfect answers, and there are usually equally effective alternatives to most well-established clinical strategies. Nevertheless, it is crucial that, where highly beneficial medical, psychological, or social strategies exist, these are made readily available to the people most likely to benefit from them, and that therapists ensure that expert consultation is facilitated wherever it is indicated.

## CONTINUING SUPPORT AND AVAILABILITY

When a major crisis arises it is important that the therapist, or the therapeutic team, provides continuing support until the crisis has been resolved. This usually entails providing 24-hour telephone contact, and at times daily problem-solving sessions. This is particularly important where the crisis is life-threatening or involves disabling health problems. It is important that the therapist attempts to gauge the optimal amount of support needed, and that additional contacts are not perceived as intrusive and irritating by participants. Once again, when such arrangements are made during mutual problem-solving discussions, they will tend to work better.

## REVIEW OF SUCCESSFUL STRATEGIES

In keeping with the principles of behavioural family therapy the therapist elicits feedback about the skills and efforts of all

151

participants throughout the period of crisis resolution. All successful strategies are highlighted, even when their success is limited. Crisis resolution usually only occurs after many sessions of problem solving and the application of a number of plans and strategies. The continual constructive review process that is a key part of structured problem solving helps people to maintain their efforts even at times when progress appears stalled, or when setbacks occur.

Once a major crisis has been resolved it may be helpful to review the entire process, and to take special note of strategies that have been of particular assistance, as well as those that were of limited value only. The crisis serves as a valuable trial which may help participants to learn more efficient strategies that can be applied more readily in future crises. Some may be specific to the particular crisis, for example, a particular medication, or advice from a housing agency; others may relate to general issues such as stress management. Where families have applied the specific communication and problem-solving methods they have learned, they may be able to define specific benefits derived from these efforts. For example, one father noted how he managed to persuade his daughter to return home after repeatedly making positive requests rather than threatening her; another household found that convening daily household meetings provided considerable support and helped them to coordinate their efforts while the mother was in hospital having major surgery. Where major deficits in communication and problem solving have been observed during the crisis period, the therapist may decide to provide further coaching and training in these skills.

Where the crises concern exacerbations of chronic health problems, this review may provide further opportunity to educate participants about the nature and clinical management of that disorder. The usual association between stress levels and the disorder, as well as the benefits of medication and other treatment strategies, may be clarified. Plans to prevent future episodes, or to respond to them earlier and more efficiently, may be refined.

## SPECIFIC CRISES AND CRISIS MANAGEMENT STRATEGIES

The previous part of this chapter outlined the generic approach to crises in families and other households. There are some crises of specific concern to those working within this context. They include household violence, emotional abuse, substance abuse, and suicide.

## Household violence

Surveys of family behaviour indicate that sporadic violent acts occur in most households. Such a high prevalence should not be taken to indicate a cultural acceptance of such acts of aggression, nor should it be employed as a spur to zealots wishing to rid society of undesirable patterns of behaviour. However, where persisting or severe violent behaviour is suspected in a household, the therapist is expected to target the issue, even when it is not clearly identified as a problem for the participants.

As with all targeted issues, the first approach is to conduct a thorough assessment. This helps to establish the most likely situations where aggressive actions may occur, including interpersonal and environmental triggers and predisposing factors. The assessment may also uncover strategies that participants are already applying that may be contributing to a reduction in the risk of such actions. It is important to look at occasions when angry impulses are controlled and to contrast them with occasions when aggression has resulted.

The principles of anger control that we have employed include the following:

- Education that anger is a natural emotion that cannot be avoided or effectively suppressed.
- The appropriate expression of anger often helps in resolving problems and achieving goals.
- Each person must take full responsibility for the origins of his or her own feelings and not blame other people's actions for *causing* their unpleasant emotional states.
- Aggressive acts can never be excused, even when the person acts under extreme provocation – there is always an alternative to violence.
- Assaults on persons or property are illegal. They should always be reported to the police, who should take responsibility for ensuring that legal procedures are adhered to, according to the laws agreed by the community in which the offender resides.

- No mental or physical disorder exonerates any citizen from any law or the appropriate legal processes. It may affect the type of sentence given to an offender at the completion of a trial.
- People caring for those with chronic disabilities are likely to feel angry with them from time to time. Their ability to express their anger appropriately may prove crucial. Some stress-reduction measures appear to advocate suppression of all expression of negative feelings towards the index patient. While this may be of limited value at the time of florid episodes in some cases, it has potential hazards for the carers if continued.

The clear aim of anger control is the appropriate expression of strong, angry feelings within a problem-solving framework. This involves the following skills:

- Pinpointing exactly what has triggered the angry feeling. This is often some aspect of a person's behaviour or a specific context, e.g. a threatening gesture, a remark or action perceived as rejecting or belittling, a crowded place, feeling cornered, etc.
- Deciding whether immediate expression of the angry feeling will lead to efficient resolution, and reduce the likelihood of its recurrence, or whether it will escalate tension.
- Avoiding expressing anger when under the influence of alcohol or drugs.
- Telling the person who is the target of your expression exactly what he or she has done that has triggered off your anger. If this is his or her own behaviour stick to that one specific behaviour and avoid broadening the discussion to other less relevant behaviour or issues. In other words, *target the problem, not the person*!
- Telling the person exactly how you feel in that situation, using appropriate non-verbal expression, e.g. eye contact, firm tone of voice. Avoid aggressive postures such as standing over a person and crowding him or her, or threatening gestures, raised voice, or sarcasm.
- Trying to suggest some ways that the person could modify his or her behaviour in future that would prevent your angry response. If necessary, be prepared to carry out a longer problem-solving discussion using the six-step method.

154

This method of expressing negative feelings is identical to that employed in the communication skills training that is a major component of the approach employed to assist participants to manage stress (see page 98). It can be employed to express any feeling in a clear, direct manner.

It is clear that learning to communicate anger in a non-aggressive way may take some time and, with the extreme provocation engendered by many mental disorders, added strategies may be needed as interim contingencies. Two useful strategies are limit setting and time out.

### Limit setting

This strategy involves negotiating with the potentially aggressive person the precise behaviours that will be tolerated by household members, and the precise behaviours that will not. The immediate response to an unacceptable aggressive action is also agreed between the participants. This usually involves removing the offender immediately from the household circle but, in keeping with the overall approach, the precise plan is left to the discretion of the household members. However, we advocate taking a very strong line on any form of violence or emotional abuse, and urge people to do likewise, if necessary assisting them to call in police or other social agencies at an early stage. Good rapport with the local police may facilitate visits from a police officer to clarify the legal consequences of such acts to a potential offender in a firm yet understanding manner. The police may need to rehearse this performance to ensure that they convey the message appropriately. However, it is our experience that police officers have excellent skills in the expression of limit setting. It is crucial that any specified example of inappropriate behaviour is managed according to the contract. Many people tend to dismiss minor offences, thereby tacitly approving them and increasing the likelihood that they will escalate to major offences. A consistent approach to setting limits is a valuable strategy in the prevention of violence.

### Time out

Many people will be familiar with the use of time out in parenting. However, when the offender is an adult it is not a simple task to frog-march him or her to the bathroom and have him or her remain there for a specified time. A variant which has proved useful with adults involves the same principle of removing the person from the provoking situation and withdrawing positive reinforcement for inappropriate behaviour. A contract is agreed: when clear warning signs appear that are prodromes of an aggressive act the person is prompted to leave the situation immediately and carry out some behaviour likely to reduce the risk of aggression. This usually involves prompting the person to take a walk or engage in some physical activity that helps them to unwind. Patients are encouraged to recognize the warning signs and to initiate this behaviour themselves to help their self-control. Once again, in order to prove effective this approach must be clearly specified and applied in a highly consistent manner. Therapists may rehearse the situation several times with patient and carers. In addition, it is useful to rehearse likely snags in its application, and problem solve how they may be handled.

A final cautionary note involves the use of drugs to promote anger control. To date no drugs have been developed that have a consistent anti-aggressive effect. However, it is common for doctors to consider that this is one benefit associated with tranquillizing drugs. It is not our policy to use any drug as a means of behaviour control. Rather, we are eager to restrict the use of drug and psychological strategies to manage specific impairments for which there is adequate scientific evidence for their specific efficacy. Thus, we would use a tranquillizing drug to reduce the perceptual disturbance that results in hallucinations and delusions or to slow manic thought processes, all of which may predispose a person to aggressive acts. Over-enthusiastic prescribing of high doses of drugs may have the paradoxical effect of reducing self-control over violent impulses or of producing toxic confusional states where the risk of violence is heightened (Curry *et al.* 1970).

### Emotional abuse

The management of emotional abuse in households is fraught with difficulty. It is defined as any recurring pattern of behaviour contributing to major distress in others. Where such abuse is associated with violence or sexual assaults, the issue is more clearly defined than where the abuse is purely emotional. Yet evidence suggests that the emotional trauma is much more destructive in the long term than the physical damage. Further, emotional abuse may not be so readily communicated in assessments, particularly when the victim is being blackmailed not to disclose the behaviour. However, when evidence of abuse is detected the therapist is advised to respond in the same firm way as recommended for other aggressive acts.

### Suicide threats

Suicide is another form of behaviour with a very low frequency of occurrence, yet it is often associated with family and relationship distress, especially bereavement, family breakup, work failure, as well as with serious mental or physical health problems. Reliable methods of determining this risk have yet to be formulated, and current studies have shown how difficult it is to predict the specific individuals who will commit suicide. The best predictor remains a statement of the victim's intentions. Whenever a person is suspected of having thoughts of suicide or self-destruction, therapists conduct a tactful and comprehensive screening that aims to develop rapport and trust, while displaying concern about current life problems. Where a potential risk of a suicide attempt is detected the following procedures are recommended without delay:

● Consult a psychiatrist.
● Ensure that the high-risk person is appropriately supervised at all times of the day and night by a carer who fully comprehends the danger and is willing to take responsibility for monitoring the person's behaviour.
● In the absence of people both capable *and willing* to undertake this monitoring responsibility, a mental health professional(s) must be assigned to carry out this task. This may necessitate admission to a hospital unit.
● Reduce access to suicide weapons in a firm, yet diplomatic, way:
  – remove all sharp knives, razors, and guns from the household;
  – remove all unused drugs;
  – remove alcohol supplies;
  – remove dangerous chemicals.

- Ensure that small doses of drugs are prescribed by the family practitioner, and that a clear note is made on the front of the chart to alert other doctors to current concerns. At times all doctors covering the practice may need to be informed of these concerns.
- Draw up a written contract in close collaboration with the high-risk person and carers, stating that he or she will agree to contact specific people or agencies before performing any self-destructive actions. This states clearly the services that will be provided to assist the person through the current crisis. The person at risk is requested to sign this statement, which is then countersigned by the key therapist. This contract is left with the person; a copy is made for his or her key carers, a copy for the family practitioner, and a copy for the mental health service.
- Reassess suicidal intention on a daily basis until risk becomes minimal.
- Begin clinical management of underlying disorder or dysfunction without delay.
- Consider all threats of self-destructive actions as potential antecedents of such actions, regardless of the manner in which they are communicated.

In summary, the key elements of management of suicidal threat include comprehensive assessment, effective monitoring of risk factors, and application of effective treatment of the underlying problems, both psychosocial and biological. Consistent with our overall approach, all household members are considered at the centre of all clinical management and their efforts to cope with the crisis are always integrated with those of the professional services.

## CONCLUSIONS

It is concluded that the BFT approach to crisis intervention employs an approach that emphasizes clear, direct communication between the therapist and all household members, and ensures that the same efficient problem-solving approach is employed in resolving the crisis. Few specific strategies have been shown to have consistent benefits in the resolution of specific crisis situations, such as violence, emotional abuse, or suicidal threats. Well-controlled research studies are extremely difficult to conduct under such circumstances. Nevertheless, common sense dictates that clear assessment of the context triggering such behaviour, with attempts to reduce any obvious risk factors, combined with intensive problem solving and careful monitoring, may help families to cope with such problems. Instead of merely coaching from the sidelines, the therapist does not hesitate to become involved in the problem-solving process, but remains cautious in giving participants false confidence in the effectiveness of his or her suggestions, unless there is clear evidence of the efficacy of these strategies from the scientific literature. It is essential that the therapist receives the support of a competent professional team during such crises, and that meetings with them also employ effective problem-solving approaches, rather than hackneyed solutions that do not account for the specific strengths and weaknesses of the household, such as immediate hospital admission, residential care, or excessive reliance on sedative drugs to control inappropriate behaviour. It may be necessary for the therapist to provide daily sessions, or even to spend extended periods with the family. Such intensive care is aided by the assistance of multidisciplinary team work.

Where crises are associated with episodes of mental disorder specific strategies to reduce the impairment may be employed. These include a range of validated biomedical and psychosocial approaches that have proven efficacy in reducing the severity of the symptoms of anxiety, depressive, manic, and schizophrenic symptoms, and should be readily provided by mental health services (Falloon and Fadden 1993).

The non-confrontational nature of BFT seeks to prevent major crises arising, while at the same time actively promoting resolution of interpersonal conflicts and life stresses. However, the therapist does not shirk responsibility when abusive behaviour is detected, nor does he or she hide behind the cloak of professional confidentiality when illegal acts are observed. Statutory agencies are contacted whenever appropriate and their powers to instigate legal procedures are supported, even when these may conflict with the philosophical views of the therapist.

# 8

# SPECIFIC STRATEGIES

## INTRODUCTION

The six-step problem solving/goal achievement method enables participants to devise plans to cope with a wide range of issues in their everyday lives. At times the experienced therapist may be aware of specific validated strategies that may have been shown to produce consistent benefits when applied to many of the issues that the family may encounter. Naturally, he or she may be tempted to introduce these strategies into the family repertoire. However, the BFT approach attempts to maximize the competence of the living group to derive their own specific methods of coping with issues and achieving their goals. These efforts may be undermined by a highly skilled therapist who is able to provide them with a standardized answer to almost every issue, rather than train them to develop novel ways to devise their own effective plans. Nevertheless, the therapist does not allow the family to struggle continually with major stresses where there are well-researched biomedical or psychosocial strategies shown to be effective in modifying those stresses. In these circumstances the family is trained to incorporate the specific strategy in the manner shown to produce maximum benefits. This chapter will highlight several therapeutic strategies that may be integrated with the BFT approach, and will outline the manner in which they are applied within the structured problem-solving method.

## CRITERIA FOR INTRODUCING A SPECIFIC THERAPEUTIC STRATEGY

The family problem-solving efforts may be supplemented by the introduction of a specific strategy when each of the following conditions exists:

- A major problem area is addressed that is associated with significant current or anticipated stress, usually involving moderate or severe impairment, disability, or handicap to one or more participants.
- Problem-solving efforts at planning a strategy to cope with this stress are observed to have major deficits, and are considered unlikely to prove effective in resolving the stress efficiently.
- There is a specific therapeutic strategy that has proved effective in replicated controlled research trials.
- The therapist has been trained in the competent application of this therapeutic strategy, or is able to seek the assistance of a colleague who has experience of this strategy (as a co-therapist or supervisor).

Unless each of these conditions is met the therapist continues to support the participants' efforts to seek effective problem resolution, and avoids any interference with this process. It is essential that all therapists keep abreast of the scientific developments in the mental health field, including both biomedical and psychosocial therapies, and that they receive effective training in the assessment and application of state-of-the-art strategies. These conditions are most accessible where therapists function as members of multidisciplinary teams and can obtain expert consultation and training from physicians, psychologists, occupational therapists, social workers, and nurse therapists.

## BIOMEDICAL STRATEGIES

It is crucial that people who are experiencing major or persisting stress receive the benefits of effective biomedical management when this is indicated. As we have noted, major stress is a common precipitant of a wide range of pathophysiological responses including excess stomach acid, muscle tension, increased adrenal and pituitary hormones, high cholesterol, and excessive gastrointestinal activity. Unchecked, these responses may lead to serious impairment, even life-threatening disorders. For this reason any complaints of symptoms should be reviewed with a physician, who may wish to provide further assessment and treatment which, in addition to the psychosocial stress management provided by the BFT, may include drug strategies targeted to counter the observed physiological impairments.

As well as the specific strategies employed to resolve general medical problems, several drug strategies have been shown to have long-term benefits in reducing the impairments associated with major mental disorders. These include the neuroleptic drugs for schizophrenic and manic episodes, tricyclic drugs for major anxiety and depressive disorders, and lithium preparations for mood swings. These drugs have consistent benefits in the acute phases of these disorders as well as in the prevention of recurrent major episodes. All practitioners of BFT should be aware of the indications for the use of these specific approaches, and not hesitate to seek expert medical consultation when they detect the early signs of any major disorder. At present there are no specific medical interventions to counter stress responses generally. In particular, the use of tranquillizing drugs, such as the benzodiazepines, in the clinical management of stress responses has been discredited (Catalan *et al.* 1984). Details of specific drug interventions are not provided in this book and the reader is referred to other texts.

Crucial components of drug therapy include education about the benefits and side effects, training in compliance, and the ability to recognize the early warning signs of impending exacerbations. These strategies are described in Chapter 4.

## RELAXATION TRAINING STRATEGIES

Relaxation training includes a number of strategies to reduce physiological arousal through psychosocial means. Although not generally considered a biomedical strategy, it aims to achieve similar effects as tranquillizing medication, and has been used extensively in conditions where muscle tension produces chronic pain, such as chronic back pain and tension headaches, and in reducing autonomic arousal associated with high blood pressure. In addition, relaxation techniques have been used to counter the effects of anxiety, nervous tension, worry, and sleep disturbance.

162

Individuals are taught strategies that promote both physical and mental relaxation. These include progressive muscle relaxation (Bernstein and Borkovec 1973), imagery techniques (Lazarus 1978), and lifestyle planning (Woolfolk and Lehrer 1984). Despite appearing straightforward, effective application of these methods is accomplished only by competently trained therapists.

Yoga and other meditation strategies aim to achieve similar benefits. They are readily available in most communities, where they are taught by lay practitioners. Although most of these approaches employ techniques similar to therapeutic relaxation training, they are usually linked to religious and mystical philosophies and may be endowed with benefits that have not been scientifically validated. Notwithstanding, many people clearly benefit from these approaches and they are often proposed as solutions during family problem solving. The principle of never taking on a role that the family can achieve competently without the therapist's intervention applies here, and participants are encouraged to try all available community resources and judge their effectiveness for themselves before resorting to similar strategies applied by the therapist and his team.

> Pamela suffered from difficulties in getting to sleep, which were worse when she was under stress. She and her mother devised a plan for her to attend a relaxation class at the local community college which employed yoga techniques. Pamela found that she could not relax in the group setting and dropped out of the class after three sessions. Her therapist offered to provide training in deep muscle relaxation. She practised this with her mother during two sessions and reported much improved sleep. The plan included strategies to be carried out when the relaxation was not effective at inducing sleep, especially at times when she was unable to relax because of excessive worrying. Her mother, who tended to worry in a similar fashion, reported that she also benefited from using a similar strategy.

## ANXIETY MANAGEMENT

Anxiety management is readily conducted within a family problem-solving framework (Mathews *et al.* 1981). Family members may assist the anxious person by coaching him or her in the day-to-day application of anxiety reducing strategies.

Anxiety manifests itself in a wide variety of responses, such as avoidance or escape from fear-inducing stimuli (e.g. crowds, spiders, social situations, etc.); fearful thoughts and obsessions (e.g. fears of dying, dirt and disease, embarrassment or losing control); and excessive physiological arousal (e.g. palpitations, breathlessness, sweating, muscle tension, etc.). Specific strategies have been developed to counter each of these specific manifestations. These include applied relaxation (Ost 1987), exposure *in-vivo* (Marks 1987), slow breathing exercises (Clark 1986), modelling and behaviour rehearsal (Falloon 1978), response prevention (Marks 1987), and a range of cognitive strategies (Beck *et al.* 1985).

The competent therapist devises a therapy plan that targets the main sources of disabling anxiety and the specific responses they induce in the anxious person, and selects one or more anxiety management strategies to counter these effects. During the sessions he or she coaches the anxious person to implement the plan whenever the anxious symptoms are experienced. Wherever possible the therapy is conducted in the settings where anxiety is most readily provoked so that the strategies can be practised with expert guidance from the therapist. It is easy to see how other members of the person's household may help in this coaching on a day-to-day basis, until the person learns to cope with the stimuli and is no longer disabled or handicapped.

## SOCIAL SKILLS TRAINING

Deficient interpersonal skills may be found in all household members. Anxiety, lack of confidence, as well as inadequate repertoire of interpersonal behaviour (e.g. dating, job interviewing), may contribute to deficient performance in the social skills required to achieve personal goals (Falloon 1978).

Social skills training employs identical methods to those employed in enhancing the communication skills training of all household members. However, the focus of the training is handling stressful interpersonal situations outside the family. A problem or goal is specified, such as joining a social club, asking the boss for time off, or making a telephone call to an old friend, alternative ways of handling the situation are listed, the advantages and disadvantages of each are highlighted, the optimal solution is agreed, careful planning which usually includes repeated rehearsals of key interpersonal communications is conducted, and the effectiveness of the approach used is reviewed. Several useful books describe details of this strategy which has wide application within a family context (Kelly 1982; Liberman *et al.* 1975; Trower *et al.* 1978) and with a wide range of mental disorders (Curran and Monti 1982; L'Abate and Milan 1985). In addition to improving deficiencies in interpersonal communication, social skills training can be a useful strategy for improving other areas of a person's functioning. Skills training has been effective in modifying outbursts of temper (Mueser *et al.* 1986), the ability to refuse drugs in social situations (Foy *et al.* 1984), depressive disorders (Becker *et al.* 1986), and acquiring community living skills in people suffering from disabling mental disorders (Wallace 1982).

Samantha had recently had her first child. Six months earlier she and her husband, Pat, had moved to a new house. They had not made any new friends since their arrival. Sam felt lonely and missed her family and friends. She lacked confidence, and feared that she would be rejected if she attempted to make friends with women in her new neighbourhood.

During the planning phase of problem solving this issue the therapist coached her in a series of role-played rehearsals in which she practised introducing herself to two neighbours who had young children. Her husband played the role of these women. She was coached to improve her eye contact and speak more slowly. After several rehearsals, which included practising how to respond to rejection, she felt able to attempt to introduce herself to the woman who had appeared most receptive. She tried this the following day, successfully inviting her neighbour to coffee. Although she found this very stressful she was pleased to have succeeded, and was warmly praised by her husband on his return from work. Later that week her neighbour invited her to go shopping with her. She felt she could not cope with this and declined the invitation. At the next BFT session they problem solved this issue and rehearsed coping with the specific situations that concerned her. Subsequently she went shopping with her neighbour and began to establish a close friendship.

165

## OPERANT CONDITIONING STRATEGIES

The provision of specific rewards for performance of specific behaviour is the basis for contingency contracting. It is based on research evidence that demonstrates that rewards or pleasing responses immediately following a person's specific behaviour lead to an increase in the frequency of that behaviour, i.e. they reinforce the behaviour positively. On the other hand, the absence of rewarding responses to a person's specific behaviour will tend to lead to a decrease in frequency of that behaviour, i.e. the behaviour will be extinguished.

These principles can be applied to a wide variety of plans. An example is the strategy known as *shaping*, whereby performance of complex behaviour is built in a series of small steps with rewards given for every small approximation to a specific desired response. The manner in which a parent encourages a baby to speak his or her first words is an example of shaping. Each attempt to make an intelligible sound is rewarded with praise, smiles, and cuddles. A disabled person may be trained to walk using identical methods.

A comprehensive operant conditioning programme may be developed for an individual with several deficits. In some cases it may be possible to award points, tokens, or money for specific behaviours rather than more tangible reinforcement from food, interpersonal contact, praise, or pleasurable activities. These tokens can then be exchanged for a range of rewards. This strategy has been called a *token economy*, and has proved particularly useful in psychiatric rehabilitation in group settings (Paul and Lentz 1977).

*Extinction* strategies involve specific avoidance of attention for specific behaviours that a person wishes to eliminate from another's repertoire. For example, an anxious person who frequently seeks reassurance from others by asking them, 'Am I going crazy?', may maintain this behaviour as long as people respond to it by saying that he or she is 'all right' and 'should not worry'. By agreeing specifically to ignore this reassurance-seeking behaviour, family members may assist the anxious person to reduce these panic-provoking thoughts that promote the distressing behaviour.

A word of warning: the unwanted behaviour will be maintained as long as it is intermittently reinforced. Thus, extinction strategies are effective only where the responses that reinforce

166

unwanted behaviours can be eliminated entirely and continuously. For this reason, such methods are not efficient ways of modifying behaviour in most family settings.

Patterson (1975; 1976) provides excellent descriptions of operant strategies applied in families. These methods have been developed into a systematic approach to train parents to cope with children with problem behaviours. These include temper tantrums, poor peer relations, academic underachievement, aggression, non-compliance, toilet training, and bedwetting (Forehand and McMahon 1981; Kelly 1982).

## TIME OUT PROCEDURES

These strategies have often been employed by families in some fashion to deal with inappropriate, aggressive, or bizarre behaviour in children. Their application in the management of household violence has been mentioned briefly in the previous chapter. The family member exhibiting the behavioural disturbance is removed from contact with other family members for a brief period. This usually involves sending the person to a setting in the home where rewards for the behaviour disturbance are minimized (e.g. bathroom) for several minutes (maximum of five minutes) with minimal fuss. A major source of reward that maintains these inappropriate responses to interpersonal stress is the attention centred upon the perpetrator, even when that attention is not clearly positive, such as threats, demands to behave appropriately, and other angry or frustrated expressions. Removal from the interpersonal setting assists in the extinction of this behaviour once the person finds that his or her disruptive behaviour does not induce any responses from others. However, the immediate removal process may lead to a temporary escalation of the disturbance, which is difficult for many people to tolerate.

The use of time out procedures is difficult to apply with disturbed adults. However, persons with a propensity for antisocial behaviour can be trained to monitor their stress and tension levels and to excuse themselves from situations where the risk of an episode of disturbed behaviour is high. Heated family discussions, stressful work, and social interactions may trigger these episodes. The person is trained to excuse him or herself and take a brief walk, visit the toilet, or engage in some

167

distracting activity in another room (e.g. watch television) until the tension abates.

Jessie and Henry had been under considerable financial stress. Whenever they attempted to carry out problem solving about this issue their discussions rapidly escalated into heated arguments. They problem solved this issue with their therapist who suggested that they tried to detect when they first began to raise their voices. Either partner was then to initiate a time out by giving the other a signal, and get up and take a 30-second break before resuming the discussion. After using this technique on a few occasions they modified it to merely signalling each other and ensuring that they were using effective communication skills at that moment.

Tom suffered recurrent panic attacks when he had to eat in restaurants. This was expected as part of his job as a sales representative. He used to stay as long as he could until he could not tolerate it any longer. He learned to recognize the early signs of an impending attack, to excuse himself, and go to the bathroom where he practised relaxation strategies for five minutes until he was able to return without embarrassment to continue the meal. On occasions he would have to repeat this process two or three times during a meal, but he found this preferable to declining all invitations, or to leaving the setting abruptly and not returning.

## SETTING LIMITS

Where household members clearly infringe the code of behaviour agreed by the family precise rules may be set up, with precisely defined consequences for non-compliance. The therapist may assist families to draw up clear plans that define the limits of specific behaviours and the punishments for stepping beyond those limits.

Susan was a teenager living with her parents and younger brother. She believed that she was overweight and mis-shapen and began to diet excessively, to the extent that she was diagnosed as having anorexia nervosa. The therapist noted that, although the family were able to make excellent plans to encourage more appropriate eating behaviour, they repeatedly failed to implement the plans. They tended to give in readily to Susan's efforts to sabotage the plans that she had agreed to. On reviewing their efforts the parents asked the therapist what they could do to ensure that the agreed plans were carried through. They rehearsed responding firmly to Susan's excuses in the sessions after the therapist had modelled an assertive approach. One session was arranged at a meal time so that the therapist could provide coaching in a real-life setting. Over four weeks Susan's pattern of eating became more appropriate and she began to regain weight.

The specific application of this method to help families cope with overt aggressive behaviour is described in Chapter 7.

## CONTINGENCY CONTRACTING

The idea that the interaction between two or more persons is governed by a set of rules that reflects a balance between mutual benefits and 'costs' (in terms of time, effort, and emotional stresses, etc.) is employed in contingency contracting. A written plan is negotiated whereby each person agrees to carry out a specific task for which he or she receives a specific reward. For example, John washes dinner dishes and receives half an hour of TV viewing of his choice; or he works for an hour in the garden and is paid £3. The contract is planned carefully within the problem solving/goal achievement framework, and is written out clearly. It is crucial that all participants agree on the terms of the contract. This agreement may be formalized through having them sign the contract.

Contracts such as these can be used in resolving many problems and in achieving a wide range of goals. They are particularly useful in providing incentives for people to increase behaviours that they do not find inherently rewarding, i.e. where any benefits are cancelled out by the effort or skill required to achieve the desired result. It is always worth considering the relative costs and benefits of any plan of action to each family participant. Unless the benefits or rewards exceed the potential 'costs' there is a high risk that the plan will not be implemented.

Contracts of greater complexity that involve a choice of rewards for a series of specific behaviours may be devised. For example, June had experienced depressed mood shortly after the birth of her first child. She and her husband had moved to a new house three months earlier and she had not developed any social or leisure activities in her neighbourhood. She thought that her mood would improve if she were able to get out and meet other young mothers but could not get herself sufficiently motivated to do this. The following contract was devised that involved gaining points for each step accomplished towards her goal. These points were exchanged for objects and activities that June found particularly rewarding:

*Goal:* To have a five-minute chat with one person in the neighbourhood every day.

| Steps | Points |
| --- | --- |
| Get out of bed | 5 |
| Take a shower | 3 |
| Get dressed | 3 |
| Dress baby Terry | 2 |
| Walk to corner shop | 5 |
| Talk to shop assistant for one minute | 7 |

An excellent account of contingency contracting for family-based problems is provided in *Marital Therapy* (Jacobson and Margolin 1979).

## MANAGEMENT OF AFFECTIVE EPISODES

Behavioural family therapy provides an excellent framework for the clinical management of depressive disorders (Follette and Jacobson 1988). Education about the nature and treatment of depression, training in effective family communication and problem solving, as well as the application of specific behavioural and cognitive strategies to increase constructive behaviour and decrease distorted thinking appear to facilitate sustained recovery (Beck *et al.* 1979). A handout employed in the educational phase of this approach is available (Falloon 1985a). Follette and Jacobson (1988) have reported on a successful application of behavioural marital therapy with depressed women. As might be expected, benefits of this approach, which

170

tended to emphasize relationship issues, were most effective in cases where marital discord was severe.

A similar approach has been employed in several cases of manic disorders but controlled clinical trials have not been completed to provide empirical support for its effectiveness (Falloon *et al.* 1988; Hole 1987). One such trial, currently in progress in Los Angeles, is examining the benefits of adding behavioural family therapy to optimal drug therapy and case management for young persons who have experienced a recent manic episode. The pilot phase of this project appeared extremely promising (Miklowitz, personal communication, 1990) and the results of the controlled phase are eagerly awaited.

Affective disturbance contributes to a wide range of problems in households, from childcare issues, lack of constructive activity, and sexual disorders, to suicide, and sleep and appetite disturbance. Some of these problems lend themselves to the application of specific strategies, and many more to the generic problem-solving methods that form the basis for BFT.

## SCHIZOPHRENIA MANAGEMENT

Behavioural family therapy has been combined with optimal neuroleptic drug therapy to reduce the clinical symptoms, social disability, and family stress associated with chronic schizophrenic disorders (Falloon 1985b; Tarrier *et al.* 1988). Schizophrenia is a complex syndrome associated with a wide variety of clinical symptoms and functional handicaps. In addition to education, and enhanced problem solving/goal achievement skills, families may be trained to apply a range of additional strategies to cope with problems such as drug compliance, 'negative' symptoms, social skills deficits, depressive and anxiety symptoms, sexual problems, and behavioural disturbances.

Delusions and hallucinations present a particular problem for many household members, particularly in cases where these symptoms persist despite optimal drug therapy (about 25 per cent of all cases). To date there is a lack of controlled research evidence to support the use of any specific behavioural strategies in the clinical management of these symptoms. A careful assessment of the contingencies surrounding these false and distorted perceptual experiences sometimes enables the skilled therapist to assist the patient and family to devise strategies that may enhance coping. Such behavioural strategies are recommended as an alternative to drug therapies for persistent psychotic symptoms, and may assist in reducing the high dosages of drugs often employed in the cases with limited benefits (Simpson *et al.* 1982).

## STRATEGIES FOR SEVERELY DISABLED PERSONS

Behavioural family therapy methods have been adapted for use with severely disabled persons, both institutionalized and developmentally disabled cases. Excessive focus of family problem solving and goal achievement on the index patient's deficits should be avoided, particularly on problems that are unlikely to be resolved, or concern unrealistic goals. The therapist assists family members to accept a slowed rate of progress, and to 'mourn' the loss of their high expectations for the severely disabled person. They are encouraged to treat the person as a 'normal' human being with major difficulties in specific areas of his or her life.

*Low attention span* is a common problem in such cases. Short family discussions (five to ten minutes) conducted more frequently (daily) may facilitate problem solving with severely disabled persons. Repetition of straightforward instructions, taken one step at a time with clear prompts and reminders, and, above all, an abundance of praise and encouragement for tiny amounts of progress, will help the disabled person to learn new skills.

The need for caregiving family members to support one another and to develop interests aside from their caring roles is crucial. The availability of a confidant in their family or social network to whom they can unburden their frustrations is a key resource. *Single parents* are particularly vulnerable to caregiving burdens. A useful strategy is to get them to invite a close friend to participate in the family therapy sessions and the weekly (or more frequent) family meetings. This may require considerable problem solving to achieve, but will usually prove worthwhile. Joining local support groups may assist in a similar way, but is no substitute for a close confiding relationship that is available on a day-to-day basis.

## MARITAL AND SEXUAL THERAPY

Marital and sexual therapy follows the same problem-solving framework. Additional specific strategies for enhancing intimate relationships may be incorporated within the problem-solving framework. Highly effective strategies have been devised to deal with several specific forms of sexual dysfunction. These specific marital and sexual strategies are described in several guidebooks (Jacobson and Margolin 1979; Liberman *et al.* 1980; Hawton 1985).

## CONCLUSIONS

This chapter outlines some of the cognitive-behavioural strategies that may be readily incorporated into the BFT approach to assist in managing the stress associated with some specific problems commonly found in mental and psychosocial disorders. It is emphasized that specific strategies are introduced by the therapist as a supplement to the household group's efforts to seek their own unique solutions to these problems. Furthermore, the strategies are incorporated into the six-step problem-solving model, and subjected to the same scrutiny and planning as any other suggestions made by participants. Of course, the therapist may have the opportunity to summarize the benefits of the specific strategies he or she suggests during the third step of problem solving, when each alternative is briefly evaluated in terms of its chief advantages and disadvantages. The planning step allows the therapist to demonstrate the strategy, to invite key people to practise it, and to discuss ways of coping with any hitches that may arise in its implementation.

Space does not permit more than a brief mention of most of the strategies, and the therapist will need to refer to detailed descriptions of these techniques in other publications. The expert behavioural family therapist will need to acquire competence in the application of all the strategies outlined here, before working with people who have experienced major mental disorders. This training is readily available in all comprehensive mental health services and departments of clinical psychology, and is increasingly becoming a core part of basic training for all mental health professionals. However, the novice behavioural family therapist should not be unduly dismayed if he or she has only limited competence in some of these strategies. All cognitive-behavioural strategies are based on the identical problem solving/ goal achievement approach described in this handbook, and once this method has been mastered the additional strategies can be quickly acquired, particularly when the therapist is working in a cohesive multidisciplinary team.

# 9

# COPING WITH PROBLEMS IN THE APPLICATION OF BEHAVIOURAL FAMILY THERAPY

Difficulties in applying behavioural family therapy arise at some stage in most families. Unlike many forms of therapy, these difficulties are considered the sole responsibility of the therapist, and at no stage are participants blamed for 'resisting' the changes that the therapist is promoting. This formulation frees therapists to consider the problems that they experience while working with the family, and to take responsibility for resolving those problems themselves, albeit often seeking the cooperation of the household members. Among the problems most commonly encountered are the following:

- poor attendance of key household members;
- participants reluctant to chair problem-solving discussions;
- low frequency of completion of real-life practice;
- poor adherence to medical and social interventions advocated by other professional agents;
- preference for discussion to active learning strategies;
- focus on content of problems rather than training in problem-solving strategies;
- destructive criticism and hostile flare-ups;
- excessive focus on one participant's goals and problems.

It is evident that these issues fall into two groups: a) compliance problems; and b) structuring interactions within the sessions. We will discuss the general approach to resolving these issues and highlight briefly some specific strategies that therapists have found consistently helpful.

## A PROBLEM-SOLVING APPROACH TO THERAPIST PROBLEMS

Behavioural family therapists use an identical approach to addressing the problems encountered in their role as therapists as they expect participants to use in dealing with their own problems. The communication skills and six-step problem-solving method are employed by therapists to address therapy problems.

A problem is defined in the same manner for the therapist as for any other participant, i.e. as a specific behaviour pattern that triggers a strong emotional response in the therapist. When such a response is triggered by the behaviour of one or more of the participants, the therapist must decide how to attempt to resolve his or her unpleasant feelings. The competent therapist will decide whether the issue is worth addressing at this point, and if he decides to respond, what form this response might take.

For example, therapist Jane had completed five sessions of communication skills training with one household. Despite repeated discussions about the rationale for holding a family meeting the participants had failed to organize one meeting, and had made very little effort to carry out the plans that they had all agreed to at the end of each session. Jane had experienced increasing feelings of frustration, but had not yet expressed them directly, choosing to make positive requests for the household group to meet. She decided that during this session she would express her frustration about this issue and request that the group assist her in resolving *her problem*. When they said they had once again failed to set up a meeting she told them:

'I am feeling very frustrated that after five weeks of my requests and discussions you have still not held a family meeting. I would be most grateful if you would spend some time this session helping me to sort this problem out. Because I see this as my problem at the moment I would be happy to chair the discussion this time. OK?'

Although initially tending to justify their lack of compliance with excuses about good intentions but too little time, the participants agreed to deal with this issue, and problem solving developed a plan that clearly addressed the issue of making the family meeting the top priority for every member of the household. Jane expressed her gratitude to the participants for their efforts

175

on her behalf, and her pleasure when they reported having convened a family meeting at the start of the next session.

In common with most household members, therapists have a tendency to note the many minor irritations that prevent the programme proceeding as smoothly as they would like. It is important that they avoid nagging the family by constantly remarking on these minor indiscretions. *Behavioural family therapy does not have to feel right to the therapist to be effective*, and therapists often need to learn that the most effective strategy is to focus feedback on the positive features, and to *do nothing* about niggling issues, unless they are serious threats to progress. When major deficits are evident it is crucial to ensure that they are dealt with using the problem-solving method. Thus, therapists learn to deal with their stresses in the same way that they are training families to do this.

This process is facilitated where therapists work in teams. They may rehearse methods of addressing therapy problems with their colleagues, as well as seek assistance with their pinpointing of key issues. There are times when personal stress may impinge on the therapists' ability to work effectively with families. Once again, the application of the stress management approach to these issues, with the support of the professional team, may prove helpful.

## SPECIFIC STRATEGIES

### Establishing and maintaining adherence to components of training

Behavioural family therapists *expect* poor compliance with all aspects of the training programme from *all participants*. Specific efforts are made to prevent this tendency throughout the programme. Most of these preventive measures form an integral part of the approach, and include providing a cognitive framework (rationale) for each aspect, careful explanation of all assignments, ensuring that all efforts are relevant to participants' personal goals, providing promptsheets and reminders, rewarding all efforts, and problem solving difficulties. However, even when all these interventions are applied competently, suboptimal compliance is common. Additional strategies that may help include the following.

*Attendance*

Training will be of limited benefit where key household members do not participate in the sessions. This includes both the therapist-led sessions and family meetings. Efforts to schedule meetings at times and locations that facilitate attendance are obvious measures. When such measures have been applied without success further behavioural analysis may be needed to pinpoint the problem. Several approaches may prove useful:

### Rewarding attendance

Attendance of participants at sessions may be rewarded in various specific ways. Some families have found that having a special meal after the session promotes good attendance. Others have targeted rewards for each household member. For example, Billy usually lost an hour's wages when he left work early to attend sessions. His father agreed to make up his lost earnings. His sister protested that she was not rewarded in a similar fashion. The family agreed to deduct £5 from her weekly rent payments to match the benefits provided to her brother. Rewards are most effective when they are clearly contingent upon attendance, are selected by the individual, and provided without delays.

It is important that non-attendance is not rewarded. Participants who miss sessions, even when they have acceptable excuses, should be expected to review all aspects covered in the sessions and make up any training they may have missed.

### Setting limits

Several households have made attendance at sessions a basic requirement for continued residence in the household. Such rules are not uncommon in residential care facilities, such as hostels, and have been adopted successfully in several family households. This limit-setting approach will be unlikely to prove effective where participants are allowed to break the rules without experiencing the threatened consequences. For such an approach to work clear plans for carrying out the adverse consequences must be made to avoid hitches.

177

*Promoting the chairperson's role*

The most common reason why participants show reluctance to perform the chairperson's role is the tendency for inexperienced therapists to take over that role during the sessions. It is crucial that therapists hand over the direction of problem-solving discussions to the family and physically remove themselves from the household group when they are not actively coaching. The household chairperson may then call for a discussion as in a family meeting. The therapist is able to reward the chairperson's efforts and provide coaching to enhance the role. This may include modelling of specific aspects of chairing problem-solving discussions, with the therapist changing places with the chairperson and demonstrating some aspect of the role, before returning to the observer role.

In addition to chairing discussions, the chairperson is expected to take responsibility for providing a weekly report of the family meeting. He or she may choose to delegate this to the secretary or another spokesperson. Once again, this is unlikely to happen if the therapist tends to dominate this part of the review process.

Some families prefer to take turns at chairing meetings. However, the role is often difficult for family members to perform, and the best results are often achieved when one member takes on the task for a six-month stint. The initial choice of chairperson should reflect the participant's strengths and weaknesses in undertaking the role, as well as motivation. We avoid any attempts to change family structure by prescribing this role to anyone whom we might wish to support in a more dominant role in the household.

*Completing real-life practice*

The transfer or generalization of skills performed during therapist-led sessions into everyday life is the key to effective BFT. In addition to ensuring that family meetings focus on goal achievement and problem solving, the completion of practice assignments of specific communication skills by all participants is the cornerstone of the BFT approach. Thus any evidence of suboptimal performance of this task is viewed as a potential crisis by the therapist, requiring immediate action.

Failure to establish compliance with this key aspect of the programme is associated with the following therapist responses:

- lack of clear rationale for real-life practice;
- lack of clear explanation of the tasks requested;
- presenting the practice as an irrelevant 'homework exercise' that participants find reminiscent of school;
- accepting excuses, such as lack of time, forgetfulness, etc.;
- not rewarding efforts by making the review of real-life practice a highlight at the beginning of each session, even when crises may distract attention from this component of the training.

When participants have not completed the real-life assignment the therapist may delay the start of the session to allow them to do so. This includes the completion of worksheets. As well as completing individual communication training assignments in this way, the therapist may request that the household convenes for the missed family meeting at this time. This use of therapy time reinforces the BFT view that the real-life practice is at least of equal value as therapist coaching.

*Adherence to medical and social interventions*

A final area where adherence to recommended strategies is considered of major importance concerns compliance with specific medical and social interventions. Behavioural family therapists attempt to integrate their efforts with those of medical and social agencies and support all recommended strategies. This may include adherence to medication or the application of welfare procedures, including legal constraints. The problem-solving approach may be employed to deal with compliance problems in a similar way to that deployed to manage poor adherence to the key components of BFT.

## ENSURING THAT THE STRUCTURE OF BFT IS MAINTAINED

The ability of therapists to ensure that the highly structured approach to sessions is established and maintained is crucial to the BFT approach. For therapists proficient in less well-organized training this may feel uncomfortable initially. However, with practice and coaching most therapists quickly overcome their discomfort. Several problems usually arise.

179

## Preference for discussion over rehearsal

Many participants and therapists may feel more comfortable discussing issues rather than practising them during the sessions. Performance of everyday skills, such as expressing feelings, in behaviour rehearsals may appear contrived and awkward, and lead to anxiety in many participants. It is crucial that the therapist resolves such difficulties at an early stage and supports participants when they engage in rehearsals. Among the strategies that may help to overcome the reluctance of participants are:

- demonstrating the skills through modelling by the therapist and other more confident participants;
- ensuring that requests to engage in behaviour rehearsals are made in the most effective manner, e.g. 'I would like you to show me how you told June that you were upset that she arrived home late.' Avoid asking people to volunteer. Instead ask each person to participate in turn, thereby setting the expectation that everyone will attempt the rehearsal;
- praising all efforts to participate, and ensuring that suggestions for enhancing performance are constructive and provided in a supportive framework;
- choosing topics for rehearsal that are clearly relevant to participants' personal goals and current problem-solving efforts, i.e. setting the rehearsal as real-life practice, not as a role-played 'exercise';
- using anxiety management strategies which may be helpful where avoidance appears associated with performance anxiety, e.g. relaxation strategies; breaking the rehearsal into a series of progressively more complex steps; and supportive prompting during performance as well as praise for all efforts, no matter how small.

## Focus on content rather than structure

The therapist-led sessions should focus on the way in which participants structure their interpersonal communication and problem-solving discussions, and not become immersed in the content of the topics addressed during practice. The aim is to teach people to use a particular way of expressing themselves when dealing with stresses in their everyday lives. The resolution of those stresses is a secondary issue that the therapists expect households to deal with in their family meetings and everyday interactions between sessions. For this reason the therapist helps the family to choose everyday topics to address during the sessions, and preferably issues that do not arouse excessive emotions in the participants. This allows participants to learn the skills more readily during the sessions. Once they have acquired the skills they are then encouraged to tackle real-life issues outside the sessions. At times the therapist may prompt participants to stay away from 'hot' issues until they have achieved a level of competence that permits them to address such issues without provoking undue stress.

Competent therapists assess the issues that are likely to provoke little stress, as well as the potential 'hot' issues. This assessment begins at the initial meetings with participants and continues throughout the sessions.

Issues raised during communication training are handled similarly. Hot issues are avoided wherever possible, and even when they are exposed inadvertently, the therapist does not permit prolonged discussion. Instead the focus is immediately shifted to the structure of the communication skill that is being trained. For example:

Lesley:   I was so pleased when you told me you liked the casserole I made last night. You've never done that before.
Samantha:   Rubbish! I'm always . . .
Therapist:   Sam, I'd like you to stop there and just tell Lesley what you liked about the way she expressed how pleased she was about what you said to her last night.
Samantha:   OK. Well, I guess it was good. But I do tell her nice things.
Therapist:   What particular steps did Lesley use when she told you how she liked your comments about her casserole? I'd like you to tell her.
Samantha:   (looking at her guide sheet) You looked at me and kind of smiled . . . You said what I had done to please you. . . . I'm not sure whether you said how you felt.
Therapist:   I thought I heard you say you were pleased, didn't you, Lesley?

This example shows how the therapist prevents a potentially heated discussion about how often Samantha has complimented

Lesley in the past and moves quickly on to examining the structure of the communication skill.

Of course, there are occasions when major crises arise that create persisting stress in households. At such times therapists may need to address these issues and ensure that they are resolved during the sessions. However, even at these times therapists may focus feedback on the structure of the problem-solving process as well as on the content of the discussion.

### Destructive criticism and hostility

Despite efforts to structure sessions around learning effective communication and problem-solving skills, participants may resort to destructive criticism and hostility from time to time. Such outbursts tend to escalate tensions and are always destructive. It is important that the therapist takes a highly directive role in resolving these outbursts immediately. The therapist should take the following steps:

1 Request that the discussion stops immediately.
2 Suggest that the session stops for a few minutes and participants take 'time out'.
3 Reconvene the session and reiterate the rules of conduct expected during sessions, in particular efforts to avoid hostility.
4 When the outburst appears to have been triggered by specific upsetting behaviour of another participant, the therapist may invite the protagonist to express his or her unpleasant feelings in an appropriate way. Where participants have learned the skills of expressing unpleasant feelings the therapist may review those steps. When the outburst precedes such training the therapist may need to guide the participant through the steps.
5 When the outburst reflects a persisting problem issue the therapist may need to convene a problem-solving discussion immediately.

Hostile communication does not always take the form of angry outbursts. More subtle expressions, such as sarcasm, rejection of a person's best efforts, and dismissal of a person's suggestions or feelings ('That's a silly idea!', 'You don't feel that way about it!'), may prove just as destructive as more overt expression. The therapist is expected to intervene on these occasions, and request that the protagonist restructures his or her communication more appropriately. It may seem that BFT aims to prevent the expression of all negative emotions. This is not the case. The clear aim is to encourage participants to express their unpleasant feelings in the way that leads to their most efficient resolution for everybody involved. It is the manner of expression that determines whether such expression is destructive and exacerbates stress, or constructive and leads to resolution of stress.

### Excessive focus on the goals and problems of one household member

Attempts to focus almost exclusively on resolving the difficulties of one member of the household are common. This is most marked where that person suffers from major disabilities, but may occur in households where one member's behaviour is defined as the main source of stress for others. This problem seldom arises where the competent therapist ensures that the focus of sessions remains that of training the family to conduct more efficient goal achievement and problem solving, rather than using the therapy as the means to target and resolve all household problems. Attempts by participants to use therapist-led sessions in this way are resisted, and therapists ensure that the issues dealt with during the sessions concern the goals and problems of each participant. In households with one or more disabled member it is likely that problem issues will tend to focus more on those members. However, the proportion of topics that address issues associated with a disabled participant should not usually exceed 50 per cent of the problem or goals chosen during training sessions.

Devoted carers of disabled people often find it difficult to realize that their exclusive concern about the people they care for may be perceived as stressful by the recipients of their care, who may feel that they have contributed to an enormous persisting burden for their carers, a burden that they feel powerless to shift. When the therapist requests that the carers take responsibility for getting on with achieving their own personal goals, allowing the disabled people to take some control over their personal aspirations themselves, this often defuses considerable tension within households. Not infrequently the carer finds that the disabled person is able to provide him or her with small but significant assistance in his or her own personal goal achievement efforts. The resulting reciprocal relationship tends to feel much more supportive to the disabled person, and less burdensome to the carer.

The process of shifting at least some of the focus away from the disabled person on to the more able carer is difficult in two-person households (e.g. single parent–single child; couples without children). Co-opting a third person, such as another relative, close friend, or neighbour, into the programme tends to facilitate communication and problem-solving training, by providing two additional pairings to rehearse communication skills, and an additional contributor to the problems and goals addressed during training sessions as well as in the weekly family meetings. It is preferable to co-opt such people from the start of the programme, and we usually try to plan this for all such households during the initial assessment phase.

## CONCLUSIONS

The strategies used by behavioural family therapists to over-come the resistance of families to adopting key aspects of efficient communication and problem-solving skills, which may lead to enhanced stress management in their households, are essentially the same skills that they expect the participants to employ to overcome their own problems and achieve their own goals. First, the therapist expresses his or her own feelings about the situation in a constructive manner, and engages the family to assist in resolving the problem issue. A few specific strategies are employed to manage outbursts of hostility or other abusive behaviour within the household. However, the behavioural approach is designed to minimize confrontation with family values or modify solutions to household living chosen by the participants by mutual consent. The focus is on the structure of the problem-solving process, and the therapist coaches the family to try alternative ways of conducting their own problem solving themselves, so that they can deal with the problems chosen in the most efficient way.

The most common difficulty is that of organizing structured household meetings that engage all members and permit the personal needs of each individual to be discussed in a colla-borative way in the absence of a skilled therapist. For many households this represents a major change of lifestyle. Therapists anticipate poor compliance with such life changes and employ compliance training strategies from the initial phase of therapy rather than waiting until lack of progress on this issue becomes a major concern. Failure to comply with this form of intervention remains the responsibility of the therapist at all times and attempts to blame the family in any way are avoided. Instead, effective education, interpersonal communication, and problem solving are employed to ensure that families find their own ways of managing the stresses in their lives effectively and achieving their personal goals.

# APPENDIX A:
# THERAPIST COMPETENCE

This appendix comprises a summary of the specific skills used by professional therapists in each session of behavioural family therapy. Each component skill is described in detail. A rating system for assessing the competence of therapists, and giving specific feedback during therapist training, is provided.

The effective application of behavioural family therapy requires careful application of several specific skills. These skills can be classified into four groups:

1 Specific behavioural skills
2 Structuring skills
3 Therapeutic alliance skills
4 Skills for dealing with therapy problems.

These skills are applied during the course of each training session. Although the content of the sessions may vary, the structure of each tends to be similar (see Table A.1). Each phase of the session may require somewhat different skills. The discrete skills that must be applied by a competent therapist will be described.

## SPECIFIC BEHAVIOURAL SKILLS

Specific skills are an integral part of behavioural family therapy and tend to be the predominant strategies applied by a therapist in every session, whether the focus is on assessment of, education in, or training stress management skills. They may be classified in five groups:

- Assessment and review
- Providing a rationale

- Coaching
- Providing feedback
- Handing over.

*Table A.1* The structure of a BFT session

| |
|---|
| 1 *Assessment* |
|    Progress towards personal goals: 2–5 minutes |
|    Report of the family meeting: 2–5 minutes |
|    Re-enactment of real-life practice: 5–10 minutes |
|    Early warning signs and health status: 5–10 minutes |
| |
| 2 *Review* |
|    Revision of continuing deicits: 5–10 minutes |
| |
| 3 *Skills training* |
|    Skills training with education and training modules: 25–35 minutes |
| |
| 4 *Real-life practice assignment* |
|    Assignment of real-life practice: 5–10 minutes |

## Assessment and review

Comprehensive, continual assessment of specific interpersonal skills is the most important feature of behavioural family therapy. All interventions are targeted to the specific strengths and weaknesses of each participant and the family group as a problem-solving unit. Before the intervention begins, during each session and at regular major review points a multilevel assessment is performed that addresses the following key areas:

1 Progress towards personal goals.
2 The effectiveness of the problem-solving functions of the household (including family meetings).
3 The effectiveness of real-life application of specific communication and problem-solving skills.
4 Observational assessment of competence of the specific skills performed during each session.
5 The assessment of each participant's mental and physical health status (whenever relevant).

With an adequate assessment the therapist develops a clear idea of the participants' progress and integration of skills into their everyday lives. He or she also identifies relevant examples of difficulties that may need to be reviewed in the next stage of the session.

The component therapist skills include:

- requesting participants to describe specific examples of their progress;
- requesting participants to re-enact specific examples of communication and problem-solving skills;
- observation of each participant's performance of specific skills throughout sessions;
- conduct of mental and physical health status screening interviews.

It is assumed that all therapists trained in this approach have completed training in basic interpersonal interviewing skills. This includes the use of specific interview schedules for screening mental and physical health problems.

Therapists are expected to employ the same structure to their requests of participants as outlined in the module on making positive requests (see pages 241–4). Thus, when asking a participant to make a specific response, the therapist uses phrases such as: 'I would like you to tell me . . .', 'I would appreciate your showing me how you . . .' At the beginning of each session the therapist makes specific requests of participants to report on their various assignments and personal goals. Open-ended requests, such as 'How have things been since we last met?' or 'What's your week been like?', are avoided. Instead the therapist opens the session with: 'I am very pleased to see you all here. I would like you all to give me a brief report on how you have been getting on with your personal goals. I'd like you to start, Bill . . .' This introduction ensures that the session follows a clear structure focusing on the specific issues that form the core of the approach.

The skill of accurate observation of specific communication and problem-solving skills employed by participants during the sessions is acquired with practice. Initially it may be helpful to audiotape sessions so that the therapist can review them later. However, it may be necessary to reinforce the use of such skills at the time they are performed, so the competent behavioural family therapist needs to acquire the ability to recognize these specific skills during the sessions. Reports and re-enactment of real-life practice provide a more straightforward assessment process.

As well as eliciting reports of specific assignments, family meetings, and progress towards achieving personal goals, the therapist is expected to elicit examples of the problem-solving strategies employed by participants in association with these specific issues. For example:

Bob and Mary had used their family meeting to plan how they would spend their free time at the weekend. They had planned to go to a concert for the first time in years. However, when Bob went to buy tickets he found that the concert was fully booked. He reported this to the therapist at the next session. The therapist asked him what they had done then. They reported that Mary had suggested they go to a movie instead, but Bob did not seem interested, so she did not take any further action. The therapist invited Bob to report his problem solving. He said that he was interested in the idea of going to a movie, and had intended to mention it to Mary later in the week, but was preoccupied with a work assignment and had forgotten. The therapist then asked them if they had discussed any other possibilities. They had not had any further discussion. The therapist noted Bob's comment that this pattern of behaviour had occurred on previous occasions and had contributed to their lack of shared leisure pursuits. He suggested that they might place this issue on the agenda of their next family meeting, and devise ways to persist with planning after encountering hitches. In addition, he noted that Mary continued to have difficulty in making clear requests of Bob, and tended to try to read his mind rather than check out his thoughts and feelings directly.

### Providing a rationale

This skill involves providing participants with a clear understanding of the benefits of a skill or strategy in resolving stresses. It is based on the assumption that sustained lifestyle changes are more likely when participants can envisage the probable beneficial results from their efforts to change. One or more early sessions are devoted entirely to outlining the likely benefits and costs (efforts, responsibilities, etc.) of the behavioural family therapy approach. In addition, when BFT is applied as part of

189

the clinical management for a stress-related health risk in one or more of the participants, additional sessions may be devoted to providing an understanding of the nature of the disorder and the rationale for its comprehensive long-term management.

The rationale for each communication or problem-solving module is provided in a similar fashion, including the reasons for emphasizing the need for real-life practice and regular family meetings.

The skills used in providing a rationale include:

- eliciting the ideas of all participants;
- active listening skills;
- communicating information;
- summarizing.

The behavioural family therapist always attempts to elicit a rationale from the participants by inviting them to express their ideas about the topic at issue. This may vary from their views on the benefits of drug treatment of panic attacks to their thoughts about the value of eye contact when making a request. Once participants have expressed their ideas about the potential value of a specific strategy, the therapist summarizes and may add any key points that have been overlooked. For example:

Therapist:   I would like to spend some time dealing with the topic of how to make clear plans once everyone has decided on the strategy to achieve a goal or resolve a problem. First, I'd like each of you to say what you think the value of clear planning might be.
Bob:   Everyone knows what they are supposed to be doing.
Therapist:   Great. That's one crucial point. What others?
Bob:   It helps get things done.
Therapist:   I'd be grateful if you could give some examples of what you mean.
Bob:   Well, it helps people to remember what they agreed to do. Especially if somebody writes the plan down.
Therapist:   I like that idea. Do you usually note down your plans?
Mary:   Quite often we do. We've both got lousy memories. I think another value about making a clear plan is that if it does not work out you can go over it and see where things went wrong.

Therapist:   That's another point I like. So you are telling me
that careful planning helps to prompt people to do the things
they have agreed to do and it helps you to review progress,
even when nothing very dramatic has happened. It may also
help to prepare you for the hitches that are most likely to
occur.

Wherever possible, the experienced behavioural family therapist
involves participants in the educational process in this manner.
Participants are prompted to describe their observations, ideas,
and understanding, with the therapist employing active listening
skills (see pages 107–10) to encourage them to express themselves, to clarify what they are trying to say, and to summarize
the key points.

The therapist will usually need to contribute specific information to rectify deficits in the understanding of the household
group. This information is provided in straightforward everyday language, often with the aid of diagrams, posters, and
specially written handouts. For example, the steps of each
communication or problem-solving skill are outlined on a guide
sheet, which is handed to every participant and may be enlarged
to form a poster or copied on to a flipchart or chalk-board. All
information is linked clearly to the vulnerability/stress model.
Discussions about irrelevant (but often very interesting) material
are minimized; for example, the value of Chinese herbal
medicine in anxiety disorders, or nineteenth-century ideas about
madness.

The therapist encourages participants to ask questions and
will answer these in a direct manner wherever possible. Where
a therapist is unsure of the answer to a factual question, such as
'Does anorexia nervosa run in families?' or 'Can stress bring on
a heart attack?' he will be expected to tell participants of his lack
of knowledge and endeavour to clarify this at the next session.
Where a specific strategy is indicated to cope with a specific
problem, the therapist may need to obtain training in the
application of this strategy, or alternately invite a competent
exponent of the strategy to contribute to one or more sessions.
*At no time does a behavioural family therapist attempt to impart any*
*information to participants that he or she is not clear about, and has not*
*adequately prepared.*

## Coaching and feedback

The third set of specific skills includes the experiential methods of skill training. The following strategies are used:

- behaviour rehearsal
- performance feedback
- modelling
- social reinforcement
- real-life practice.

*Behaviour rehearsal*

Behaviour rehearsal involves requesting participants to perform a specific communication or problem-solving skill within the session. The manner in which the therapist initiates behaviour rehearsals contributes to their effectiveness. The following skills characterize effective performance:

1 Therapist makes a positive request (see pages 101–3) of each participant in turn. For example, 'Bob, I would like you to show us exactly how you told Mary that you were pleased with the dinner she cooked last night.'
2 Therapist helps participants to re-enact the scenario in a way that replicates the real-life performance. Wherever feasible, the rehearsal takes place with the participants in the setting where the communication or problem solving occurred, or is likely to occur. This may entail moving around the house, and even at times to locations in the immediate neighbourhood.
3 The topics rehearsed involve practice of communication and problem-solving skills relevant to the achievement of the personal goals of each participant. Whenever possible, the therapist tailors the topic to current problem-solving efforts described during the assessment and review phase of the session. For example, when Mary said that she was concerned about Bob working exceptionally long hours, the therapist noted this and suggested that she express her concern to him later in the session when they were practising expressing unpleasant feelings.
4 The therapist prompts participants to follow the guidelines for the specific skill being rehearsed. This may be aided by using the guide sheets or posters as prompts during the performance.

5 Rehearsals are kept brief and are complete as soon as the target participant has attempted to perform the specified skill as instructed. The other participants' responses in the rehearsal to the target person merely address his or her performance of the steps of the skill, not the content. For example, Mary told Bob that she was very concerned that his long hours of work might be detrimental to his health. He began to justify the current need to work longer than usual, but the therapist cut him off saying: 'Bob, I'd like you to discuss that with Mary later. At the moment I'd be grateful if you could concentrate on giving her feedback on how she followed the steps of expressing an unpleasant feeling.'

*Performance feedback*

Performance feedback is provided after each rehearsal. The aim is to specify those steps of a specific skill that were performed competently, and those major deficits where further training may prove beneficial. Feedback is given in a consistent manner using the following steps:

1 The therapist asks the participants to tell the target person what they liked about the rehearsed performance, and in particular, to point out which steps were followed competently. For example, he or she might say: 'Bob, I would like you to tell Mary what you liked about the way she expressed her pleasure to you.'
2 Once all the participants have told the target person what they liked about the way the steps of the skill were performed, the therapist invites them to suggest any major ways the performance of the skill could be enhanced. For example: 'Bob, I would like you to tell Mary if there are any major improvements that you could suggest. Is there any way that you could have expressed your pleasant feeling differently, that might make it even better?'
3 The therapist may add his own specific feedback when major strengths and weaknesses are overlooked by the participants.
4 Attempts by the target person to respond to the feed-back, especially attempts to justify his or her best efforts, are discouraged by the therapist. He may point out that, when a person is attempting to defend his or her efforts, he or she is not usually concentrating on the feedback being

given, and may not take in some helpful ideas. On the other hand, it is important to explain that it is not essential to respond to all suggestions for alternative performance in exactly the manner outlined; rather the target person is encouraged to consider all the advice and to base any major changes on formulation of the 'best alternatives'.

The therapist trains all participants to provide feedback consistently. All the positive aspects are reinforced before any corrective feedback is given. Prompting participants to express their pleasure at rehearsal of relatively straightforward skills, and to restrict criticism to constructive suggestions for change only where major deficits are evident, helps to create a supportive therapeutic environment, where people may feel able to express themselves freely, and try out alternative interpersonal skills without excessive fear of failure. It may take some time for participants to experience pleasure when observing the deficient performances of other members of their household. However, with practice almost everybody can learn to feel pleased with others' efforts to enhance their skills, even when competence is minimal. It may help to draw the analogy of observing a baby take his or her first steps – an insignificant achievement for mankind, but a major accomplishment for that child and his family!

*Modelling*

Modelling simply means demonstrating a specific skill or component of a skill. The therapist performs the following steps:

1 The therapist chooses a participant to demonstrate a specific element of performance; this participant must have previously demonstrated his or her competence in the performance of that specific element. The therapist may choose himself as a model if no other participant is clearly competent, or other participants express their discomfort in demonstrating their competence. The most effective models are those who are not vastly more competent in their performance than the target person.
2 The therapist invites the target person to change places with the designated model.

3 The therapist sets the scene for the modelled performance making it clear that the setting is identical to the one rehearsed earlier by the target person, and the model is performing a role similar to that of the target person in the setting.
4 The therapist gives clear instructions about the specific element of the model's performance that he would like the target person to focus on. For example, 'I would like you to note the way Bob looks directly at me.'
5 When the modelled performance is completed the therapist invites the target person to provide feedback on what he or she liked about the *specific elements* of the modelled performance. The target person is invited to consider whether the model's performance of the *specific elements* had any specific advantages that might be incorporated into his or her own subsequent performance. Discussion of other topics, particularly more competent aspects of the model's performance, is avoided.
6 The therapist instructs the target person to resume his role by changing back to his original position, and to repeat a rehearsal of the brief sequence, while attempting to imitate the *specific element* of communication that was modelled. Participants are reminded to incorporate the modelling into their own style of communicating in a way that feels comfortable to them, not merely to repeat the model's performance 'parrot-fashion'.
7 All efforts to incorporate some specific elements of the modelling are praised by participants immediately after the repeated rehearsal.

Modelling is used in the following situations:

- to demonstrate each specific communication skill;
- to coach participants in the steps of problem solving;
- whenever verbal instructions prove ineffective or cumbersome in conveying alternative performance: 'I would like to show you what I mean . . .' or 'I would like you to show us what you mean . . .'

In addition to overt modelling, the therapist employs all the communication and problem-solving skills that he or she is encouraging the household members to use throughout the programme. The consistent application of these specific skills is thought to make a substantial contribution to the therapeutic alliance and facilitate changes in household stress management.

## Social reinforcement

Social reinforcement in the form of praise from other participants is a major component of the skills training approach. After feedback has been given for behaviour rehearsal the target person attempts to incorporate suggested (or modelled) changes into repeated rehearsals. After each rehearsal praise is provided for all (a) *efforts* to make changes, and (b) *any small improvements* observed by participants. The therapist prompts participants to express the pleasant feelings they experience when they observe the target person making what at times may seem only tiny steps towards competent performance. For example:

> The therapist had noted that Bob had a major deficit in making requests. Although he expressed himself clearly, his voice tone was harsh and came across as demanding. Mary tended to interpret this as anger. After suggesting that he might try to speak in a softer voice, Bob repeated the request.
>
> Therapist: Mary, what did you like about the way Bob tried to speak in a more friendly tone when he made that request?
> Mary: He still sounded angry to me.
> Therapist: Did you notice *any* change in his tone?
> Mary: Well, I suppose he spoke a little softer.
> Therapist: I'm glad you noticed that little change. I'd like you to give Bob some feedback about his efforts.
> Mary: I was pleased that you tried to speak a little softer. If you could do that a little more it would be even better.
> Bob: Thanks. I was trying very hard, but I guess I'm so used to speaking that way it's hard to change.
> Therapist: I am pleased that you were able to praise Bob's efforts, even though he may have a long way to go before he can make a request that doesn't sound like an order. A little praise for each tiny step encourages people to keep trying, even when progress is very slow. I'd like you to try to make that same request again, Bob, and to try to speak in an even softer tone.
> Bob: OK. I'll give it a go.

It is important to note that therapists discourage the use of value-laden expressions such as 'That was good!', 'That was great!' Such expressions sometimes seem patronizing and may remind participants of receiving grades at school. Instead, persons giving feedback are encouraged to express their own feelings of pleasure about specific aspects of the performance. This sincere expression of genuine feelings carries much greater impact than vague compliments.

### Real-life practice

Real-life practice is assigned at the completion of the coaching phase of skill training. Each participant is asked to complete a weekly assignment that promotes further practice of the communication or problem-solving skills in everyday situations. The following key elements are displayed by competent therapists:

1 The therapist provides a rationale for the value of real-life practice in acquiring efficient stress management skills.
2 Participants are clearly instructed about each assignment, and the therapist checks that they have fully understood all details.
3 Participants are given specific worksheets on which to record their efforts. The value and use of such records are outlined and each participant practises completion of the worksheet during the session.
4 The therapist helps participants to plan how they are going to undertake real-life practice, including devising prompting strategies, allocating specific times, and locating worksheets, etc.
5 The therapist ensures that real-life practice is reviewed extensively at the beginning of the next session, and forms the basis for further training. Feedback is given emphasizing positive efforts. Partial success in achieving optimal benefits results in further problem solving and planning to ensure continuing progress.
6 The therapist takes immediate and firm action whenever assignments or worksheets are not completed (see pages 178–9).

## Handing over

Throughout the intervention programme therapists ensure that participants remain in control of their own stress management. Although at times the therapist may seek to impose some structure and guidelines to assist family members to structure their efforts, he or she avoids taking an active role in the actual communication or problem solving. The therapist expects to become dispensable as a coach as soon as possible. This handing over process is most evident in the efforts made to ensure that skills are practised in real life. However, it may be seen that the coaching style employed by competent therapists ensures that they avoid becoming embroiled in the content of personal or household issues.

There are rare occasions when the therapist may become directly involved in family issues. These include problems associated with physical and emotional abuse, and suboptimal compliance with critical aspects of therapies (see Chapter 9). However, even when dealing with these issues the therapist aims to hand over responsibility for problem resolution to the household group at the earliest possible time.

## STRUCTURING SKILLS

It is evident that a competent exponent of BFT must acquire considerable skill at providing a clear structure for each session. This includes the ability to carry out the following procedures:

- setting an agenda;
- prioritizing key relevant issues;
- keeping participants on task;
- time keeping;
- focus on skill training rather than content issues.

The therapist makes it clear to participants at the start of therapy that each session will be clearly structured, is business-like in his ability to ensure that sessions begin and end on time, and demonstrates that all key issues are dealt with in a highly efficient and effective problem-solving manner. It is crucial to maintain a consistent approach to the structuring of sessions. This skill is most difficult for therapists who have been trained in less structured therapy approaches, and who tend to structure sessions haphazardly. This is arguably the most crucial skill in determining therapist competence in this approach.

## THERAPEUTIC ALLIANCE SKILLS AND DEALING WITH DIFFICULTIES

The specific skills used to develop and maintain an effective therapeutic alliance with all participants and to deal with therapeutic difficulties are described in detail in Chapters 3 and 9. These include a wide range of assessment, educational, and skill training procedures to ensure that at all stages of the programme participants consider that the benefits of the approach exceed the efforts they are expected to make. The ability of therapists to use the same effective communication and problem-solving skills that they are training participants to use appears to have a major impact on the therapeutic relationship.

## ASSESSMENT OF THERAPIST COMPETENCE

An important aspect of behavioural family therapy involves the training of therapists to a clear criterion of competence. A standardized scale has been developed enabling tutors to measure reliably the competence of a therapist during a session of behavioural family therapy (Laporta *et al.* 1989). The scale has been devised not merely to measure competence in performing the skills outlined here, but also to facilitate supervisory feedback. In addition, therapists may use the scale themselves to review their own sessions using audio or video recordings. The Behavioural Family Therapy Skills assessment (BFTS) has improved our understanding of the core components of BFT. It is being used in research settings where BFT is employed to evaluate therapist training, and to ensure treatment adherence in intervention studies, including the NIMH Treatment Study of Schizophrenia which compares behavioural and supportive approaches in the psychosocial treatment of schizophrenia. The BFTS scale is outlined on pages 200–3.

## CONCLUSIONS

Training therapists to conduct behavioural family therapy competently is facilitated by the clear definition of therapist skills. A relatively small number of specific skills are core components of a wide range of treatment strategies. Training is conducted in a series of experiential workshops which employ the same training strategies used in the therapy. In addition to 30–40 hours of workshop training the trainee receives supervision on at least 30 assessment and treatment sessions. Each session is rated on the BFTS and once the trainee has been rated as 'satisfactory' on 30 sessions he or she is considered competent to practise this approach. Over 1,000 therapists have completed training in the specific BFT approach outlined here, and many others have been trained in similar approaches worldwide.

## BEHAVIOURAL FAMILY THERAPY SKILLS ASSESSMENT (BFTS)

### 1. Assessment and review

*Personal goals:* steps achieved, problems encountered, effectiveness of problem-solving efforts.

*Family meeting:* report from chairperson; effectiveness of problem-solving efforts.

*Real-life practice of skills:* reported performance; observed performance (e.g. re-enactment; problem-solving test at 0, 3, 6 months, etc.).

*Knowledge and understanding:* knowledge and understanding of effects of stress on individuals; specific disorders and their clinical management, including emergence of specific early warning signs or symptoms.

*Identify participants' strengths and weaknesses:* may be incorporated into current and subsequent sessions.

### 2. Rationale and teaching

Develop a cognitive framework for stress management using the vulnerability/stress/problem-solving approach. May include rationale for:

- assessment procedures;
- all intervention strategies (including education about specific disorders and their clinical management);
- setting agenda and goals of session;

- specific skill modules and steps involved;
- other specific therapeutic strategies when needed;
- carrying out real-life practice.

Competent performance involves:

- Assessment of current understanding of participants;
- Presentation of information clearly and accurately;
- Use of teaching aids effectively;
- Answering questions clearly; admitting ignorance and problem-solving provision of effective answers;
- Checking understanding after information presented;
- Making use of all opportunities for continued education throughout programme.

### 3. Rehearsal and coaching

Assess participants' current performance of specific skills.

Use effective communication skills: active listening, positive requests, praise, prompts, directions, etc.

Behaviour rehearsals of specific skills:

- Outline steps of skill; include modelled demonstration;
- Elicit a clear description of behaviour to be rehearsed;
- Structure the rehearsal clearly;
- Elicit positive feedback; praise efforts, suggest/demonstrate changes, focus on one deficit at a time;
- Further rehearsal and feedback until competent performance.

### 4. Feedback

Elicit praise for clearly specified efforts (rather than achievements) from participants whenever possible.

Elicit specific suggestions for changes that may improve performances.

Discourage participants' justification for suboptimal performances.

### 5. Handing over

Prompt participants to re-enact specific situations whenever possible.

Prompt full participation in all aspects of BFT: assessment, information, review, behaviour rehearsals, etc.

Hand over to family chairperson as much control over the session as possible at each stage: review, choice of issues, structuring, etc.

Prompt and review clearly understood real-life practice assignments, including weekly family meetings.

## 6. Structuring

Follow the consistent structure for each session: assessment, review, skill training, real-life practice assignment.

Efficient use of time; keep participants on task; ensure that rehearsals are brief; deal assertively with interruptions; start and end sessions effectively; avoid 'chat' during sessions.

Integrate assessment, education, communication skills, goal achievement/problem-solving training, real-life practice.

## 7. Relationship

Engage all household members to attend sessions regularly.

Outline clearly the specific responsibilities of the therapist and participants.

Maintain a low stress therapeutic environment; use effective communication and problem-solving skills throughout; use straightforward, jargon-free expressions congruent with household expressions; self-disclosure and humour where appropriate.

## 8. Dealing with therapeutic difficulties

Deal assertively with hostility or antisocial behaviour.

Problem solving to deal with difficulties in therapy, e.g. poor compliance, inadequate attendance, emerging crises.

Employ specific strategies for specific disabilities, e.g. attentional difficulties, persisting anxiety, perceptual deficits, etc.

## 9. Overall impression of BFT skills

A rating is made of the overall competence of the therapist in employing the specific BFT skills throughout the session.

---

Behavioural Family Therapy Skills Assessment (BFTS)

Therapist: _____  Participants present: _____

Session date: _____  Rating date: _____

Session no./module: _____  Rater: _____

| 1 | 2 | 3 | 4 | 5 |
|---|---|---|---|---|
| very poor | poor | satisfactory | very good | excellent |

1. Assessment and review

    1    2    3    4    5

2. Rationale and teaching

    1    2    3    4    5

3. Rehearsal and coaching

    1    2    3    4    5

4. Feedback and reinforcement

    1    2    3    4    5

5. Handing over

    1    2    3    4    5

6. Structuring of session

    1    2    3    4    5

7. Relationship

    1    2    3    4    5

8. Dealing with therapeutic difficulty

    1    2    3    4    5

9. Overall impression of skills

    1    2    3    4    5

---

# APPENDIX B:
# SESSION GUIDES I–V

Summaries of the specific aspects of each component of behavioural family therapy are provided in a modular form for therapists to use as guidelines during sessions. Guide sheets and worksheets to be given to participants are incorporated. The modules include:

I    Behavioural Assessment of the Family Unit
II   Guidelines for Family-Based Treatment
III  Educating Families about Mental Disorders (including Bibliography of Educational Materials)
IV  Specific Communication Skills
    A. Expressing Pleasant Feelings
    B. Making Positive Requests
    C. Expressing Unpleasant Feelings
    D. Active Listening
V   Specific Problem-solving Skills
    A. Introduction to Six-Step Method
    B. Pinpointing Problems and Goals
    C. Brainstorming
    D. Evaluating Alternatives
    E. Choosing Optimal Solution
    F. Planning
    G. Review of Implementation

# SESSION GUIDE I: BEHAVIOURAL ASSESSMENT OF THE FAMILY UNIT

*Goal:* To pinpoint the specific strengths and weaknesses of the family unit as a resource for solving the problems and achieving the goals of individual family members and the family as a whole.

*Subgoals:*
1. Specify the assets and deficits of each family member.
2. Specify the short-term goals of each family member.
3. Specify the collective assistance/problems of the family unit in achieving these individual goals.
4. Examine the assets and deficits of current family problem-solving efforts.
5. Formulate how family resources can be deployed efficiently to enhance family problem-solving to achieve all functional family goals.

*Structure:*
1. Interview each family member.
2. Conduct at least one home visit.
3. Observe family problem solving.
4. Complete brief formulation summary.

## Family member interview

This is a semi-structured interview which was designed to elicit specific information about the current goals, problems, and problem-solving functions of each family member. The relative contribution of the family unit to these goals, problems, and problem-solving functions is also assessed. The specific probes listed below are to be used flexibly so as to facilitate the efficient acquisition of all relevant details.

*Introduction*: 'I would like to spend some time getting to know you better. I am going to ask you about situations that you find stressful in your life, and how your family helps you to overcome these problems. Also, I would like to get an idea of your own goals, and how your family helps you to achieve these. This will help me to decide the best way we can help your family to work together for everyone's benefit. Do you have any questions before we start?'

MANAGING STRESS IN FAMILIES

1. *Background information* (Please record information as requested on page 30, Individual family member interview: summary sheet.)
2. *Knowledge of index patient's disorder* (See page 31.)
   What do you understand about _____'s disorder?
   What is it called?
   What do you think causes it?
   What do you do that seems to help?
   What do you do that seems to make things worse?
   What do you know about the medication he or she is currently receiving (e.g. type, dosage)?
   What do you see as the benefits of the medication?
   What are the undesirable effects of the medication?
3. *Coping and burden*
   What are the main difficulties you have had with the patient/ you have experienced (i.e. when the person interviewed is the index patient)?
   How do you cope with his/her (your) symptoms or behaviour (as described by above answer)?
   All things considered, how much of a burden is the patient to you (how much of a burden is your illness)?
4. *Reinforcement survey* (See page 33.)
   *Suggested probes*:
   What activities take up most of your time? (e.g. work, chores, hobbies, doing nothing, etc.)
   What activities would you like to spend more time doing?
   What prevents you from doing the things you like?
   Where do you spend most of your time? (e.g. work, home, bedroom, garden, parks, etc.)
   Where would you like to be able to spend more time?
   Who do you spend most of your time with? (e.g. workmates, friends, family, alone, etc.)
   Who would you like to be able to spend more time with?
   Do you have a person you can discuss your problems with? How often?
   Do you need more privacy? Do you have your own bedroom?
   Do you have a sexual partner? (Choose appropriate wording.)

206

How would you like your friendships to be better? (more/less intimate)

What situations (activities, people, places) do you dislike/avoid?

Does anyone in the family bother/concern you? How much time do you spend with him or her? How would you like him or her to be different?

5. *Personal goals* (See page 34.)

   If your current problems were removed or reduced, what would you like to be doing in three months' time? (pinpoint 1–2 goals)

   What people (family, friends, etc.) could help you to achieve this goal? (specify)

   What may prevent you from achieving this goal? (specify)

   What steps have you achieved already? (specify)

6. *Other problems*

   What other problems do you have in your everyday life? Specify problems that may not be identified by the family member as current limitations of functioning, e.g. marital conflict, medical or psychiatric symptoms, lack of friendship, social skills deficits, substance abuse, financial stress, housing problems, work-related problems, cultural conflicts, etc.

### Family problem solving

1. *Reported problem solving* (See Family assessment: summary, page 38.)

   Describe examples of family efforts at solving problems reported during family member interviews. Make note of:
   (a) Family members involved/social network involved?
   (b) Setting of discussion;
   (c) Communication style (e.g. critical/supportive, intrusive/ direct, excitable/calm, dominant/democratic, confused/ clear);
   (d) Range of alternatives acknowledged;
   (e) Consensus on 'best' alternative;
   (f) Clear planning;
   (g) Review; continued efforts;
   (h) Long-term stress level – reduced/increased/unchanged.

2. *Observed problem solving* (See page 41.)
   (a) Choose an example of an everyday current problem

described by at least one family member that concerns all household members.

(b)  Convene *all* household members.

(c)  Describe the problem issue clearly and briefly.

(d)  Tell the family: 'I would now like you to discuss this problem as a family for ten minutes. Tell each other how you see the problem and try to come up with a plan of how you are going to resolve the problem. I am going to record your discussion so that I can listen to it later. I will not interrupt you. Do you have any questions?'

(e)  Initiate tape recording and withdraw from family group.

(f)  Avoid any efforts to engage in the discussion until ten minutes have elapsed. Switch off tape recorder and remark on positive features of the discussion.

(g)  Listen to tape later to identify assets and deficits of family communication and problem solving. Complete the communication and problem-solving checklist, designating evidence of baseline competence in each skill with a zero in the criteria B boxes.

3. *Formulation* (See page 46.)

A succinct summary (maximum one page, single-spaced) of the family resources that can be deployed to enhance family problem solving, and assist family members to achieve their specific functional goals. Focus on observable or reported specific behaviours rather than making excess use of inference. Note discrepancies in reported goals and problems of family members, and any specific problems you consider relevant to family problem-solving functions.

**Family assessment: summary**

Index patient:_____ Date (month/year):_____

Household members and relationship to index patient:

_____

_____

_____

_____

_____

Home address:_____

_____

_____

Telephone number:_____

Family history (summary):_____

_____

_____

_____

_____

_____

_____

_____

_____

_____

_____

_____

_____

_____

_____

FORMULATION

Summarize the goals, resources, and limitations of the family unit. Note reported and observed evidence of family problem-solving and coping skills (including evidence of misunderstanding of nature of index patient's disorder).

_____

_____

_____

_____

_____

_____

_____

_____

_____

_____

_____

_____

_____

_____

_____

_____

_____

_____

_____

_____

_____

_____

_____

_____

# Individual family member interview: summary sheet

**PART 1: BACKGROUND INFORMATION**

Name of index patient:_____

Name of family member:_____

Relationship to patient:_____

Address:_____

_____

_____

Telephone number:_____

Age:_____ Sex:_____ Marital status:_____

Education (highest level completed):_____

Current occupation:_____

Highest occupational level:_____

Medical treatment:

    Current:_____

    _____

    Past:_____

    _____

Psychiatric treatment:

    Current:_____

    _____

    Past:_____

    _____

Other background details:

_____

_____

_____

_____

_____

---

**PART 2: KNOWLEDGE OF INDEX PATIENT'S DISORDER**

*Name of disorder:*_____
What is is called? What do you understand about the disorder?

Cause(s):_____

_____

_____

_____

_____

_____

*Detrimental factors:*
What seems to make the disorder worse?_____

_____

_____

*Beneficial factors:*
What seems to help?

_____

_____

*Prognosis:*
What do you think will happen with the disorder?

_____

_____

*Medication:* Type:_____

Benefits:_____

Side effects:_____

Compliance history:_____

_____

**PART 3: COPING AND BURDEN**

*Main difficulties:*_____
What main difficulties do you have with the disorder?

_____

_____

---

212

*Ways of coping with difficulties:*_____
How do you cope with difficulties/your symptoms (above)?

_____

*Burden of illness:*_____
All things considered, how much of a burden is the patient/illness to you?

_____

**PART 4: REINFORCEMENT SURVEY**

*Activities:*     *Current:*   1. _____
What activities take up most of your time?   2. _____

3. _____

4. _____

*Desired:*   1. _____
Are there any things that you would like to be doing?   2. _____

*Locations:*    *Current:*   1. _____
Where do you spend most of your time?   2. _____

3. _____

4. _____

*Desired:*   1. _____
Is there anywhere you would like to spend more time?   2. _____

*People:*    *Current:*   1. _____
Who do you spend most of your time with?   2. _____

3. _____

4. _____

*Desired:*   1. _____
Who would you like to spend more time with?   2. _____

*Supportive persons (current or potential):*
Do you have someone to discuss your problems with? How often?

_____

*Aversive (activities, people, places):*
What situations (activities, people, places) do you dislike/avoid?

_____

Does anyone in your family bother or concern you?_____

## PART 5: SUBJECT'S FUNCTIONAL GOALS RELEVANT TO INDIVIDUAL AND FAMILY NEEDS

**If the current problem was removed/reduced what would you like to be doing in three months?**

*GOAL* (specify exactly):_____

_____

*Steps already achieved:*_____
What steps have you already achieved?

_____

*Problems encountered or anticipated:*_____
What may prevent you achieving this goal?

_____

*Family support versus conflict:*_____
*What people would help you to achieve this goal/prevent you (why)?*

_____

*GOAL* (specify exactly):_____

_____

*Steps already achieved:*_____

_____

*Problems encountered or anticipated:*_____

_____

*Family support versus conflict:*_____

_____

## PART 6: OTHER PROBLEMS

**What other problems do you have in your everyday life? e.g. marital, friendship, finances, work, housing.**

_____

_____

_____

**Family assessment**

**Reported problem solving** (from individual and family discussions

**Problem**

Description:_____

_____

_____

_____

_____

_____

_____

Coping strategies:_____

_____

_____

_____

_____

_____

_____

_____

_____

Coping Effectiveness Scale (CES):

| 0 | 1 | 2 | 3 | 4 |
|---|---|---|---|---|
| No active coping | Ineffective | Marginally effective | Moderately effective | Highly effective |

**Observed problem solving**
10–15-minute discussion of a current problem or goal audiotaped by therapist and rated on communication and problem-solving checklist.

**Family meeting time**
Note time(s) when family usually meet to discuss problems/goals.

**Communication training**

1 Able to receive and process verbal communication.

2 Able to express specific positive feelings.

3 Able to request specific behaviour change in a constructive way.

4 Able to express specific negative feelings for specific behaviour.

5 Able to listen actively
   - non-verbal attentiveness
   - clarifying questions/check content, feelings.

**Problem-solving training**

1 *Family unit* is able to pinpoint a specific problem issue.

2 *Family unit* is able to generate five or more alternative solutions.

3 *Family unit* is able to acknowledge all suggested alternatives (i.e. make note of each).

4 *Family unit* is able to evaluate pros and cons of each alternative.

5 *Family unit* is able to agree on 'best' solution.

6 *Family unit* is able to plan strategies for implementing 'best' solution.

7 *Family unit* is able to implement plans.

8 *Family unit* is able to review outcome of 'problem' in constructive manner.

## Communication and problem-solving checklist

**Criterion A**                    **Criterion B**

* FM _____    FM _____

\* FM = Family Member. Note each by initial of first name at top of column.

Criterion A – Spontaneous evidence in session/reported interaction at home.
Criterion B – Prompted by therapist within session.

217

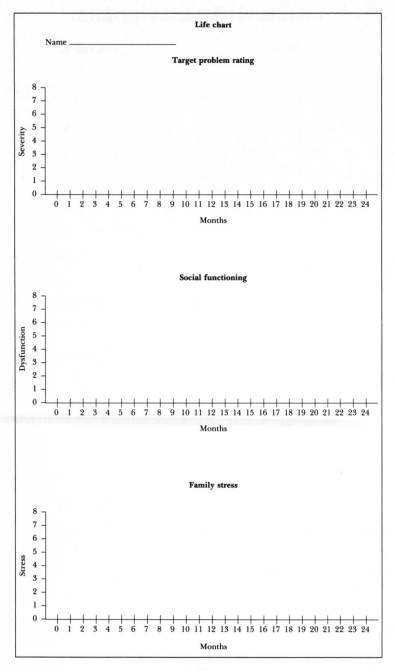

### Early warning signs

Name: _____

I have a risk of developing episodes of a _____
disorder.

My early warning signs are:

1. _____

2. _____

3. _____

Whenever I experience *any* of these signs I will respond by:

a) _____

b) _____

c) _____

My doctor is: _____ Phone: _____

My home contact is: _____ Phone: _____

If I have any concerns about my disorder I will contact

_____ immediately.

## Medication record

Name _____

| Date | Drugs | Dosage | % taken | Comments |
|------|-------|--------|---------|----------|
|      |       |        |         |          |

## Family goal achievement record

Family name _____

|  | Expected | Achieved |
|---|---|---|
| *Dates* | | |

FM _____

1 _____

2 _____


FM _____

1 _____

2 _____


FM _____

1 _____

2 _____


FM _____

1 _____

2 _____


FM _____

1 _____

2 _____


FM _____

1 _____

2 _____

## Family intervention summary

| Date | Session no.* | Comments |
|------|--------------|----------|
|      |              |          |
|      |              |          |
|      |              |          |
|      |              |          |
|      |              |          |
|      |              |          |
|      |              |          |
|      |              |          |
|      |              |          |
|      |              |          |
|      |              |          |
|      |              |          |
|      |              |          |
|      |              |          |
|      |              |          |
|      |              |          |
|      |              |          |
|      |              |          |
|      |              |          |

* Include *additional* emergency sessions; number as 'E'.

## SESSION GUIDE II: GUIDELINES FOR FAMILY-BASED TREATMENT

The goals of this form of treatment are to help all participants to cope more efficiently with all forms of stress that they may experience in their lives from day to day, and as a result to be able to reach their personal goals with less difficulty.

Stress is associated with a wide range of health and social problems. Where you are living in a household with one or more people who have developed disorders that are made worse by stress it is helpful for every member of that living group to develop highly effective and efficient methods of managing stress. This is of particular benefit to the sufferers of stress-related disorders. Recovery from major illness is almost always facilitated by effective stress management, often accompanied by specific medical treatments and other changes in a person's lifestyle that have been shown to be particularly helpful for each type of illness.

This guidesheet will outline some of the methods that we will use in our work with you. They will be explained in much greater detail by your therapist, who will be pleased to answer any questions that you may have at all times.

### The main steps of the treatment

The approach we use consists of several steps. These are:

- assessment of current ways of dealing with stress, and current personal goals
- education about specific disorders
- enhancing communication about problems and goals
- enhancing problem solving as a household group
- specific strategies for dealing with difficult problems.

*Assessment*    Before we begin treatment we like to meet with each member of the household to get to know them and to find out how they cope with the various stresses in their lives. This will include finding out what each person knows about any major disorders that people have been suffering from in the household, and particular difficulties that may have arisen. We will also be interested in knowing what goals you may be trying to achieve in your lives. These may include efforts to improve aspects of your home, family, work, social or leisure activities. Once we know your goals and problems we will meet with everybody in the household and try and get an idea of how you help each other to deal with everyday things that people find stressful. You may notice that we are particularly interested in learning about the ways of dealing with stresses that you have found work well for you, as well as getting some ideas about suggestions that we may be able to make that may help you to be even more successful.

*Education about specific disorders*   Where one or more members of your household has a major health or social problem we will discuss all aspects of that particular disorder with you all. This helps everyone to understand how they can help those people recover from their problems and stay well. Even when people are unlikely to recover fully you may still be able to help them to lead a full life. We always aim to encourage sufferers and their carers to become key partners with the treatment team.

*Enhancing communication*   An important part of solving problems and achieving goals involves discussions with other people. When people are under stress they often find it difficult to communicate their concerns and feelings with others in a clear manner. Some people become very emotional and others tend to clam up. We will help you to be able to discuss important issues with each other in a clear, open manner so that you will be able to get help to sort them out as quickly as possible with the least amount of stress.

*Problem solving*   The first step in solving problems and achieving goals is to get a clear idea of the exact problem or goal. Once the problem or goal has been agreed plans must be made to resolve it. We will help you to develop a way to discuss problems and goals in your household that enables both everyday issues as well as major crises to be resolved effectively.

A key aspect of this approach is to hold a weekly *Family Meeting*. This meeting is arranged by yourselves, so that you have the opportunity to discuss your problems and goals with each other regularly. This is in addition to the treatment sessions that your therapist will organise. All household members are expected to attend. The meeting is scheduled to last 30 minutes, and is arranged at a regular time and location, and is run in a business-like manner.

A Chairperson and a Secretary are elected from among yourselves. The duties of these people are described in the guidesheet (page 229). It is hoped that these meetings will become a part of your family life and will continue long after the training has been completed. The family meeting may not seem necessary when you are having weekly treatment sessions. But it is crucial that you get into the habit of meeting in this way in your household as soon as possible.

*Specific strategies*   You will find that once you have begun to use a more structured way of solving problems most of the everyday issues will be sorted out without too much stress. Your therapist will encourage you to continue to find your own solutions to problems unless you become stuck, or experience a major crisis. However, at times you may experience a problem where one particular treatment strategy has been shown to have major advantages over the kinds of solutions you have come up with. On these occasions your therapist may teach you to use those effective strategies. But more often he or she will act more like a coach, and help you to become more and more efficient at finding your own answers to your own problems.

### The format for treatment sessions

1 The *duration* of sessions is expected to be one hour. This may vary according to need. For example, where a major crisis is being resolved the session may be extended until an effective plan has been agreed.
2 *Attendance* of all household members is expected at all meetings. Close friends or other relatives may be invited to participate where this is considered helpful.
3 *Location* of sessions will be in your own home whenever this is possible. This helps you to practice strategies in the situation where many will be used.
4 The *structure* of each session consists of essentially four parts:
   i) Assessment of progress and difficulties with personal goals is made at the beginning of every session. This is followed by the Secretary's report of your family meeting. Any specific disorders may be reviewed by the therapist. Every three months one session will be devoted entirely to a more detailed review of your progress.
   ii) Review of real-life practice based on the practice assignments set during the previous sessions. As well as obtaining a report of your efforts, the therapist will invite you to show the group exactly how you performed. All your

efforts will be praised, and you will receive further training for any major difficulties.

iii) Training in specific skills. Your therapist will help you to
learn more effective strategies to enhance your communication and problem-solving skills. You will be expected to
practice these skills in the sessions, with encouragement
and coaching from all participants.

iv) Real-life practice of those skills is essential to enable them
to be incorporated into your everyday life. Your therapist
will place special emphasis on your efforts to do this, and
will give you worksheets to record all your efforts to try
these strategies between the sessions.

### Crisis sessions

Your therapist will be available for extra sessions when a crisis
arises. These sessions will follow the format of regular sessions,
with your therapist encouraging you to use your own skills to
resolve the crisis. However, your therapist will usually become
more involved in helping you find the most efficient way to
resolve the crisis, and may schedule daily problem-solving
sessions, when necessary.

### Session rules

Several rules are suggested for sessions. They include:

- no person should attend sessions under the influence of drugs
  or alcohol;
- violent acts or threats will not be tolerated;
- any participant who finds the session becoming too stressful
  may request a *time out* break for a few minutes to relax and
  regain their composure;
- sessions will begin and end at the specified times, wherever
  possible;
- the Chairperson will be expected to ensure that all rules are
  approved and applied in an appropriate manner thoughout.

### Completion of treatment

At the completion of the initial assessment your therapist will
contract to provide a specific number of weekly treatment

sessions with you. The number will depend on your current skills in managing the stresses experienced by participants. Where participants suffer from major disorders this will usually extend to at least ten sessions over a three-month period. At the end of the contracted period further review will help you and your therapist decide on how many more sessions may be beneficial. Once the training has been completed your therapist may advise further follow-up sessions (usually monthly) to help you to maintain efficient stress managment. For many people this support may need to continue indefinitely.

## The family meeting

### *Rationale*

1 Invite family members to suggest ways in which they could ensure that the methods they learn in the treatment sessions to enhance the efficiency of their problem solving/goal achieving functions will be employed in everyday family life.
2 Summarise:

'The value of learning more efficient ways of achieving goals and resolving problems is greatest when you can apply these methods on an everyday basis as if they are second nature. This usually requires a good deal of practice, far more than is possible in the time we spend together in these sessions, which cannot continue for ever.

'I would like you to arrange a time to meet each week to discuss your goals and problems when I am not here. Families who meet each week for 30 minutes or so in this way seem to learn these methods much quicker and continue to use them well after the treatment sessions have finished. You may feel that this is not necessary while you are having treatment meetings with me every week, but this course will go quite quickly, so I would like you to be in the habit of meeting by the time we finish.

'Does anyone have any questions about that?'

### *Review current skill levels*

1 Review behavioural assessment reports of problem solving/ goal achievement skills, with special reference to the context in which they currently perform these skills.

- Do they tend to meet regularly already to discuss issues of concern?
- Are *all* household members included?
- Are the meetings usually at a specific time and place (e.g. around the dinner table, at the kitchen sink, etc.)?
- Who usually organizes the meetings? Who 'chairs' the discussions?
- How structured are the discussions?

2 Give feedback on the *strengths* of the structure of existing family meetings.

*Outline steps of skill*

1 Invite family members to convene a 30-minute meeting before the next treatment session.

---

**The family meeting**

1 Select a day and a time for a weekly family meeting of 30 minutes' duration.

2 Elect a secretary to organize the family meetings. Duties may include:

- collecting items for discussion
- prompting attendance by household members
- keeping notes on items discussed.

3 Elect a chairperson to structure the discussions during the family meeting. Duties may include:

- ensuring that meetings begin and end on time
- prompting people to keep discussions to the point
- ensuring that every person has his or her say
- ensuring that people behave appropriately.

4 Give a brief report of each meeting to your therapist at the beginning of the next treatment session.

---

2 Instruct them to set the following agenda:
  a) Day and time for weekly family meetings.
  b) Elect a 'secretary' to organize weekly family meetings, to collect agenda items, to prompt attendance by all house-hold members, to keep notes on topics discussed.
  c) Elect a 'chairperson' to structure the discussions during family meetings, to ensure that people keep to the agenda topics, that everybody is able to express themselves freely, that behaviour is appropriate, that meetings begin and end on time.
3 Invite family members to report the results of their delibera-tions to the therapist at the next treatment session.

## SESSION GUIDE III: EDUCATING FAMILIES ABOUT MENTAL DISORDERS

Recent developments in the management of mental disorders have included systematic education of patients and their carers, to enhance their understanding of the disorders and their treatment. Numerous information guides have been written for a lay readership. A list of these titles and their current cost is provided at the end of this section. We will focus on the style of presentation not the content.

### Goals

1 *Give a rationale for treatment:* Facilitate understanding about the specific disorder and its drug/psychosocial management as applied to each patient and family.
2 *Enhance self-management:* Assist the index patient and family to assume an active role in the management of the mental disorder. The index patient is designated an 'expert' in the experience of his or her disorder and its treatment.
3 *Develop a therapeutic alliance:* The therapist establishes him or herself as an honest, straightforward, supportive person, who is knowledgeable about mental disorders and their state-of-the-art management.
4 *Assessment of family problem-solving functions:* All educational meetings with the family contribute to the baseline assessment of family problem-solving skills. Any communication or prob-lem-solving skills *observed* are recorded with an 'O' on the CPC checklist.

*Assess index patient's symptom profile and past treatment*

Ensure that you know the profile of major symptoms that the index patient has experienced, the drug and psychosocial treatment he or she has received, and the reported responses to that treatment, including major side effects.

*Assess family history of disorder*

Clarify whether other family members have experienced any mental disorders or stress-related physical disorders, e.g. peptic ulcers, migraine attacks, asthma.

*Choice of time for family education*

Although education is a process that should be carried out at all phases of a disorder, the main input may occur in two- or three-hour long sessions. These are best conducted soon after the index patient has recovered from a major episode of the disorder; all family members should be capable of attending to the discussion, and be capable of processing the information provided. If this is not feasible (e.g. index patient persistently disabled) then input may need to be presented in a briefer, simpler manner over a longer period.

Lengthy workshops (e.g. three to six hours) should take account of the information processing of all participants (e.g. attention span, concentration), and do not usually suit patients in the early phase of recovery from a mental disorder.

Avoid conducting sessions when family members are tired (e.g. nights) or have potential sources of interruption (e.g. cooking meals, telephone calls expected, friends visiting, drinking beverages, eating snacks, etc.).

## Methods

*A. Preparing for education sessions*

### Assessment of family knowledge

Review individual family member interviews to define the levels of knowledge of each family member. Note assets as well as deficits, so that you can plan your presentation to allow know-ledgeable family members to display their understanding, as well as correct misinformation.

### Inform yourself

Digest information on all handouts you are planning to use. Read material on family education, e.g. Chapter 8 of *Family Care of Schizophrenia* (Falloon *et al.* 1984); Dorothy Rowe's book on depression (see page 235).

### Select handouts carefully

Select written materials consistent with the information you plan to impart. Ensure they are written in a way that the family will comprehend. If handouts are not available, prepare your own materials.

Take care in recommending professional communications to families, e.g. books, journal articles. They may misinterpret some aspects of such materials.

### Use of visual aids

Summarize the main points on a chalk-board, flipchart, overhead projector or other visual aid.

### B. *Conduct of sessions*

### Structure sessions

Tell the family how you plan to structure the session time at the start of the session. Minimize digression from main points. Maximize the time spent on discussion about those issues of specific relevance to that family.

### Clear presentation

Discuss issues in everyday language. Avoid technical detail, medical jargon, complex explanations. Avoid debates about diagnosis, causes, alternative therapies, etc. Freely admit lack of knowledge; offer to consult experts; make sure you do just that.

Use simple visual aids (see above).

### Index patient as co-presenter

Invite the index patient to share the presentation by describing his or her first-hand experiences of the disorder and its treatment. Continue encouraging a reluctant patient throughout the session. Praise all his or her efforts, no matter how small.

Prompt by describing general features of an issue and inviting patient to describe his or her specific experiences.

### Maintain attention

Present each issue in no more that five-minute segments, without interruption. Then ask patient/family to describe their own experiences and concerns, or ask questions. Encourage family members to summarize the key points they have understood at the end of each issue.

'Now we have discussed the characteristic features of depression, I would like you to tell us what you have understood them to be, Jane. You can refer to the handout if you like.'

Involve all family members by directing questions to each in turn throughout the session.

Repeat key points throughout the session.

### Control emotional climate

Present in a calm, neutral manner. Avoid taking sides or debating issues. Acknowledge all constructive, empathic exchanges clearly.

*Halt accusatory, hostile, histrionic exchanges immediately.*

### Homework task/family meeting

Ask family to study handouts and identify questions for clarification at the start of the next session. Suggest they discuss the content of the session during their weekly family meeting.

Start the next session with question and answer discussion. Raise main points of previous session. Review important issues that have not been clearly understood.

Continuing education

Encourage continued clarification during *all* subsequent sessions. This is especially important at times of suboptimal compliance with any aspect of treatment.

A detailed assessment of understanding of the disorder is conducted at each ten-session/three-month assessment. If deficits persist it may be necessary to repeat sessions or refer back to handouts.

## Detecting warning signs of mental disorders

The outcome of most mental disorders is better where episodes are treated optimally at the earliest possible time. The ability to recognize the earliest signs of an impending episode is a key component to effective management. Patients and their carers may then initiate crisis management with minimal delay.

The early signs of many disorders are similar. Most are the signs of excessive stress which threatens to overwhelm the coping capacity of the patient. Sleep and appetite disturbances, muscle tension pains, irritability, and social avoidance are among the common prodromal features of depressive, manic, anxiety, and schizophrenic disorders.

Each person tends to have his or her own patterns of signs that warn of an impending episode of the disorder to which he or she is most vulnerable.

After a clearly recognized major stressful event, the patient may be able to recognize excessive levels of stress before the onset of an early warning sign. Such stress may be recognized in terms of thoughts of potential negative consequences, dysphoric mood, and physiological changes such as increased heart rate, blood pressure, or muscle tension. Again, these stress responses tend to be specific to each individual, with one person experiencing a rapid heart rate, another muscle tension in a specific muscle group, and yet another an apprehensive mood.

In some disorders the effects of overwhelming stress act as triggers to an acute episode. This is characteristic of schizophrenic and manic episodes, where overwhelming stress may result in an episode within a few days. Episodes of other disorders, such as depression and anxiety, tend to develop over longer periods of exposure to high stress levels, usually weeks or months.

233

Discrete life events, such as bereavement, loss of job, relationship breakup, accident, are superimposed upon background stress in the environment. High levels of everyday stress are often associated with unemployment, poverty, hunger, family tension, or substance abuse. In such instances relatively small increases in stress levels may overwhelm a person's coping capacity and place him or her at high risk of an episode of their disorder.

### Modifying factors

Two main forms of intervention appear to reduce the impact of environmental stress: 1. stress management and 2. drug treatment. If patients can be trained to recognize early warning signs and initiate urgent responses to these signs, major episodes of mental disorders may be averted.

1. *Stress management* is effective if it proves capable of resolving the major threatening impact of a stressful event within a week of its occurrence. This usually necessitates highly efficient problem solving by the patient and carers, with additional assistance from medical health professionals on a crisis basis.
2. *Drug treatment* serves as a buffer against the effects of stress and may delay the onset of an episode. However, drugs do not actually resolve stress and do not have lasting benefits in the continued presence of high levels of unresolved stress. Furthermore, some drugs appear to detract from efficient psychological stress management (e.g. minor tranquillizers).

For these reasons it is probably best to initiate immediate stress management, and then to add drugs only when these initial efforts do not succeed in reducing the stress to manageable levels within one week. The levels of early warning signs are good indicators of the effectiveness of these interventions.

If there is *any doubt*, start (or increase) drugs without delay.

### Completing the early warning signs card (see page 219)

Each patient is provided with a wallet-sized card to carry at all times. On this card they record the following:

1. Name of main disorder to which they are vulnerable.
2. One to three clearly specified early warning signs of that disorder.
3. The specific steps they must take when any of these signs are evident.
4. Names and phone numbers of their doctor, therapist, and home contact person (key family member).
5. Name of the person they contact to get advice on any concerns about their disorder, usually their therapist.

- Patients and their home contacts are invited to review this card at their weekly family meetings.
- Therapists review this card at the beginning of early therapy sessions.
- Copies of this information are inserted in the GP's medical records as well as the outpatient medical records.
- A copy of this information is given to the home contact to display in a prominent place in the home.

## Bibliography of educational materials

### Anxiety disorders

Butler, G. (1985) *Managing Anxiety*. Oxford University Press, Oxford.
Marks, I. M. (1978) *Living with Fear*. McGraw Hill, New York.

### Depressive disorders

Blackburn, I. M. (1987) *Coping with Depression*. W. R. Chambers, Edinburgh.
Falloon, I. R. H. (1985) *Coping with Depression*. Buckingham Mental Health Service, Buckingham, UK.
Rowe, D. (1983) *Depression: The Way Out of Your Prison*. Routledge & Kegan Paul, London and New York.

### Schizophrenic disorders

Birchwood, M. and Smith, J. (1985) *Understanding Schizophrenia*. West Birmingham Health Authority Mental Health Series, Birmingham, UK.

Falloon, I. R. H., McGill, C. W. and Boyd, J. L. (1980) *What is Schizophrenia?* and *Treatment of Schizophrenia: Medication*. University of Southern California, Los Angeles (videotape also available).
Seeman, M. V., Littman, S. K., Plummer, E., Thornton, J. F. and Jeffries, J. J. (1982) *Living and Working with Schizophrenia*. University of Toronto Press, Toronto.

### Manic disorders

Hole, V. and Falloon, I. R. H. (1987) *What is a Manic Episode?* and *Coping with a Manic Episode*. Buckingham Mental Health Service, Buckingham UK.

### Childhood behaviour disorders

Patterson, G. R. (1971) *Families: Applications of Social Learning to Family Life*, Research Press, Champaign, IL.

### Dementing disorders

Mace, N. L., Rabins, P. V., Castleton, B. A. *et al.* (1985) *The 36–Hour Day: Caring at Home for Confused Elderly People*. Hodder & Stoughton, London.

## SESSION GUIDE IV: SPECIFIC COMMUNICATION SKILLS MODULE A: EXPRESSING PLEASANT FEELINGS

### Review of progress

*Personal goals:* note steps achieved and all problem solving/goal achievement efforts – praise efforts.
*Family meeting:* note organization and problem-solving skills.
*Real-life practice:* review previous session, e.g. educational or assessment issues.
*Revision of continuing deficits:* education (including checks on early warning signs and current mental status); communication and problem-solving skills; and use of specific strategies or crisis management.

## Work on training module

### *Rationale*

1. Invite family members to suggest how clear, frequent expressions of feelings about other people's pleasing behaviours might help to solve problems and achieve goals.
2. Summarize: 'When people have encountered a series of difficulties they tend to focus on the problems around them and forget to notice the good things that other people do. Telling people about the little things they do that please you helps to encourage them to keep trying when things are difficult, improves morale in the family, and creates an atmosphere where people are more able to work together to solve problems.'

### *Review current skill levels*

1. Review behavioural assessment reports and observations of family members' skills in expressing pleasant feelings (communication and problem-solving checklist).
2. Elicit recent examples of expression of pleasant feelings.
3. Give feedback on *strengths* of their performance.

### *Outline steps of skill*

1. Look at person and use appropriate non-verbal expression – smiles, touch, gestures, etc.
2. Tell the person exactly what things he or she did that pleased you.
3. Tell the person exactly how it made you feel when he or she performed that pleasing behaviour.

### *Skill training*

1. Demonstrate use of the skill to participants by expressing a pleasant feeling to them about some aspect of their recent performance in the sessions, e.g. attendance, time-keeping, participation, etc.
2. Observe each family member attempting to perform skills.
3. Elicit feedback from other participants on specific steps

performed competently. 'What did you like about the way . . . expressed his or her pleasant feelings?'

4. Coach family members to overcome major deficits. Use repeated rehearsal, praise for small improvements, verbal instructions, specific modelling by competent family members and therapist, simple verbal and non-verbal prompts.

### Real-life practice

1. Give rationale concerning (a) need for practice; (b) feedback for therapist.
2. Outline worksheet 'Catch a person pleasing you' (see page 240).
3. Complete entry for one example practised during session.
4. Promptsheets: display guide sheets on 'Expressing pleasant feelings' on noticeboards, etc.
5. Family meeting: prompt weekly discussion time.

### Behavioural assessment

1. Update CPC.
2. Update family goal achievement record.
3. Note *new* goals/problems mentioned in session.

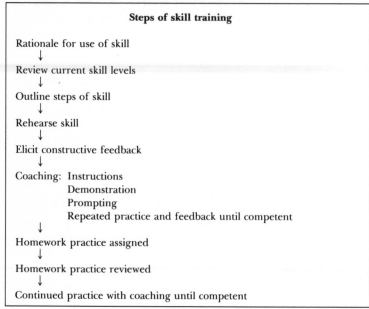

**Steps of skill training**

Rationale for use of skill
↓
Review current skill levels
↓
Outline steps of skill
↓
Rehearse skill
↓
Elicit constructive feedback
↓
Coaching: Instructions
Demonstration
Prompting
Repeated practice and feedback until competent
↓
Homework practice assigned
↓
Homework practice reviewed
↓
Continued practice with coaching until competent

---

### Non-verbal skills

- Gaze, eye contact

- Facial expression

- Gestures and posture

- Voice tone, volume, stress, timing

- Appearance

- Personal space

- Bodily contact

---

### Expressing pleasant feelings

- Look at the person and speak in a warm tone

- Tell him or her exactly what he or she did that pleased you

- Tell him or her how it made you feel

# Catch a person pleasing you

| Day | Person who pleased you | What exactly did he or she do that pleased you? | What did you say to him or her? |
|---|---|---|---|
| Mon | | | |
| Tues | | | |
| Wed | | | |
| Thurs | | | |
| Fri | | | |
| Sat | | | |
| Sun | | | |

*Examples:*

Looking good
Being on time
Helping at home
Cooking meals

Work in garden
Being pleasant
Having chat
Making a suggestion

Going to work
Offering to help
Tidying up
Making bed

Being considerate
Going out
Showing interest
Taking medicine

Attending treatment
Making phone call

# MODULE B: MAKING POSITIVE REQUESTS

## Review of progress

*Personal goals:* note steps achieved and all problem solving/goal achievement efforts – praise efforts.

*Family meeting:* note organization and problem-solving skills.

*Real-life practice:* review worksheet reports of skills used; re-enact one scenario for each participant.

*Revision of continuing deficits:* education (including checks on early warning signs and current mental status); communication and problem-solving skills; and use of specific strategies or crisis management.

## Work on training module

### Rationale

1. Invite family members to suggest how a constructive request for a person to do something, or to change his or her behaviour, may be more effective than nagging, threats, or demands in solving problems and achieving goals.
2. Summarize: 'Situations often arise when you would like to ask another person to do something, or change his or her behaviour in some way. A request made in a nagging, demanding, or threatening way does not encourage the person to do what you would like. There are no guarantees that people will do exactly what you request, but a friendly atmosphere is preserved.'

### Review current skill levels

1. Review communication and problem-solving checklist.
2. Elicit recent examples of requests.
3. Give feedback on *strengths* of their performance.

### Outline steps of skill

1. Look at person and use appropriate non-verbal expression (smile, friendly voice tone, posture, and gestures).
2. Describe exactly what you would like the person to do.

3. Tell the person how you expect to feel when he or she performs that behaviour.

### Skill training

1. Demonstrate the skill by making a request to one or more of the participants concerning something you would like them to do, e.g. complete real-life practice, attend on time, etc.
2. Observe each family member attempting to perform skill as outlined.
3. Get participants to give feedback on specific steps performed competently. 'What did you like about the way . . . made that request?'
4. Coach participants to overcome major deficits. Use repeated rehearsals, praise for small improvements, verbal instructions, modelling by family and therapist, simple prompts.

## Real-life practice

1. Brief rationale (a) practice; (b) feedback for therapist.
2. Outline worksheet 'Making positive requests'.

---

**Making a positive request**

- Look at the person and speak in a warm tone

- Tell him or her exactly what you would like him or her to do

- Tell him or her how you expect to feel when he or she has done that

- Use phrases like:

    'I would like you to . . .'

    'I would be pleased if you would . . .'

    'I would be grateful if you . . .'

---

# Making positive requests

- Look at the person
- Say exactly what you would like him or her to do
- Tell him or her how it will make you feel

| Day | Person to whom request made | What exactly did you request? |
|---|---|---|
| Mon | | |
| Tues | | |
| Wed | | |
| Thurs | | |
| Fri | | |
| Sat | | |
| Sun | | |

In making **positive requests**, use phrases like:
- 'I would like you to . . .'
- 'I would appreciate it if you would . . .'
- 'I would be pleased if you would . . .'

3. Complete entry for one example practised during session.
4. Promptsheets: display guide sheets on noticeboards, etc.
5. Family meeting: prompt weekly discussion time.

### Behavioural assessment

1. Update CPC.
2. Update family goal achievement record.
3. Note *new* problems/goals mentioned in session.

## MODULE C: EXPRESSING UNPLEASANT FEELINGS

### Review of progress

*Personal goals:* note steps achieved and all problem solving/goal achievement efforts – praise efforts.
*Family meeting:* note organization and problem-solving skills.
*Real-life practice:* review worksheet reports of skills used; re-enact one scenario for each participant.
*Revision of continuing deficits:* education (including checks on early warning signs and current mental status); communication and problem-solving skills; and use of specific strategies or crisis management.

### Work on training module

#### *Rationale*

1. Invite family members to suggest how clear, direct expression of unpleasant feelings may help to solve problems/achieve goals.
2. Summarize: 'The first step in solving a problem involves knowing exactly what the problem is. To introduce a discussion about a problem it is necessary to describe the situation causing you stress and to tell the person whom you wish to include in the discussion exactly how you feel about it.

   'A problem may make you feel anxious, angry, sad, disappointed, frustrated, worried or some other sort of unpleasant feeling.

   'It is important to realize that these are *your own* feelings about the problem and that the most efficient way of resolving them is to solve the problem. The situation may be eased with the constructive help of others, particularly when it is *their behaviour* that triggers off these unpleasant feelings in you.

'Blaming, threatening, and nagging people will tend to produce bad feelings in them, and will often produce hostile arguments. Making clear, direct statements of how you feel about a specific situation tends to minimize hostility and clears the way for effective problem solving.'

## Review current skill levels

1. Review behavioural assessment reports and observations of family members' skills in expressing unpleasant feelings (CPC). Identify 'hot issues' that would be best avoided during session.
2. Elicit recent examples of expression of unpleasant feelings.
3. Give feedback on strengths of performance.

## Outline steps of skill

1. Look at the person. Speak calmly and firmly. Use posture and gesture appropriate to your feelings.
2. Say exactly what triggered off your unpleasant feeling.
3. Tell the person how you felt.
4. Suggest how this might be resolved. Either by making a positive request for change or by arranging a problem-solving discussion, i.e. *take responsibility for resolving your own distress.*

## Skill training

1. Demonstrate expressing an unpleasant feeling to participants by choosing a relevant example of your own unpleasant feelings triggered by the behaviour of one or more participants, e.g. lateness, poor compliance, etc. (Take care to choose an issue that will be likely to lead to improved therapeutic alliance with participants.)
2. Observe each family member attempting to perform skill (choosing an everyday/minor problem issue).
3. Get participants to give feedback on specific steps performed

245

competently. 'What did you like about the way . . . expressed that feeling?'

4. Coach participants to overcome major deficits. Use repeated rehearsals, praise for small improvements, verbal instructions, modelling by family and therapist, simple prompts. *Modelling* may be especially useful where tension is high.

### Real-life practice

1. Brief rationale (a) practice; (b) feedback for therapist.
2. Outline worksheet: 'Expressing unpleasant feelings' (see page 247).
3. Complete entry for one example practised during session.
4. Promptsheets: display guide sheets on noticeboards, etc.
5. Family meeting: prompt weekly discussion time. Suggest that any issues raised requiring further problem solving be placed on the agenda for meeting.

### Behavioural assessment

1. Update CPC.
2. Update family goal achievement record.
3. Note *new* goals/problem issues mentioned in session.

---

### WARNING!

- Stop all hostile exchanges immediately.
- Focus on *structure* of expression, not content of problems.
- Be prepared to conduct crisis problem solving using six-step method if a major crisis erupts.

---

**Expressing unpleasant feelings**

- Look at the person and speak firmly
- Tell him or her exactly what triggered your unpleasant feeling
- Tell him or her how you are feeling
- Suggest ways in which he or she might help you to get rid of that feeling (Make a positive request or arrange a problem-solving discussion)

**Expressing unpleasant feelings**

● Say exactly what displeased you ● Tell the person how it made you feel ● Suggest how this could be avoided in future

| Day | Person who displeased you | What exactly did he or she do that displeased you? | How did you feel? (angry, sad, etc.) | What did you ask him or her to do in future? |
|---|---|---|---|---|
| Mon | | | | |
| Tues | | | | |
| Wed | | | | |
| Thurs | | | | |
| Fri | | | | |
| Sat | | | | |
| Sun | | | | |

**Examples:**

'I feel angry that you shouted at me, Tom. I'd like it better if you spoke more quietly next time.'

'I'm very sad that you did not get that job. I'd like to sit down and discuss some other possibilities with you after dinner.'

'I feel very anxious when you tell me I should get a job. It would help me a lot if you didn't nag me about it.'

## MODULE D: ACTIVE LISTENING

### Review of progress

*Personal goals:* note steps achieved and all problem solving/goal achievement efforts – praise efforts.

*Family meeting:* note organization and problem-solving skills.

*Real-life practice:* review worksheet reports of skills used; re-enact one scenario for each participant.

*Revision of continuing deficits:* education (including checks on early warning signs and current mental status); communication and problem-solving skills; and use of specific strategies or crisis management.

### Work on training module

#### *Rationale*

1. Invite participants to suggest how helping a person to clarify the exact nature of a goal or problem may assist in achieving that goal or resolving that problem.
2. Summarize: 'It is not always easy to say exactly what is troubling us or what goals we would like to achieve. Active listening by other people helps us to state our problems and goals more clearly. This makes it easier for us to find solutions and make plans to improve our lives.'

#### *Review current skill levels*

1. Review behavioural assessment reports and observations of family members' listening skills (CPC).
2. Elicit recent examples of listening skills.
3. Give feedback on strengths of skills.

#### *Outline steps of skill*

1. Look at speaker; adopt appropriate posture.
2. Attend to what is being said; minimize distraction.
3. Nod your head; say 'uh-huh', etc., to indicate clear reception of information.
4. Ask clarifying questions to improve your understanding of what is being said.

5. Check your understanding by summarizing what you have heard, then asking the speaker if that was his or her intended message.

*Skill training*

1. Demonstrate use of active listening to participants. Choose an issue that you would like to clarify with one or more participants.
2. Observe each family member attempting to perform the skill in a five-minute discussion with another family member about a relevant goal or problem issue.
3. Elicit feedback on specific steps performed competently: 'What did you like about the way . . . used the steps of active listening?'
4. Coach family members to overcome major deficits.
5. Use *modelling* by competent family members and therapist, rather than lengthy instructions, e.g. 'I'd like you to watch the way I ask questions to clarify what Joan is telling me.'

## Real-life practice

1. Brief rationale (a) practice; (b) feedback for therapist.
2. Outline worksheet 'Active listening' (see page 251). To be used to record number of clarifying questions asked by each family member during a 10–15-minute discussion that attempts to produce an *exact* description of a goal or problem.
3. Practise using the worksheet during rehearsals in the session, so that the key participants are familiar with its use.
4. Promptsheets: display guide sheets prominently in home.
5. Family meeting: indicate that family may wish to continue discussion about achieving the goal or problem they have defined in a specific manner with their active listening task (see above).

## Behavioural assessment

1. Update CPC.
2. Update family goal achievement record.
3. Note *new* problems/goals mentioned in session.

---

**Active listening**

● Look at the speaker; move close

● Attend to what he or she says

● Show interest; nod head, say 'uh-huh'

● Ask clarifying questions

● Check out what you heard

---

# SESSION GUIDE V : SPECIFIC PROBLEM-SOLVING SKILLS

## MODULE A: INTRODUCTION TO SIX-STEP METHOD

### Review of progress

*Personal goals:* note steps achieved and all problem solving/goal achievement efforts – praise efforts.

*Family meeting:* note organization and problem-solving skills.

*Real-life practice:* review worksheet reports of skills used; re-enact one scenario for each participant.

*Revision of continuing deficits:* education (including checks on early warning signs and current mental status); communication and problem-solving skills; and use of specific strategies or crisis management.

# Active listening

Check the number of times each family member asks a question to clarify the ideas and feelings of other family members during a family problem-solving discussion.

| | Family member 1 ___(name)___ | Family member 2 ___(name)___ | Family member 3 ___(name)___ | Family member 4 ___(name)___ | Family member 5 ___(name)___ |
|---|---|---|---|---|---|
| Number of clarifying questions | | | | | |

Person checking: _____

## Work on training module

### *Rationale*

1. Invite family members to suggest how they could improve their efficiency at resolving everyday problems and achieving everyday goals.
2. Summarize: 'In addition to being able to express your feelings about problems and goals, it is helpful to sit down and have a discussion with people who are concerned about you, such as your family and close friends. Such a discussion is most useful when it allows us to focus on one particular problem or goal, and helps us to develop a clear plan of how to cope with the problem or achieve the goal.

   'During the next few sessions I would like to teach you a way to structure your regular problem-solving discussions which many households have found helpful, both in reducing stresses and achieving personal goals.'

### *Review current skill levels*

1. Review behavioural assessment reports and observation of problem solving/goal achievement skills (see CPC).
2. Review your notes on effectiveness of weekly family meetings.
3. Repeat assessment of problem solving (reported and observed) if necessary.
4. Give feedback on the *strengths* of their performance.

### *Outline steps of skill*

Introduce the six-step method, with solving problems and achieving goals worksheets.

1. *Pinpoint the problem or goal* as precisely as you can. Take several minutes to discuss it. Use active listening to clarify exact problem/goal. Use other communication skills appropriately such as expression of unpleasant feelings or positive requests, to introduce a problem issue or propose a goal; praise all contributions.

   Try to get everyone's agreement on the description of the problem/goal (chairperson).

252

Then write down (secretary) *exactly* what the problem/goal is.

2. *List all possible solutions/ideas.* All ideas, both good and bad, are written down, with minimal comment about their merits or discussion about their application. Every participant is invited to suggest an idea. *Every* idea is acknowledged and added to the list. *At least five* ideas are listed.

3. *Evaluate each possible solution/idea.* Each idea is *briefly* evaluated in terms of its advantages and disadvantages as a solution. The main good points are highlighted, then the main bad points. Every solution has some good and some bad. Avoid lengthy discussions or debates at this stage. *Do NOT write down comments.*

4. *Choose the 'best' solution.* This is not usually the 'ideal' solution, merely the one that can be applied most readily with the present available resources, and that will be likely to go at least some way to achieving the goal/resolving the problem. Good communication skills (listening, expression of feelings) will assist where a debate is needed to achieve agreement.

5. *Plan how to carry out the solution.* A step-by-step plan of action is created describing the precise activities of each person involved with the solution.

   Who does what? To whom? How? When?

   Major problems that might arise are considered. A plan is devised for monitoring each step. A time is agreed for a discussion to review the plan.

6. *Review.* At the review meeting the success of the plan is noted. Where complete problem resolution/goal achievement has been achieved, the successful components are highlighted for future reference. Where incomplete resolution is achieved, those steps that have proved beneficial are highlighted, and the limiting steps reviewed in a constructive fashion.

   *All efforts* of family members, no matter how small or how successful, are praised.

   Problem solving is continued until the goals have been achieved.

### Skill training

1. Describe how a family has used the problem solving/goal achievement method to deal with a *straightforward* issue.

2. Invite the family to choose an *everyday issue* that they would like to resolve. *Guide them to choose a non-emotional issue.*

3. Instruct the family to consider that they are convening a family meeting, with their chairperson and secretary assuming their duties. Clarify any queries.

4. Tell the family that you are handing over to their chair-person. Tell them that you will be observing their efforts and will provide feedback when they have completed their discussion. *Leave the group* and observe the family employ the six–step method.

5. Intervene only where gross misunderstandings are observed, or emotional tension is high.

6. Once the discussion is completed elicit feedback on the strengths of the performance.

7. Target major deficits for coaching in future sessions.

### Real-life practice

Request that the family convene their weekly family meeting to discuss another everyday issue using the six-step structure, with the worksheet. Tell them you would like to review their efforts at the beginning of the next session.

### Behavioural assessment

1. Update CPC.
2. Update family goal achievement record.
3. Note any *new* goals/problems mentioned during session.

---

**Problem solving and goal achievement**

- Pinpoint the problem or goal

- List all possible solutions

- Highlight likely consequences

- Agree on 'best' strategy

- Plan and implement

- Review results

---

**Solving problems and achieving goals**

STEP 1: WHAT IS THE PROBLEM/GOAL?
Talk about the problem/goal, listen carefully, ask questions, get everybody's opinion. Then write down *exactly* what the problem/goal is.

_____

_____

STEP 2: LIST ALL POSSIBLE SOLUTIONS.
Put down *all* ideas, even bad ones. Get everybody to come up with at least one possible solution. List the solutions *without discussion* at this stage.

1) _____
2) _____
3) _____
4) _____
5) _____
6) _____

STEP 3: DISCUSS EACH POSSIBLE SOLUTION.
*Quickly* go down the list of possible solutions and highlight the *main* advantages and disadvantages of each one.

STEP 4: CHOOSE THE 'BEST' SOLUTION.
Choose the solution that can be carried out most easily to solve the problem or achieve the goal.

_____

_____

STEP 5: PLAN HOW TO CARRY OUT THE BEST SOLUTION.
Resources needed. Major pitfalls to overcome. Practise difficult steps. Time for review.

Step 1) _____
Step 2) _____
Step 3) _____
Step 4) _____

STEP 6: REVIEW IMPLEMENTATION AND PRAISE *ALL* EFFORTS.
Focus on *achievement first. Review plan. Revise as necessary.*

# MODULE B: PINPOINTING PROBLEMS AND GOALS

## Review of progress

*Personal goals:* note steps achieved and all problem solving/goal achievement efforts – praise efforts.

*Family meeting:* note organization and problem-solving skills.

*Real-life practice:* review worksheet reports of skills used; re-enact one scenario for each participant.

*Revision of continuing deficits:* education (including checks on early warning signs and current mental status); communication and problem-solving skills; and use of specific strategies or crisis management.

## Work on training module

### *Rationale*

1. Invite family members to suggest the benefits of accurate description of problems and goals.
2. Summarize: 'An exact description of a problem or a goal has the following benefits:

   (a) It helps everyone to focus on the same issue.
   (b) It makes it easier to know when the goal has been achieved.
   (c) It helps people to set clear-cut, realistic goals, rather than vague, unattainable goals.

### *Review current skill levels*

1. Report on strengths noted on behavioural assessments, in particular in recent sessions and reports of weekly meetings.
2. Suggest family discuss a current everyday issue for five minutes, with the goal of pinpointing the problem.

### *Outline steps of skill*

1. *Key person introduces issue.* This is either a personal goal: 'I would like to have the house looking neat and tidy'; or a personal problem: 'I do not like the way the house is so messy.'

256

2. *Other participants give their views* on the problem or goal. 'I agree that the house is untidy'; 'I disagree. I like it the way it is.' Goals are easier to define than problems – think in terms of what goal would indicate that the problem had been resolved, e.g. 'A messy lounge' becomes 'A tidy lounge, with books on bookshelves, records in record cupboards, shoes and clothes in bedrooms'. Or 'having no friends' becomes 'making one friend of same sex, to meet once a week and go to a sports club'.

3. *Active listening* enables family members to ask clarifying questions, check out other people's views.

4. The chairperson invites the key person to *summarize the problem/goal definition* at the end of the discussion (or after an agreed time limit of five minutes).

5. The *definition is noted on the worksheet* (secretary).

6. Chairperson introduces next phase of problem solving.

### Skill training

1. Revise key skills, e.g. expressing pleasant and unpleasant feelings; active listening.

2. Repeated five-minute practice of employing skills to pinpoint problem or goal.

3. Constructive coaching to overcome major deficits with praise for small improvements.

4. Demonstrate skills by taking the role of a family member (often the chairperson) while that person watches, then attempts to emulate one key aspect of your performance.

5. Observe family group performing skill for 5–10 minutes.

6. Give feedback on specific steps performed competently.

7. Coach family members to overcome major deficits. Repeat brief (two minutes) segments, with praise for small improvements, further verbal instructions, modelling by competent family members and therapist, simple verbal and non-verbal prompts.

### Real-life practice

1. Brief rationale (a) practice; (b) feedback for therapist.

2. Choose one major deficit, e.g. listening skills, expression of unpleasant feelings, active directions from chairperson.

3. Hand out appropriate worksheet and revise.
4. Family meeting: instruct family to practise pinpointing two or three problem/goal issues at family meeting. Instruct chairperson to ensure that family members employ the steps practised in the session.
5. Review the definitions of two or three problems or goals written on solving problems and achieving goals worksheets. Review other worksheets assigned, e.g. Active listening.

### Behavioural assessment

1. Update CPC.
2. Update family goal achievement record.
3. Note *new* problems/goals mentioned during session.

## MODULE C: BRAINSTORMING

### Review of progress

*Personal goals:* note steps achieved and all problem solving/goal achievement efforts – praise efforts.
*Family meeting:* note organization and problem-solving skills.
*Real-life practice:* review worksheet reports of skills used; re-enact one scenario for each participant.
*Revision of continuing deficits:* education (including checks on early warning signs and current mental status); communication and problem-solving skills; and use of specific strategies or crisis management.

### Work on training module

#### Rationale

1. Invite family members to suggest the benefits of listing all possible solutions to a problem/goal in a non-judgemental way.
2. Summarize: 'Brainstorming is a method that helps us to come up with new ideas in order to sort out difficult problems or achieve important goals. Rather than focusing on the best or ideal solutions, we relax and list any ideas that come into our minds. These may seem to be good ideas or bad ideas – it

258

doesn't matter. Each idea is blurted out and listed *without comment*. Everyone is encouraged to come up with an idea no matter how ridiculous it may sound. This helps us to come up with new ideas. Often an idea that at first sight looks ridiculous can lead us to a much better solution than the more obvious answers that we've tried and failed with before.'

### *Review current skill levels*

1. Note whether brainstorming methods have been employed by the family in reports and observations of the problem-solving efforts to date.
2. Give feedback on strengths of their performance.

### *Outline steps of skill*

1. Chairperson tells participants to think of all possible ideas about how the problem can be solved or the goal achieved. He or she invites them to list both good and bad ideas without evaluating their merits.
2. Secretary lists each idea suggested, thanking each person for providing a suggestion.
3. Chairperson prompts every member to make a suggestion, and discourages members from dominating.
4. Chairperson stops discussion of the relative merits of ideas. Reminds family that that occurs in the next phase of problem solving.
5. When five or six ideas have been listed the chairperson introduces the next phase of problem solving.

### *Skill training*

1. Observe family performing skill for five minutes.
2. Give feedback on specific steps performed competently.
3. Coach participants to overcome major deficits, e.g. dominance of members, reluctance of other members to suggest ideas, put-downs for 'silly' ideas, comments about merits of ideas, lack of structuring by chairperson.
4. Repear brief (two minutes) rehearsals, with praise for small improvements, verbal instructions, modelling, prompts.
5. *Note. Therapist avoids participation*, except to model overtly a

259

specific step. It may help to model suggesting 'bad' or outrageous ideas, e.g. by playing the devil's advocate or suggesting the idea of 'doing nothing'.

### Real-life practice

1. Brief rationale (a) practice; (b) feedback for therapist.
2. Choose one major deficit and ask the family to employ the methods used in the session to overcome this deficit in their problem solving/goal discussions at their weekly family meeting.
3. Review their solving problems and achieving goals worksheets at beginning of next session for evidence of improvement. Praise efforts.

### Behavioural assessment

1. Update CPC.
2. Update family goal achievement record.
3. Note *new* problems/goals mentioned during session.

## MODULE D: EVALUATING ALTERNATIVES

### Review of progress

*Personal goals:* note steps achieved and all problem solving/goal achievement efforts – praise efforts.
*Family meeting:* note organization and problem-solving skills.
*Real-life practice:* review worksheet reports of skills used; re-enact the step being practised during past week.
*Revision of continuing deficits:* education (including checks on early warning signs and current mental status); communication and problem-solving skills; and use of specific strategies or crisis management.

### Work on training module

#### *Rationale*

1. Invite family members to suggest the benefits of briefly highlighting the advantages and disadvantages of every suggested solution.

2. Summarize: 'Briefly highlighting the potential advantages and disadvantages of each idea suggested as a possible solution to a problem enables the family to decide which solution might be best for them. Of course, no solution is ideal; every good idea has its faults – for example it may cost money, it may require expert skills. On the other hand, every apparently 'bad' idea has some good points. It may be easy to apply, and it may solve the problem. For example, robbing a bank may achieve the goal of getting money for a bus pass, but has major disadvantages!'

### Review current skill levels

1. Feed back to family on the specific strengths you have noted in their performance during past sessions.
2. Target *major* deficits for skill training.

### Outline steps of skill

1. Chairperson introduces this phase of problem solving. Requests secretary to report each idea in turn. Tells family to highlight the main advantages and disadvantages of each idea in turn.
2. Chairperson ensures that the advantages are noted first, then the disadvantages.

   – at least one advantage and one disadvantage are noted for each idea.
   – discussion is brief, debates avoided.
   – detailed planning is left to the planning phase.
   – each participant is involved, dominance avoided.

3. No written notes are made of the pros and cons, merely mental notes of the highlights.
4. Chairperson introduces the next phase of problem solving.

### Skill training

1. Therapist observes family performance for two minutes.
2. Feedback elicited on competence.
3. Coach family to overcome major deficits.
4. Repeat brief (one to two minutes) rehearsals, with praise

261

for small improvements, verbal instructions, modelling, prompts.

5. *Note*: Therapist avoids active participation, coaches at the *end* of each brief rehearsal.

### Real-life practice

1. Brief rationale (a) practice; (b) feedback for therapist.
2. Choose one major deficit for family to work on during their weekly family meeting.
3. Review their solving problems and achieving goals worksheets at beginning of next session, and request specific reports of implementation of this phase of problem solving.

### Behavioural assessment

1. Update CPC.
2. Update family goal achievement record.
3. Note *new* problems/goals mentioned during session.

## MODULE E: CHOOSING OPTIMAL SOLUTION

### Review of progress

*Personal goals:* note steps achieved and all problem solving/goal achievement efforts – praise efforts.

*Family meeting:* note organization and problem-solving skills.

*Real-life practice:* review worksheet reports of skills used; re-enact the step being practised during past week.

*Revision of continuing deficits:* education (including checks on early warning signs and current mental status); communication and problem-solving skills; and use of specific strategies or crisis management.

### Work on training module

#### Rationale

1. Invite participants to suggest the benefits of agreeing an optimal solution together.
2. Summarize: 'Agreeing on the solution to solve a particular problem or achieve a goal may take some time. We find that

this is most easily achieved when you try to choose the solution that can most readily be used. This is not necessarily the ideal solution, rather the one you can get started on right away with the resources you have at the moment. It may not solve the problem completely, but at least it may make a difference now, not next month or next year.'

### *Review current skill levels*

1. Give family feedback on the specific skills you have noted that are relevant to this phase of problem solving, e.g. active listening, negotiating skills, a willingness to compromise, expression of positive and unpleasant feelings.

### *Outline steps of skill*

1. Chairperson introduces this phase with brief instructions to family.
2. A discussion about the pros and cons of one or more of the listed solutions directed towards finding the solution that best fits the problem/goal and existing family resources (skills, finances, materials, time, etc.).
3. Active listening and competent expression of feelings.
4. Compromise: where two or more family members strongly favour differing solutions, compromise is reached by deciding to try one solution first followed by the second, if necessary. The manner in which this is negotiated may require further problem solving itself.
5. Solution is recorded on worksheet (secretary).
6. Chairperson introduces next phase of problem solving.

### *Skill training*

1. Observe family performance for two to five minutes.
2. Give feedback on specific steps performed competently.
3. Coach family members to overcome major deficits. Repeat brief (two minutes) segments, with praise for small improvements, verbal instructions, modelling, and prompts.

## Behavioural assessment

1. Update CPC.
2. Update family goal achievement record.
3. Note *new* problems/goals mentioned during session.

# MODULE F: PLANNING

## Review of progress

*Personal goals:* note steps achieved and all problem solving/goal achievement efforts – praise efforts.

*Family meeting:* note organization and problem-solving skills.

*Real-life practice:* review worksheet reports of skills used; re-enact the step being practised during past week.

*Revision of continuing deficits:* education (including checks on early warning signs and current mental status); communication and problem-solving skills; and use of specific strategies or crisis management.

## Work on training module

### *Rationale*

1. Invite participants to suggest the benefits of devising a step-by-step plan of action.
2. Summarize: 'Careful planning of the exact steps everyone is going to take in putting the best solution into action ensures that the problem is resolved efficiently. Many good solutions are not put into practice because there is a lack of planning.

    'It is worth spending sufficient time to make detailed plans, particularly when the solution requires the cooperation of several participants.'

### *Review current skill levels*

1. Feedback to family the specific strengths you have noted in their planning skills.
2. Target *major* deficits for skill training.

*Outline steps of skill*

1. Chairperson introduces planning, with a brief reminder of the key points.
2. Key points include:
   - write down who will do what and when.
   - go over the steps and consider likely hitches; devise ways of coping with these.
   - rehearse or role play situations that may prove difficult, e.g. meeting people, interviews.
   - nominate one person to monitor the steps of the plan.
   - write down a specific time and place to review progress.
3. Chairperson ensures that discussion proceeds efficiently and concludes problem solving/goal achievement by requesting secretary to read out the plan for final approval by the family.

*Skill training*

1. Therapist hands each family member a guide sheet, 'Planning checklist' (see page 266). He reviews steps of planning.
2. Choose a problem/goal that family attempted to resolve but failed to implement because of deficient planning.
3. Therapist observes family performance for five minutes.
4. Feedback elicited on competence.
5. Coach family to overcome major deficits.
6. Repeat deficient aspects, with praise for small improvements, verbal instructions, modelling, prompts.

**Real-life practice**

1. Brief rationale (a) practice; (b) feedback for therapist.
2. Request family to focus on planning at their weekly family meeting.
3. Give the chairperson two 'Planning checklist' worksheets and request that he or she checks that all steps are carried out in planning the solutions to two problems/goals.
4. Review planning efforts from worksheets at beginning of next session.

**Behavioural assessment**

1. Update CPC.
2. Update family goal achievement record.
3. Note *new* problems/goals mentioned in session.

| Planning checklist | Yes | No |
|---|---|---|
| 1. Are all resources (time, skills, materials, money) needed to carry out the solution available? | | |
| 2. Has person(s) agreed to arrange necessary resources (time, skills, materials, money)? | | |
| 3. Have all the steps in the plan been arranged so that everybody knows what they are doing and when they are doing it? | | |
| 4. Have the steps been checked to highlight specific likely hitches? | | |
| 5. Have specific plans been made to cope with likely hitches? | | |
| 6. Have people practised difficult parts of the plan (e.g. meetings, interviews, phone calls)? | | |
| 7. Has one person agreed to check that people do what they have agreed to do at the right time? | | |
| 8. Have a time and place been agreed when overall progress with the plan will be discussed? | | |

## MODULE G: REVIEW OF IMPLEMENTATION

### Review of progress

*Personal goals:* note steps achieved and all problem solving/goal achievement efforts – praise efforts.

*Family meeting:* note organization and problem-solving skills.

*Real-life practice:* review worksheet reports of skills used; re-enact the step being practised during past week.

*Revision of continuing deficits:* education (including checks on early warning signs and current mental status); communication and problem-solving skills; and use of specific strategies or crisis management.

## Work on training module

### *Rationale*

1. Invite participants to suggest the benefits of a detailed review of the implementation of a specific plan.
2. Summarize: 'Solving difficult problems or achieving personal goals is rarely possible after only one attempt. It is helpful to review progress at regular intervals to see how your plans are progressing. Steps may need to be changed or new ones added. Most important of all, everyone needs to be praised for their specific efforts, regardless of how successful they have been so far.'

### *Review current skill levels*

1. Feed back to family the specific strengths you have noted in their reviewing skills.
2. Target *major* deficits for skill training.

### *Outline steps of skill*

1. Specific time set for review.
2. Chairperson and secretary ensure review is carried out.
3. Each step of the plan on the worksheet is discussed in terms of:

   (a) success: partial or complete
   (b) difficulties encountered
   (c) modifications devised to cope with difficulties
   (d) subsequent success: partial or complete
   (e) what has been learned?
   (f) praise for *all* efforts, no matter how small or how successful.

4. A revised plan is developed. This may require a review of one or more of the phases of the original problem solving/ goal achievement. At times the entire process may be repeated.

267

*Skill training*

1. Therapist observes family performance for five minutes.
2. Elicit feedback given on competence.
3. Coach family to overcome major deficits.
4. Repeat brief rehearsals (one to two minutes), with praise for small improvements, verbal instructions, modelling, prompts.
5. *Note*: Therapist avoids active participation; coaches at the end of each brief rehearsal.

## Real-life practice

1. Brief rationale (a) practice; (b) feedback for therapist.
2. Choose one major deficit for family to work on during weekly family meeting.
3. Review their reports of a review of implementation at the beginning of the next session.

## Behavioural assessment

1. Update CPC.
2. Update family goal achievement record.
3. Note *new* problems/goals mentioned in session.

# BIBLIOGRAPHY

Alexander, J. F. and Parsons, B. V. (1982) *Functional Family Therapy*. Brooks/Cole, Monterey, Ca.

Ambelas, A. (1987) Life events and mania: a special relationship? *British Journal of Psychiatry, 150*, 235–240.

Anderson, C. M., Reiss, D. J. and Hogarty, G. E. (1986) *Schizophrenia and the Family*. Guilford Press, New York.

Bandura, A. (1977) Self-efficacy: toward a unifying theory of behavioral change. *Psychological Review, 84*, 191–215.

Barrowclough, C., Tarrier, N., Watts, S., Vaughn, C., Bamrah, J. S. and Freeman, H. (1987) Assessing the functional value of relatives' knowledge about schizophrenia: a preliminary report. *British Journal of Psychiatry, 151*, 1–8.

Beck, A. T., Emery, G. and Greenberg, R. (1985) *Anxiety Disorders and Phobias*. Basic Books, New York.

Beck, A. T., Rush, A. J., Shaw, B. F. and Emery, G. (1979) *Cognitive Therapy of Depression*. Guilford Press, New York.

Becker, R. E., Heimberg, R. G. and Bellack, A. S. (1986) *Social Skills Treatment for Depression*. Pergamon Press, New York.

Berkowitz, R., Eberlein-Vries, R., Kuipers, L. and Leff, J. (1984) Educating relatives about schizophrenia. *Schizophrenia Bulletin, 10*, 418–429.

Bernstein, D.A. and Borkovec, T.D. (1973) *Progressive Relaxation Training*. Research Press, Champaign, IL.

Billings, A.G. and Moos, R. H. (1981) The role of coping responses and social resources in attenuating the stress of life events. *Journal of Behavioral Medicine, 4*, 139–157.

Birchler, G. R. (1988) Handling resistance to change. In I. R. H. Falloon (ed.) *Handbook of Behavioral Family Therapy*. Guilford Press, New York.

Birchwood, M., Smith, J., MacMillan, F., Hogg, B., Prasad, R., Harvey, C. and Bering, S. (1989) Predicting relapse in schizophrenia: the development and implementation of an early signs monitoring system using patients and families as observers – a preliminary investigation. *Psychological Medicine, 19*, 649–656.

Brady, J. P. (1984) Social skills training for psychiatric patients. I:

Concepts, methods, and clinical results. *American Journal of Psychiatry*, *141*, 333–340.

Brown, G. W. and Birley, J. L. T. (1968) Crises and life changes and the onset of schizophrenia. *Journal of Health and Social Behaviour*, *9*, 203–214.

Brown, G. W. and Harris, T. O. (1978) *Social Origins of Depression: A Study of Psychiatric Disorder in Women*. Tavistock, London.

Brown, G. W. and Rutter, M. (1966) The measurement of family activities and relationships: a methodological study. *Human Relations*, *19*, 241–263.

Catalan, J., Gath, D., Edmonds, G. and Ennis, J. (1984) The effects of non-prescribing in general practice. *British Journal of Psychiatry*, *144*, 593–603.

Christensen, A, (1979) Naturalistic observation of families: a system for random audio recordings in the home. *Behavior Therapy*, *10*, 418–422.

Clark, D. M. (1986) Cognitive therapy of anxiety. *Behavioural Psychotherapy*, *14*, 283–294.

Cobb, L. A. and Rose, R. M. (1973) Hypertension, peptic ulcer and diabetes in air traffic controllers. *JAMA*, *224*, 489–492.

Cooper, C. L., Cooper, R. and Faragher, B. (1985) Stress and life events methodology. *Stress Medicine*, *1*, 287–289.

Cozolino, L. J. and Goldstein, M. J. (1986) Family education as a component of extended family-orientated treatment programmes for schizophrenia. In M. J. Goldstein *et al.* (eds) *Treatment of Schizophrenia: Family Assessment and Intervention*. Springer Verlag, Berlin.

Creer, C. and Wing, J. (1974) *Schizophrenia at Home*. National Schizophrenia Fellowship, Surbiton, England.

Curran, J. P. and Monti, P. M. (eds) (1982) *Social Skills Training*. Guilford Press, New York.

Curry, S. H., Marshall, J. H. L., Davis, J. S. and Janowsky, D. J. (1970) Chlorpromazine plasma levels and effects. *Archives of General Psychiatry*, *22*, 289–296.

DeLongis, A., Coyne, J. C., Dakof, G., Folkman, S. and Lazarus, R. S. (1982) Relationship of daily hassles, uplifts and major life events to health status. *Health Psychology*, *1*, 119–136.

Doane, J. A. (1978) *Affective Style Coding Manual*. UCLA Department of Psychology, Los Angeles.

Doane, J. A., Goldstein, M. J., Miklowitz, D. J. and Falloon, I. R. H. (1986) The impact of individual and family treatment on the affective climate of families of schizophrenics. *British Journal of Psychiatry*, *148*, 279.

D'Zurilla, T. J. (1986) *Problem Solving Therapy*. Springer, New York.

D'Zurilla, T. J. and Goldfried, M. R. (1971) Problem solving and behavior modification. *Journal of Abnormal Psychology*, *78*, 107–126.

Edwards, J. R. and Cooper, C. L. (1988) Research in stress, coping, and health: theoretical and methodological issues. *Psychological Medicine*, *18*, 15–20.

Fadden, G., Bebbington, P. and Kuipers, L. (1987) Caring and its burdens: a study of the spouses of depressed patients. *British Journal of Psychiatry*, *151*, 660–667.

Falloon, I. R. H. (1978) Social skills training for community living. *Psychiatric Clinics of North America*, *1*, 291–305.

Falloon, I. R. H. (1984) Developing and maintaining adherence to long-term drug regimens. *Schizophrenia Bulletin*, *10*, 412–417.

Falloon, I. R. H. (1985a) *Coping with Depression*. Buckingham Hospital, Buckingham, UK (xeroxed handout available on request).

Falloon, I. R. H. (1985b) *Family Management of Schizophrenia*. Johns Hopkins University Press, Baltimore.

Falloon, I. R. H. (1988) *Handbook of Behavioural Family Therapy*. Guilford Press, New York.

Falloon, I. R. H. (1991) Behavioral family therapy. In A. S. Gurman and D. Kniskern (eds) *Handbook of Family Therapy*. Brunner/Mazel, New York.

Falloon, I. R. H. and Fadden, G. (1993) *Integrated Mental Health Care*. Cambridge University Press, Cambridge.

Falloon, I. R. H. and McGill, C. W. (1985) Family stress and the course of schizophrenia: a review. In I. R. H. Falloon (ed.) *Family Management of Schizophrenia*. John Hopkins University Press, Baltimore.

Falloon, I. R. H., Boyd, J. L. and McGill, C. W. (1984) *Family Care of Schizophrenia*, Guilford Press, New York.

Falloon, I. R. H., Hole, V., Pembleton, T. and Norris, L. (1988) Behavioral family therapy in the management of major affective disorders. In J. F. Clarkin, G. Haas and I. D. Glick (eds) *Family Intervention in Affective Illness*. Guilford Press, New York.

Falloon, I. R. H., Liberman, R. P., Lillie, F. J. and Vaughn, C. E. (1981) Family therapy of schizophrenics with high risk of relapse. *Family Process*, *20*, 211–221.

Fava, G. A. and Kellner, R. (1991) Prodromal symptoms in affective disorders. *American Journal of Psychiatry*, *148*, 823–830.

Follette, W. and Jacobson, N. (1988). Behavioural family therapy for depression. In I. R. H. Falloon (ed.) *Handbook of Behavioural Family Therapy*. Guilford Press, New York.

Forehand, R. and McMahon, R. J. (1981) *Helping the Non-compliant Child: A Clinical Guide to Parent Training*. Guilford Press, New York.

Foster, S. L., Prinz, R. J. and O'Leary, K. D. (1983) Impact of problem-solving, communication training and generalization procedures on family conflict. *Child and Family Behavior Therapy*, *5*, 1–23.

Foy, D. W., Nun, L. B. and Rychtarik, R. G. (1984) Broad-spectrum behavioural treatment for chronic alcoholics: effects of training controlled drinking skills. *Journal of Consulting Counselling Psychology*, *52*, 218–230.

Friedman, M. and Rosenman, R. H. (1959) Association of overt behavior pattern with blood and cardiovascular findings. *JAMA*, *169*, 1286–1296.

Goldstein, M. J., Rodnick, E. H., Evans, J. R., May, P. R. A. and Steinberg, M. (1968) A method for studying social influence and coping patterns within families of disturbed adolescents. *Journal of Nervous and Mental Disease*, *147*, 233–251.

Grad, J. and Sainsbury, P. (1963) Mental illness and the family. *Lancet*, 544–547.

Griest, D. L. and Wells, K. C. (1983) Behavioral family therapy with conduct disorders in children. *Behavior Therapy*, *14*, 37–53.

Hahlweg, K., Baucom, D. H. and Markman, H. (1988) Recent advances in behavioral marital therapy and in preventing marital distress. In I. R. H. Falloon (ed.). *Handbook of Behavioral Family Therapy*. Guilford Press, New York.

Hahlweg, K., Revenstorf, D. and Schindler, L. (1984) Effects of behavioral marital therapy on couples' communication and problem solving skills. *Journal of Consulting & Clinical Psychology*, *52*, 553–566.

Hahlweg, K., Reisner, L., Kohli, G., Vollmer, M., Schindler, L. and Revenstorf, D. (1984) Development and validity of a new system to analyse interpersonal communication (KPI). In K. Hahlweg, and N. S. Jacobson (eds) *Marital Interaction: Analysis and Modification*. Guilford Press, New York.

Harris, S. L. (1983) *Families of the Developmentally Disabled: A Guide to Behavioral Intervention*. Pergamon, New York.

Hatfield, A. (1981) Coping effectiveness in families of the mentally ill: an exploration study. *Journal of Psychiatric Treatment and Evaluation*, *3*, 11–19.

Hatfield, A. B. (1990) *Family Education in Mental Illness*. Guilford Press, New York.

Hawton, K. (1985) *Sex Therapy*. Oxford University Press, Oxford.

Herz, M. and Melville, C. (1980) Relapse in schizophrenia. *American Journal of Psychiatry*, *137*, 801–805.

Hoffman, L. (1981) *Foundations of Family Therapy*. Basic Books, New York.

Holden, D. and Lewine, R. (1982) How families evaluate mental health professionals, resources and effects of illness. *Schizophrenia Bulletin*, *10*, 626–633.

Hole, V. (1987) *Coping with a Manic Episode*. Buckingham Hospital, Buckingham, UK (xeroxed educational materials available on request).

Holmes, T.H. and Masuda, M. (1973) Life change and illness susceptibility. In J. P. Scott and E. C. Senay (eds) *Separation and Depression*. American Association for the Advancement of Science, Washington DC.

Jacobson, N. S. and Margolin, G. (1979) *Marital Therapy: Strategies Based on Social Learning and Behavior Exchange Principles*. Brunner/Mazel, New York.

Kelly, J. A. (1982) *Social Skills Training: A Practical Guide for Interventions*. Springer, New York.

Kelly, J. A., Laughlin, C., Clairborne, M. and Patterson, J. (1979) A group procedure for teaching job interviewing skills to formerly hospitalized psychiatric patients. *Behaviour Therapy*, *10*, 299–310.

Kety, S. S. (1984) Interactions between stress and genetic processes. In M. R. Zales (ed.) *Stress in Health and Disease*. Brunner/Mazel, New York.

L'Abate, L. and Milan, M. A. (eds) (1985) *Handbook of Social Skills Training and Research*. Wiley, New York.

Laporta, M., Falloon, I. R. H., Shanahan, W. and Graham-Hole, V. (1989) The NIMH behaviour family therapy skill assessment: reliability and validity. Paper presented at the World Congress of Psychiatry, Athens.

Lazarus, A. A. (1978) *In the Mind's Eyes*. Rawson, New York.

Leff, J. P. and Vaughn, C. E. (1985) *Expressed Emotion in Families*. Guilford Press, New York.

Leff, J., Kuipers, L., Berkowitz, R., Eberlein-Fries, R. and Sturgeon, D. (1982) A controlled trial of social intervention in the families of schizophrenic patients. *British Journal of Pychiatry, 141*, 121–134.

Ley, P. (1988) Communicating with patients: improving communication, satisfaction and compliance. Croom Helm, London.

Liberman, R. P. (1970) Behavioral approaches to family and couple therapy. *American Journal of Orthopsychiatry, 40*, 106–118.

Liberman, R. P., King, L. W., DeRisi, W. J. and McCann, M. (1975) *Personal Effectiveness: Guiding People to Assert Themselves and Improve Their Social Skills*. Research Press, Champaign, IL.

Liberman, R. P., Wheeler, E. G., DeVisser, L. A. J. M., Kuehnel, J. and Kuehnel, T. (1980) *Handbook of Martial Therapy*. Plenum, New York.

McCubbin, H. I., Joy, C. B., Cauble, A. E., Comeau, J. K., Patterson, J. M. and Needle, R. H. (1980) Family stress and coping: a decade review. *Journal of Marriage and the Family*, 855–871.

McGill, C., Falloon, I., Boyd, J. and Wood-Siverio, C. (1983) Family educational intervention in the treatment of schizophrenia. *Hospital and Community Psychiatry, 34*, 934–938.

Markman, H. J. and Floyd, F. (1980) Possibilities for the prevention of marital discord: a behavioral perspective. *American Journal of Family Therapy, 8*, 29–48.

Marks, I. M. (1987) *Fears, Phobias and Rituals*. Wiley, New York.

Mathews, A. M., Gelder, M. G. and Johnson, D. W. (1981) *Agoraphobia: Nature and Treatment*. Guilford Press, New York.

Miklowitz, D. J., Goldstein, M. J., Nuechterlein, K. H., Snyder, K. S. and Mintz, J. (1988) Family factors and the course of bipolar affective disorder. *Archives of General Psychiatry, 45*, 225–231.

Mueser, K. T., Foy, D. W. and Carter, M. J. (1986) Social skills training for job maintenance in a psychiatric patient. *Journal of Counselling Psychology, 33*, 360–362.

Ost, L. G. (1987) Applied relaxation: description of a coping technique and review of controlled studies. *Behaviour, Research and Therapy, 25*, 397–410.

Patterson, G. R. (1971) *Families: Applications of Social Learning to Family Life*. Research Press, Champaign, IL.

Patterson, G. R. (1975) *Families*. Research Press, Champaign, IL.

Patterson, G. R. (1976) *Living with Children*. Research Press, Champaign, IL.

Patterson, G. R. (1988) Foreword. In I. R. H. Falloon (ed.) *Handbook of Behavioural Family Therapy*. Guilford Press, New York.

Paul, G. L. and Lentz, R. J. (1977) *Psychosocial Treatment of Chronic Mental Patients*. Harvard University Press, Cambridge.

Pearlin, L. I. and Schooler, C. (1978) The structure of coping. *Journal of Health and Social Behavior, 19*, 2–21.

Robin, A. L., Kent, R., O'Leary, K. D., Foster, S. and Prinz, R. (1977) An approach to teaching parents and adolescents problem-solving communication skills: a preliminary report. *Behavior Therapy, 8*, 639–643.

Simpson, G. M., Pi, E. H. and Sramek, J. J. (1982) Adverse effects of antipsychotic agents. *Australasian Drug Information Series*.

Smith, J. (1984) The development and assessment of an educational package for families of schizophrenic patients. MSc thesis, Department of Clinical Psychology, University of Birmingham.

Smith, J. V. and Birchwood, M. (1987) Specific and non-specific effects of education intervention with families living with a schizophrenic relative. *British Journal of Psychiatry, 150*, 645–652.

Spivack, G., Platt, J. J. and Shure, M. B. (1976) *The Problem-solving Approach to Adjustment*. Jossey-Bass, San Francisco.

Stuart, R. B. (1969) Operant-interpersonal treatment for marital discord. *Journal of Consulting and Clinical Psychology, 33*, 675–682.

Tarrier, N. and Barrowclough, C. (1986) Providing information to relatives about schizophrenia: some comments. *British Journal of Psychiatry, 149*, 458–463.

Tarrier, N., Barrowclough, C., Vaughn, C., Bamrah, J. S., Porceddu, K., Watts, S. and Freeman, H. (1988) The community management of schizophrenia: a controlled trial of behavioural intervention with families to reduce relapse. *British Journal of Psychiatry, 153*, 532.

Tennant, C. and Andrews, G. (1978) The pathogenic quality of life event stress in neurotic impairment. *Archives of General Psychiatry, 35*, 859–863.

Thibaut, J. W. and Kelley, H. H. (1959) *The Social Psychology of Groups*. Wiley, New York.

Trower, P., Bryant, B. and Argyle, M. (1978) *Social Skills and Mental Health*. Methuen, London.

Vaughn, C. E. and Leff, J. P. (1976a) The influence of family and social factors on the course of psychiatric illness. A comparison of schizophrenic and depressed neurotic patients. *British Journal of Psychiatry, 129*, 125–137.

Vaughn, C. E. and Leff, J. P. (1976b) The measurement of expressed emotion in families of psychiatric patients. *British Journal of Social and Clinical Psychology, 15*, 157–165.

Wallace, C. J. (1982) The social skills training project of the mental health clinical research centre for the study of schizophrenia. In J. P. Curran and P. M. Monti (eds) *Social Skills Training*, pp. 57–89. Guilford Press, New York.

Weiss, R. L. (1980) Strategic behavioral marital therapy: toward a model for assessment and intervention. In J. P. Vincent (ed.) *Advances in Family Intervention, Assessment, and Theory. Volume 1*. JAI Press, Greenwich, New York.

Weiss, R. L., Hops, H. and Patterson, G. R. (1973) A framework for conceptualising marital conflict, a technology for altering it, some data for evaluating it. In L. A. Hamerlynck, L. C. Handy and E. J. Mash (eds) *Behavior Change: Methodology, Concepts and Practice*. Research Press, Champaign, IL.

Woolfolk, R. L. and Lehrer, P. M. (eds) (1984) *Principles and Practice of Stress Management*. Guilford Press, New York.

Zarit, S. H. and Zarit, J. M. (1982) Families under stress: interventions for caregivers of senile dementia patients. *Psychotherapy: Theory, Research and Practice*, *19*, 461–471.

# NAME INDEX

# SUBJECT INDEX

abuse: emotional 106, 156–7; physical 106
adolescent conflict 8
affective episodes, management of 170–1
ambient stress 2, 4, 7
anger, control of 153–6
anxiety disorders 71, 72, 233
anxiety management 9, 163–4
assessment processes 8–9, 16, 26–56, 187–9, 200, 223–4; in crisis situations 147–50; *see also* behavioural assessment
attendance at therapy sessions 17, 18–19, 177, 225
attentional problems 108, 109–10, 172
audiovisual aids 70–1, 191

behaviour modification strategies 7
behaviour rehearsal 83–5, 87–8, 139, 180, 192–3, 201
behavioural assessment 26, 28–9, 117, 122–3, 148, 204–22
behavioural family therapy: development of 6–9; engaging families in 13–25; problems in application of 174–85
behavioural problems in childhood 6–7, 8, 167
behavioural responses to stress 1
between-session work assignments *see* homework; real-life practice

biomedical strategies 161–2; *see also* drug therapy; medication
booster sessions 21
brainstorming 8, 113, 124, 133–4, 258–60
'bug-in-the-ear' device 89

Camberwell Family Interview 45
children: attendance at training sessions 18; behavioural problems in 6–7, 8, 167
clinical management 15–16
coaching 88, 192–7, 201
cognitive restructuring 9
'cognitive safety-net' 139–40
communication 4, 5; enhancement of 8, 11, 27, 224; of feelings 98–101, 103–7, 236–40, 244–7; hostile 182–3; non-verbal 99, 102–3, 108, 109; structure of 39
communication and problem-solving checklist (CPC) 40–1, 43, 44, 54–5, 80, 97, 216–17
communication skills: assessment of 80; core curriculum of 97–110
communication training 77–110, 195
competence of therapists 9, 186–203
confidentiality 16, 75
contingency contracting 166, 169–70

278

marital distress 8
marital inventories 45
marital therapy 7, 170–1, 172–3
medication: adherence to 179; tranquillizing 156, 162; *see also* drug therapy
medication record 52, 54, 220
meditation 163
mental disorders 2, 8, 159; drug therapy for 162, 172; early warning signs 71–5, 233–5; genetic factors 68; impact on household of 31–3; misconceptions about 65; understanding of 31
mental health education 57–76, 224, 228–36; content of 67–9; purpose of 58–9; skills employed in 62–7; timing of 60–2
mental health status 48–9
modelling 89–91, 121, 194–6

negative/unpleasant feelings, expression of 103–7, 154–5, 244–7
non-verbal communication 99, 102–3, 108, 109
number of therapy sessions 17

observed problem-solving 41–4, 46, 49, 51, 55–6, 207–8
operant conditioning strategies 166–7

performance feedback 85–7, 88, 120, 193–4, 201
physical disorders 2, 4; *see also* disability
physiological responses to stress 1, 2
planning 136–40, 264–5, 266–8
planning checklists 136–7, 266
pleasant/positive feelings, expression of 98–101, 236–40
positive requests 101–3, 188, 241–4
premarital counselling 8
problem analysis 32

problem behaviour in childhood 6–7, 8, 167
problem definition 128–33, 256–8
problem-solving 7, 8, 11, 16–17, 26–7, 33, 38–56, 111–16, 224; collaborative 115–16; observed 41–4, 46, 49, 51, 55–6, 207–8; planning phase 136–40, 264–5; reported 38–9, 49, 207; structured 39, 112–13, 118–42, 250–5; for therapist problems 175–6; *see also* solutions
problem-solving training 116–43
promptsheets 94
psychological responses to stress 1, 2

rationale, provision of 189–91, 200–1
real-life practice 20, 91–6, 178–9, 197
reciprocity concepts 7
re-enactment of real-life performance 20
rehearsal *see* behaviour rehearsal
reinforcement survey 33–4, 55, 206
relationships, interpersonal 4
relaxation training 162–3
reported problem-solving 38–9, 49, 207
requests, positive 101–3, 188, 241–4
responses to stress 1–2
review sessions 55–6
role play 20, 139

schizophrenia management 171–2
schizophrenic disorders 71, 72, 233
self-monitoring 44
setting limits 155, 168–9, 177
sexual therapy 172–3
shaping 166
size of training groups 18
social intervention, adherence to 179
social reinforcement in skills training 196–7